THE SERVANTS' CHURCH

Faith Evangelical Free Church
1920-2020

Michael J. Young

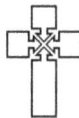

Faith Evangelical Free Church
Acton, Massachusetts

To my wonderful wife, friend, and life partner, Kate.
I love you only, still, more.

Table of Contents

Ordinary People, Extraordinary Impact

Reminiscences

Preface

*Those who do not treasure up the memory of their
ancestors do not deserve to be remembered by
posterity.*

EDMUND BURKE

I found the above quote by Edmund Burke in a family history book
while researching my family tree, and it has always stuck with me. I was
reminded of it because this is a family history book. It is the history of
the family known as Faith Evangelical Free Church (FEFC) of Acton,
Massachusetts, originally the Norwegian Zion Evangelical Free Church
of Concord. It is being produced as part of a 2020 celebration of the
100th anniversary of the church's founding. More precisely, it is the
history of the first 141 years of this 100-year-old church. The
anniversary celebrates that time when a small group of Norwegian
believers from Concord, Massachusetts began worshiping in their own
building which they had constructed on a vacant lot on Lang Street. But
the construction of a building was not the beginning. A recognizable
church had been gestating for over thirty years before that blessed day.
And like all faithful churches, they were building on what had been
handed down by followers of Christ since the first-century apostles.
Indeed, when Jesus prayed for all those who would believe through the
apostles' word (John 17:20), He was praying for us.

Over the years, the church has described its origins in various
historical sketches published in booklets commemorating the twenty-
fifth, fiftieth, and seventy-fifth anniversary celebrations of the church.
All these sketches have a common origin in a two-page sketch published
in 1932 in a small booklet entitled *Church Manual*, and later expanded
into a three-page typewritten report which documents the early

"nucleus" years of the church. It appears to be a summary of the collective memory of the early members, and was written while many of the charter members were still alive. However, those charter members, for the most part, joined the movement later in the course of events, and my research showed some factual errors in the report, especially for the earliest years before 1893. So, I began to dig deeper. This book is the result of that research.

I have attempted to corroborate and supplement the original report based on inspection of contemporaneous sources such as the archives of Trinitarian Congregational Church, the FEFC archives, and various articles from local newspapers through the years. I also will attempt to extend the record to provide some historical and cultural context, and give annual highlights where appropriate, updating the record to the present time. This is not intended to be a scholarly work, but I have included a number of notes and annotations of my sources for various facts, with the hope that those who come after us will be able to verify what is written here, and perhaps gain a jumping off point for further research. My notes are collected at the end of the book to avoid interrupting the flow of the narrative for those who are not interested in the details.

Why write such a book? For that matter, why should the church celebrate its history and anniversary at all? Why look backward? Shouldn't we rather look forward? Why is it important to remember the past? Multiple answers come to mind:

1. It is an act of worship. Scripture is replete with examples of people recounting the mighty deeds of God on their behalf. God told the Israelites to remember that they were once slaves in Egypt (Dt 5:15), to remember that the Lord delivered them from Pharaoh with a mighty hand (Ex 13:3). Songs were sung extolling events so that they would be remembered. As often as we celebrate the Lord's Supper, we do it in remembrance, and proclaim His death until he comes (1 Cor 11:23-26). The Song of Moses will be sung in heaven along with the Song of the Lamb (Rev 15:3).

2. Remembering God's work in us should invoke in us gratitude and a desire to serve. Paul never forgot what he was before he met Christ (a persecutor of the church), and what Christ had

done in his life, and it motivated him to work harder for Christ's glory (1 Cor 15:8-10).

3. By remembering God's faithfulness in the past, we are encouraged (i.e., given courage) to trust Him in future trials (Ps 63:5-8)

4. Remembering and acknowledging not only the successes but also the mistakes of our past helps those who follow avoid making the same mistakes (1 Cor 10:6,11).

5. Remembering the goals and aspirations of our forebears anchors our current plans and helps prevent mission drift. We are told to remember God's commandments, to do them. If we truly want to be a Great Commandment/Great Commission church, we must remember what that means.

One of the purposes for writing this book is that the reader might appreciate the tremendous heritage passed down to us by those who worked so hard to build the Church of Jesus Christ as it is embodied today at Faith Evangelical Free Church. The reader will notice that this book is filled with names. Most of the names will be unfamiliar to anyone who has attended the church for fewer than thirty years. They were ordinary people like the rest of us, yet in many ways they are giants on whose shoulders we stand today. Like all people, they were imperfect. Even the best of men are men at best. Yet for love of the Lord and His church, they made themselves available to Him as instruments to build and sustain the church when they were most needed. We honor them because they were faithful, and God honored their labors on our behalf. We owe them a huge debt because they were the ones who had the vision and perseverance to establish and endow this local body of believers, to carry on the work and hand it down to us.

We are also reminded that Christ is Lord of His church, and the gates of hell cannot stand against it. Through the history of our church, we may perceive the many ways Christ nourished, protected, and guided His church through trials and perils, often in spite of our worst mistakes. Although we owe a debt to those who went before, our trust is in Christ alone, and He alone deserves the glory for what He has done through us.

And yet, the Church's holiness is more important to Christ than its earthly successes or reputation, and He is not afraid to chastise and scourge His Bride so that He might one day present her to Himself in splendor, without spot or wrinkle or any such thing (Eph 5:27).

And so, in addition to celebrating the past, we will also take an unflinching look at the health of the church through the years, rejoicing in our successes, and hopefully learning from our mistakes. The leadership of this church carries a huge responsibility as Christ's under-shepherds and stewards, to learn from the successes and mistakes of our forebears, to avoid the landmines that the enemy sows around us, to pray for guidance, and to trust in the Lord of the Church to lead us, as we lead the congregation in a way that is pleasing to Him.

Sometimes we fail, but we must learn from those mistakes. The mistakes recorded here are not intended to embarrass or denigrate anyone, but to make sure that the lessons they learned are not forgotten by us or those who follow us.

Memories fade over time. What is forgotten cannot instruct. The last of those who founded the church passed on to glory in the 1970s. There remain only three active members who worshiped in the Lang Street Church, and none who actually live in Concord center itself, where the church resided for so many years.

Another goal for this book is to provide some insight into the historical and cultural context of our story and help us to see how the culture impacted the congregation and how they responded to the world around them.

My final goal in the writing of this book is to see if our own experience as a daughter church can teach us how to be better church planters, as we undertake to start a new church in the coming years.

The title of this book, *The Servants' Church,* is a reference to a nickname given to the church by some of the townspeople of Concord, recalling the socio-economic class of the immigrant community that founded the church. Most of the early Norwegian immigrants to Concord were employed as farm hands and domestic servants for the wealthier, established people of the town. Although the townsfolk were happy to support such an endeavor for the benefit of the poorer classes, they would not be willing to attend such a church themselves. This attitude was borne out in time as the church was unable to break out of its reputation as an immigrant church, and eventually needed to reinvent itself in nearby Acton. The church was willing, even anxious, to expand its influence beyond the Norwegian community, but not at the expense of their commitment to the Gospel of Jesus Christ. God has honored that faithfulness of His people with His own faithfulness—He called those who would eventually build the church. It was through His providence that the congregation came to fruition, and it is through His faithful sustenance that the church has survived and thrived for over a century. As one looks back on the meager resources of those who committed their lives to the church, one cannot help but recognize that it was truly a work of God, not of man. Therefore, this book is not about the faith or faithfulness of the church or of its people. Rather, this book is a testimony to the faithfulness of the Lord Whose we are, and Whom we serve. We are humbly thankful for the reminder that, although no church is more than a generation from extinction, Jesus Christ remains Lord of His Church. As His hand was visibly guiding His local flock over the past 100 years, we can be confident that, if we are faithful, He will continue to guide us, enable us, and use us in the coming years until He comes again in glory.

Soli Deo Gloria, 2019

Introduction

The Evangelical Free Churches stand for the unity of all Christians. This is a very important point. Once I heard P. Waldenström remark very strikingly that "a Lutheran church is a gathering of Lutheran Christians – a Methodist church is a gathering of Methodist Christians – a Baptist church is a gathering of Baptist Christians – but a Free Church is a gathering of all Christians."

REV. L.J. PEDERSEN

Faith Evangelical Free Church is celebrating a birthday. Birthdays are always fun and exciting. But this birthday is special: this little flock of believers is about to turn 100 years old! In an age where "newer" is always "better," and technology is obsolete almost before we bring it home from the store, it's hard to believe that anything or anyone this old could still be relevant. And, truth be told, it is unlikely that anyone who was around for the founding of the church in 1920 would have believed that it would still be alive and kicking a century later, if only because they believed the Lord would have returned long before!

1

So who are we, and how did we get here?

Currently worshiping at 54 Hosmer Street, Acton, Massachusetts, Faith Evangelical Free Church (often referred to in this book as Faith EFC, FEFC or just Faith) was formally organized in 1920 as the Norwegian Zion Evangelical Free Church in historic Concord, Massachusetts, ministering primarily to the Norwegian immigrant community in the area. From the beginning it has been a Bible-centered, Christ-centered community of believers affiliated with what is now known as the Evangelical Free Church of America. The church's aim, as proclaimed in the original constitution, was to "spread the Gospel both home and abroad, and as far as possible support the home and foreign missions." This aim, while restated differently at various times, is still the focus of the church. Today it plays out through a mission to "present everyone mature in Christ" (Colossians 1:28) through:

- Exalting God in
  - passionate worship
  - Bible-centered, relevant, expository preaching that proclaims the whole counsel of God
  - loving relationships

- Equipping the Saints for the work of ministry by
  - intentional disciple-making
  - leadership development
  - development and discovery of spiritual gifts
  - Bible instruction through Sunday School programs for all ages
  - Small groups that promote mutual support and accountability

- Evangelizing the world by
  - reaching our neighbors and friends for Christ
  - investing resources to plant churches
  - supporting home and foreign missions with money, prayer and personal involvement
  - comprehensive ministries to youth in the church and the community

Faith Evangelical Free Church strives to be faithful to the Great Commandment and Great Commission. We wish to teach everyone how to love the Lord with all our heart, soul, mind and strength, to love our neighbors as ourselves, and to devote ourselves to making disciples at home and abroad, baptizing and teaching everyone to do everything He commands of us.

The church currently hosts two worship services on Sundays, featuring a mix of traditional hymns and contemporary worship songs, as well as Bible-based expository preaching. More information may be found at https://www.faithevfree.org.

So how did we get here? And what have we learned along the way?

In the following chapters we will survey the events and people who played a vital role in the birth and life of Faith. Much of what we do, and how we do it, is a direct result of our experiences through the years. We are far from perfect, but we are a community that strives to grow in Christ's love and glorify Him in all we do.

This work is organized in three parts. Part One covers the history of the movement in chapters that reflect the major epochs of the church's life. Each chapter covers a period defined by the various names which the church held—the name by which we were called was indicative of the way we wished to be known in the community. Part Two looks specifically at the various people and organizations that played an important part in the birth of the church, drawing lessons from the church's time as an infant church to learn how to be a better mother church in the present-day church planting ministries of Faith. The last part takes a hard look at the health of the church throughout its history, celebrating successes and hopefully exposing lessons that can be learned from mistakes and missteps, helping future leadership avoid these pitfalls.

Prologue:
Fertile Soil at Home and Abroad[1]

Nothing happens in a vacuum. Even seemingly small, local activities can affect, or be affected by, national and global movements of history. People may think they are acting in isolation, but they are still affected by the culture around them and the people they encounter. So, in order to understand the little "Servants' Church" in Concord, Massachusetts, we first need to make a couple of transatlantic trips back in time.

Norway, 1750-1859

In early nineteenth century Norway, there was only one accepted church, the state-sponsored Evangelical Lutheran Church. A law from 1741 had decreed that no religious meetings or activities could occur without the supervision, and preferably the presence, of the local Lutheran pastor. Shortly before the turn of the century, a farmer's son from Østfold named Hans Nielsen Hauge (1772-1824) began to break this law by preaching directly to people about their need to be awakened to a consciousness of their sins and dependence upon the grace of God for salvation. His message of personal salvation and the pre-eminence of the Word of God in the life of the believer put him at loggerheads with the state church, resulting in his frequent imprisonment.

In spite of all this, Hauge was able to travel extensively throughout Norway, and won followers from all over Norway. By the time of his death, there were Haugean groups among the farmers and craftsmen in many rural areas, towns and villages throughout the country, and even small cities such as Stavanger, Bergen, and Trondheim. He and his followers did not leave the state church—in fact they were diligent in their church attendance, had their children baptized in the church, and participated in the Lord's Supper along with everyone else. However, they also met privately with each other for fellowship, worship, and prayer which was technically still illegal. Hauge kept the scattered groups together through extensive correspondence and some printed material that was circulated between communities.

In 1845, well after Hauge's death, the so-called Dissenters Law was enacted, allowing other Christian churches to operate alongside the official state church. Haugeans continued their loose association of pietistic communities, but never formed their own churches.

After the Dissenters Law was passed, there was a time of great revival throughout Norway, led mainly by lay preachers, but helped by some state church clergymen, including Gustav Adolph Lammers of Skien, who became one of the first Lutheran clergymen to withdraw from the state church to form his own "free" congregation. These so-called "mission" churches began to spring up in various places around the country. The revival also swept through the Lutheran church, and Lammers eventually re-entered the state church, although many of his followers did not join him, remaining instead in the mission churches.

Boston and Chicago, 1855-1865

Back across the Atlantic, Dwight L. Moody (1837-1899) was working in Boston in his uncle's shoe store. In 1855 he was converted when his Sunday School teacher spoke to him about the love of Christ. He moved to Chicago to start his own shoe business, but soon felt the call to hold a Sunday School class for the city's youth, while doing volunteer work at the local YMCA (eventually becoming its president!). By 1864 his Mission Sunday School had become the Illinois Street Church. Although Moody founded the church, he was never its senior pastor.

England, 1867

In 1867, Moody visited England, during which time he became acquainted with the Plymouth Brethren, founded by John Nelson Darby. Moody embraced the Brethren view of the imminent, premillennial return of Christ, and their ardent love for the lost and commitment to Scripture. Moody became one of the first great revivalists who held to premillennial views. Most previous evangelists of the First and Second Great Awakenings, like Jonathan Edwards and George Whitefield, had believed they were helping to usher in the millennial kingdom, after which Christ would return in glory (post-millennialism), or else they chose to ignore the idea of a millennial kingdom (Wesley).

Moody was by no means a trained theologian. But there were four signature doctrines that were important to him and guided all of his work: 1) a love for the lost and the need for personal faith in Christ to be saved; 2) a strong belief in the inerrancy and verbal inspiration of all of Scripture; 3) the unity of all believers in the universal church (regardless of denomination); 4) and that only believers were members of the true Church (believers only). Moody would work with any church in an effort to win the lost, but not every church would work with him.

The fifth major theological belief that guided his methods was his belief in the imminent premillennial return of Christ, including a secret rapture of the true Church before the tribulation. But although he preached on the return of Christ at every revival, he did not allow disagreement about eschatology to divide believers or prevent them from working together to reach the lost.

Chicago, 1868-1880

The Illinois Street Church was destroyed in the Great Chicago Fire of 1871, after which the congregation immediately raised funds to rebuild on the corner of Chicago Avenue and LaSalle Street. The new Chicago Avenue Church[2] was dedicated in the summer of 1876 with an auditorium that could hold up to 10,000. While the church was being rebuilt, Moody devoted his life to the Lord's work with renewed vigor and began his evangelistic work in earnest. He teamed up with his friend, singer/songwriter Ira Sankey and began conducting evangelistic meetings together. In 1873 he began a two-year campaign in the British Isles which made Moody's name a household word there.

Fredrik Franson, a Swede, attended and worked at Moody's church from 1875 through 1879. He learned and perfected Moody's revival techniques and held many revivals among the Scandinavian community there. He translated many of Moody's sermons into Swedish and Norwegian, and published them widely in Scandinavia as well as in America. So, although he never set foot in any Scandinavian country, Moody's influence and reputation there were considerable.

By 1875 many of Moody's sermons and Sankey's songs had been published by devoted followers, and were soon translated into Swedish and Norwegian.

During the time Franson was in Chicago, Moody and Sankey were holding evangelistic campaigns all over the United States, including a four-month campaign in Boston and the surrounding towns in the first half of 1877.[3]

Norway, 1880-1890

In 1881, Moody was invited to go to Sweden, but he declined, preferring to work in places where he did not need a translator. Fredrik Franson was invited in his place, and using the same techniques that he had learned from Moody, met with great success.

In 1883, after a successful tour of Sweden, Franson arrived in Kristiania, Norway (today's Oslo) for a year and a half of revival meetings targeting the scattered Norwegian free church congregations that came out of the earlier Lammers revival back in the 1850s. The result of his work: the formation of the Norwegian Mission Covenant association in Norway. These associations bore marks of Franson's techniques and theology, which he learned from Moody, including: 1) Millenarianism, specifically what today is known as dispensational premillennialism; 2) a literalist interpretation of Scripture; 3) and a view of the importance of the invisible, universal Church made up of those who were born again of the Spirit and would be taken up in the secret rapture. He also followed Moody's practice of minimizing the importance of denominational differences. Franson, like his mentor, would work with any denomination, including Rome, to reach as many individuals as possible.

The Mission churches operated as independent congregations outside the state church structure. In 1884, Marcus Whitman Montgomery gave a report to the American Home Missionary Society about the progress of the Gospel among the Scandinavians. Of his stay in Kristiania, he wrote the following:

> My professional guide insisted that there was no " Free Mission " church in Kristiania; it was impossible, or he should have known of it; but I knew better, and directed him to find the residence of Mr. M. Hanson. He was at home; was "leader" of the Mission church; introduced to me an excellent interpreter, in sympathy with my work, Mr. Neils A. S. Eie, and so the professional lost his situation. Mr. Eie was of much service to me and would have no compensation. I attended the service of the Mission friends at 6 p.m. on Bedja Dag. They were just laying the foundations of a house of worship, and were worshiping in a gymnasium, where a great audience was present. Their singing was hearty and joyous. The first song was "Wonderful Words of Life," translated into their own language, but keeping the same tune. How it thrilled me to hear in that far-off land, and so unexpectedly, that song burst forth from hundreds of worshiping tongues! The sermon was by Rev. S. K. Didrickson, a Norwegian youth of about twenty-two years, fine looking, robust, earnest, humble, consecrated, who had enjoyed little training. When he had closed they invited me to speak, and I gave them a brief account of the history and present strength of their Congregational brethren in England and America. This greatly astonished them, and awakened many audible responses. When I told them that some of our forefathers in England had suffered martyrdom for the sake of a New Testament church, untrammeled by State power, many expressions of sympathy came from the audience.[4]

Montgomery had visited the Bethlehem Church in Kristiania, which predated Franson's visit in 1883. Didriksen had been preaching there for a number of years, and had worked with Franson while he was in Norway in 1883. Although he had no formal training, he threw his whole heart and soul into preaching, and was consumed with a burning desire to preach the gospel to the unsaved. Later, Olai Johansen recounted the impact of his preaching: "The remark was made by one who attended: 'He preaches so that I cannot sleep at night.'"[5]

Boston (and Concord), 1880-1895

Severin K Didriksen's brother David came to Boston in 1882, followed shortly thereafter by his roommate and lifelong friend Olai Johansen. Together they attended the local Norwegian Lutheran churches but were disappointed with the pastors' unwillingness to stress the need for personal conversion.

> No food for the soul was served up on Sundays, and as far as I could discern, not one of the church membership was saved.[6]

They considered joining with the Swedish Mission Friends, but decided they would rather do something with the Norwegians of Boston. With the encouragement of David and his friend Olai, Severin left Norway for Boston, and soon they had organized the Norwegian Evangelical Free Church of Boston (Roxbury) Massachusetts. Severin became the new church's full time pastor from 1885 to 1886. But he soon became convinced of his need for more training, so he left for a time to attend Chicago Theological Seminary. Upon graduation and ordination in 1890, he returned to Roxbury and served there until 1894. While serving in Roxbury he had a major hand in supporting the fledgling group in Concord and organizing it into the Scandinavian Branch. The Roxbury Free Church was often called the "mother church" of the Eastern Norwegian Free Church Association, not only because it was the first to organize, but because it provided encouragement and nurture to many other churches, including Concord.

During the time that Severin Didriksen was at Chicago Theological Seminary, a number of missionaries from the Massachusetts Home Missionary Society helped the Roxbury church. One of these men, Gustav Dahl, served there for about six months, during which time he also encouraged the group in Concord through evangelistic meetings. In December 1890, after Didriksen returned, Dahl was asked to conduct a series of evangelistic meetings in Jersey City, NJ, among a group of Norwegian evangelicals who had been meeting in a German Methodist Church. As a result of these meetings the Norwegian Evangelical Free Church of Jersey City was organized on the first Sunday of January 1891. Rev. Dahl was called to be their first pastor, serving from 1891 to 1897, after which he went to Brooklyn, NY for another series of meetings which resulted in the organization of the First Evangelical

Free Church of Brooklyn. These two churches would also turn out to be a great encouragement to the Concord flock.

Chicago, 1880-1895

Meanwhile, back in Chicago, Rev. Peter Christian Trandberg, an itinerant evangelist who had worked among the Danish free churches since the middle of the nineteenth century, came to Warren, Pennsylvania in 1882 to work with the Danes who had settled there. He did not stay there long, for his reputation as an effective evangelist to the Scandinavian people preceded him. That same year, Dr. Frederick Ernest (F.E.) Emrich had accepted the call to become pastor of the Tabernacle Congregational Church of Chicago. Finding himself in a parish that included people from many nationalities, which included Scandinavians who had only recently arrived in America, he sought out Trandberg, inviting him in 1883 to come to Chicago to hold afternoon meetings for Scandinavians in their own languages on Sunday afternoons. He also took it upon himself to learn Danish, Swedish, and Norwegian. While in Chicago, he had the opportunity to see Moody and Sankey in action. He shared many of Moody's views, while still holding generally to Lutheran theology. In 1883 he was approached to head a new Dano-Norwegian department at the Chicago Theological Seminary (Congregational). In 1884 he began teaching with one student, Otto Christopher Grauer. Grauer was originally from Skien, Norway, and his mother was a charter member of the free church that was organized there after the Lammers revival. Grauer went on to become a major instrument in the foundation of the Western Norwegian-Danish Evangelical Free Church Association. He eventually returned to Chicago Theological Seminary, where he taught for twenty-five years, with students that included at least four pastors that served the Scandinavian Branch in Concord. These students and others worked, prayed, and fellowshipped together, and their churches kept in regular contact through annual conferences. From the beginning, the small group of Norwegian believers in Concord were embedded in the fellowship.

Dr. Emrich was also an instructor for the Dano-Norwegian department at Chicago Theological Seminary while he pastored at Tabernacle Church (1882-1889), before taking the pulpit at South

Framingham Congregational Church (present-day Plymouth Church) in Massachusetts. He participated in the ordination council for Ole O. Thorpe in 1894, and became Secretary of the Massachusetts Home Missions Society from 1903 to 1923, where he continued to be of great help to the Concord church.

The church in Concord was built on the shoulders of great men, who were used by God for something much larger than themselves. Few of these people were trained theologians—Moody himself was a lay preacher, as was Hauge. Most of the earliest preachers of the free church movement on both sides of the Atlantic had no more than the equivalent of an undergraduate theological education at best. But they were deep thinkers, meditating on the Word of God, and listening to His Spirit leading them. They were willing to be expended for the Kingdom. Many of these people devoted themselves to multiple simultaneous ministries that would exhaust anyone today! Yet nothing was too much for God's Church, and they knew that God was working. That was enough for them.

These global movements, while seemingly remote from rural Massachusetts, provided the fertile soil out of which the little church in Concord germinated. One can also see how the signature distinctives of the Free Church movement in America were already being formed by the time the Spirit began moving in Boston and Concord:

> "These included Anglo-American revivalism of the Moody tradition, resistance to liberal Biblical scholarship, belief in the imminent Second Advent of Christ as interpreted by John Nelson Darby, and a denigration of various adiaphora which have divided Protestants since the Reformation."[7]

In the fertile soil of this new movement we can now trace the germination and growth of the Servants' Church.

Part One: History

The Journey of Faith

Chapter 1:
The Scandinavian Mission Society

(1879-1893)

Old Wright Tavern today.

It is now over sixty years since the first Norwegians came to Concord. They were two young women who came over in the summer of 1872 to take positions as servants. In the following spring a group of eight arrived, two young men and six young women. The two men, who are still living, are both Christians.

Following these came many other Norwegians, Swedes and Danes.

At first these newcomers made no church connections. Then an American woman, Mrs. William Hunt, became interested in these young people, and after studying the Norwegian language she gathered a group of eight or ten which met as a Sunday School class in the Congregational Church. In 1879 came a young man from Norway who had a real Christian experience, and when Mrs. Hunt that winter became ill, this young man, Ole O. Thorpe, took charge. He soon turned it into a preaching service which most of the Scandinavians attended...[1]

The above quote from the 1932 *Church Manual* reflects the oral history of the earliest beginnings of the church. It was written twelve years after the formal organization of the church, while many of the charter members were still alive. However, only a few of the charter members had immigrated to the United States prior to 1890, and the collective memory of the time prior to the Scandinavian Branch might have become fuzzy. So, while the broad brush-strokes of the account are probably correct, we will flesh out the details from other sources.

Norwegians in Concord

In the second half of the nineteenth century, Norwegian immigration to the United States grew from a trickle to a flood. Those arriving in the early 1800s (especially Quakers and other non-conformists) were often seeking relief from persecution by the official Norwegian state church. This began to change with passage of the 1845 Dissenters' Law, giving tolerance to non-Lutheran Christian gatherings. But by the second half of the nineteenth century the primary motivation was economic, driven in part by the aftermath of famines in Europe and especially the great Finnish and Swedish famines in the 1860s.

Sweden, Denmark, and Norway at this time formed a "united kingdom" under King Oscar II. On 26 October 1905, Norway peacefully won their independence which was celebrated annually thereafter by Norwegians in Concord.

For most people, mention of Scandinavian immigration to the United States brings to mind the settlers of the American Midwest, especially Minnesota. However, many of those seeking a new life in America came through New York and Massachusetts, and a number of them settled there. Some, who had made their living by the sea in the old country, employed themselves as seamen and ship builders. Others were attracted to the relatively fertile farms in rural Massachusetts, such as those found in the area around Concord at that time.

The 1870 US Federal Census of Concord shows no residents who were born in Norway (other than one person who was incarcerated in the Concord prison). Rather than Scandinavia, many of the domestic servants and farm laborers in town had come from Ireland. But during the summer of 1872, two young Norwegian women arrived in Concord and took positions as domestic servants. By the next spring an additional eight arrived (two young men and six young women) and the influx of Norwegians, Swedes, and Danes began in earnest. Some found work on farms or as domestic servants, and a number who were leatherworkers made their living as cobblers. Scandinavians quickly gained a reputation as honest, reliable workers, and were sought out by many families and employers in town. Most of the early Norwegians in Concord were from what is today the Norwegian county of Hedmark, a mainly rural, landbound district with fertile fields and extensive forests.

Among the early Norwegian immigrants were Lars Petersen from Åmot, Hedmark, Norway, and Martinus Helsjier (Martin Helsher) from Helgøya, near Hamar, the administrative seat of Hedmark. Both arrived in 1873 and quickly settled in as farm laborers. Lars' brother, Rudolph, and their mother, Olena, arrived around 1878.

> Two able girls wanted—(Cook and second girl). Scandinavian preferred; used to working together preferred...
>
> —Help wanted ad from *Concord Enterprise*, 28 March 1906, p4.

One farm that made good use of Norwegian labor was that of William H. and Elizabeth Hunt. In 1873, Daniel Hunt, William's father,

Farm hands at the Hunt Farm on Punkatasset Hill. Most Hunt's farm hands and domestic servants were Norwegians. Photo courtesy of National Park Service, Minute Man Historical Park archives.

died leaving him in full possession of the Hunt farmlands on Punkatasset Hill. Shortly thereafter, Elizabeth's father, Dr. Thomas McEwan (McEuan), passed away leaving her with a sizeable inheritance. This allowed the Hunts to invest in new equipment and hire outside labor to work the farm. Many of these new laborers and domestic servants were Norwegian immigrants. William was a good employer, well liked and respected by the hired help, and he worked hard alongside them while he was able. Elizabeth, who was later described by her husband's niece, Mary Jacobs, as "a very cultivated woman with an unusual education for those days,[2]" apparently also took an interest in her domestic servants, to the extent of learning enough Norwegian so she could communicate with them more effectively.

During this time Methodism was rapidly growing in North America, partly due to a large emphasis on home missions beginning during the Civil War. They saw fertile soil among the many immigrants coming to America, including Scandinavian sailors who were such an important part of international trade at the time. According to the diary of Methodist preacher Rev. Samuel C. Charlton, he conducted the first

Scandinavian religious service for twenty-five people gathered in the vestry of Trinitarian Congregational Church on the evening of 26 October, 1875.[3] We have no records that show what, if anything, came of this meeting.

On 8 May 1877 William and Elizabeth Hunt applied for their passport[4] and shortly after they took an extended trip to Europe lasting two years, leaving the farm in the capable hands of the hired help. Allen French believed that the trip was from 1878-1880.[5] However, these recollections of Mr. Hunt to Mr. French were more than forty years removed from the events, so the dates may not be exact. It is conceivable that they could have left as early as the summer of 1877, returning the spring of 1879. A search of border crossings and passenger lists in this timeframe turned up nothing conclusive.

During the summer of 1879 a Sabbath School class was held at Trinitarian Congregational Church.[6] Neither the teacher's nor the students' names are listed, but the attendance records show a weekly Norwegian-language class meeting from 15 June through at least 21 September 1879. The average attendance (including the teacher) was between ten and eighteen people. After 21 September the class is no longer included in the weekly reports.

This is almost certainly the Sunday School class described in the *Church Manual* quoted above. Was Mrs. William Hunt the teacher? It is not impossible that the Hunts had returned home from the trip to Europe by this time. Although we cannot be sure, we do know that fond memories of Mrs. Hunt remained in the collective memory of the early members of the church. We know that she had the ability and the motive to do this, and even if she was not involved in this class, it is certain that she and her husband were involved in the lives of the Norwegian community until her death in 1903. In fact, her husband vouched for Anton Hoff, one of the church's charter members, when he took the oath of citizenship in 1901.

Who was Elizabeth Hunt? How did God prepare her to be such an encouragement to the Norwegians? She remains in many ways an enigmatic, private person, but through the research of Leslie Perrin Wilson, intriguing details have emerged. What we see is a woman who knew what it was like to be in a strange place away from home, to have no friends she could count on, and who developed the courage to rebuild her life from scratch. The back-story to this remarkable woman who played such an important role in the history of the church is recounted in Appendix A.

On 18 September 1879, Mr. Ole O. Thorpe arrived in Boston from Grue, Hedmark, Norway.[7] From there he took a train to Concord, where he was met by Lars Petersen. Thus began a friendship that lasted the rest of their lives. Thorpe arrived shortly before the last recorded Norwegian-language Sabbath School class. He quickly established a shoe store and repair shop on the south side of the Mill Dam, in a building owned by George B. Davis on Main Street between what is now known as Walden and Lexington Streets. His fiancée, Pauline Evarsdatter Bekkevold, arrived shortly thereafter, and they were married by Rev. H.M. Grout at Trinitarian Congregational Church in 1880[8], after which they joined Trinitarian as members in July 1881.[9] They made their home on Hubbard Street in a lovely Italianate house built by George Penniman around 1876. [10] Their home, which may still be seen at 94 Hubbard Street, was a short walk from Trinitarian Congregational Church, and sits just around the corner from the William Hunt Recreation Center.[11]

Although the records are sketchy on this point, it is clear from the promptness with which Thorpe joined Trinitarian and the fervor with which he served, that he had a vibrant spiritual life and strongly held beliefs, and that his relationship with Christ and the church was very important to him. But we have no way of knowing if or how he was influenced by the various movements going on in Norway prior to coming to America.

Meetings at Wright Tavern

What is clear is that Mr. Thorpe had a gift for preaching and teaching, and he soon took on a leadership role in the small Norwegian group, transforming their meetings into fruitful Norwegian-language preaching services, at which many were converted to Christ. It wasn't long before they felt the need for better organization and a place to meet, so they formed what later became known as the Scandinavian Mission Society. They rented a room in the old Wright Tavern[12] at the center of town where they held their services and social gatherings, and which they kept open during evenings as a reading room.

"Doing Business on the Mill Dam," circa 1907. Lars Andersen stands at far left, in front of what would later become Andersen's Market (still in the Andersen family as Main Streets Market). Next to him is Charles Towle, from whom Lars would buy the business. To his right, N.A. Davis talks with Leslie Anderson, then Frank Pierce, owner of the shoe shop. Ole Thorpe stands on the right, although his shoe store is across the street on the south side of the Mill Dam. Courtesy Concord Free Public Library.

By 1880 the number of Norwegians in Concord had grown tremendously. The US Federal Census of Concord (excluding residents of the prison) listed forty-four Norwegian immigrants out of a total population of 3,174. Apart from Ole O. Thorpe's shoe store, every one of them were listed as either hired farm laborers or domestic servants.

Meanwhile, Boston was also becoming home to many Scandinavian immigrants. Sometime in 1882 David M. Didriksen arrived from Norway and settled in Boston. His friend, Olai Johansen, came shortly thereafter in 1883. In 1884 (sometime after Rev. Montgomery saw him preach in Kristiania)[13], David and Olai convinced David's brother, Severin K. Didriksen, to come to Boston and help them plant a church.

Shortly after his arrival in Boston in September 1884, S.K. Didriksen wrote home to his friends in Kristiania:

> ... I live and feel pretty good here, better than I expected, because I made no big thought of thriving in America when I traveled here. During the time I have been here, I have

sought to approach my countrymen with the Word of God. Boston has probably been the place where I have worked most, but I have also been to various other places. There are countrymen in almost every field, but in general they live very scattered; and not many are found on these edges, who bear testimony that they live with God. However, I have not met so few who are in need of salvation and peace, and for whom it has been my joy to witness Jesus' great love for sinners, and some have also accepted the Word and thank God who took them to grace. It is sad to see how many are using all their powers to resist the Lord and close their ears to the calling voice of the bans. In particular, it is the youth who seek to silence the voice of conscience through worldly pleasures and societies. God pursues them with His grace. Be waiting for the Lord to come with power among us and save sinners. Here is a small flock that seeks to build us up in the Lord and work what we can to the salvation of souls...[14]

From his letter we cannot tell if Didriksen had yet visited Concord, but his description of the spiritual landscape was accurate.

In January 1885, the Norwegian Evangelical Free Church of Boston (Roxbury) was born, and Severin became its first pastor, serving from 1885 until 1886 when he left for further training at Chicago Theological Seminary. In his absence, his brother David served as pastor for a time (with help from Severin during his summer vacation from CTS) until David also departed for CTS for further training. After this, Rev. Ludwig Ellingsen served in Boston from March to October of 1889[15]. At this point the Boston church was not yet self-supporting, and their pastors were paid in part by the Massachusetts Home Missionary Society.[16]

While the Roxbury Free Church was still gestating, the Methodists renewed their outreach efforts in Concord, as evidenced by the records of the Trinitarian Church:

21 March 1884: At a regular church meeting, Jens F. Anderson and Hellen E. Anderson, his wife, applied for letters of dismission and recommendation to the Methodist Episcopal Church, Boston, of which Mr. Olsen is pastor (This looks as if it might be the commencement of a movement to organize a Methodist Church among the Scandinavians in Concord.)[17]

The Methodist Episcopal Church was already the largest single denomination in America and had also become the largest of the free church movements in Norway, having been introduced to Norway in the 1850s by seamen who converted while in American ports.

Like all free and mission churches, they stressed personal conversion, but with a twist:

> Methodists preached free will and free grace: God had given everyone the ability to respond to the gospel. Every sinner could receive assurance of personal salvation, and from there could confidently go on to seek the "second blessing" of entire sanctification. He would be cleansed of all sin and would gain power to fulfill the commandment to love God with heart, soul, and mind, and one's neighbor as oneself. Free will, universal atonement, and the promise of perfectibility - these were the optimistic doctrines on which Methodism's growth rested.[18]

The people of the Scandinavian Mission Society were split about evenly between adherence to Methodist doctrine on one side and Lutheran or Congregational (primarily Calvinist) views on the other.

In time, about half of the Society decided to affiliate with the Methodist movement, and organized the Norwegian-Danish Methodist Episcopal Church on 6 February 1887 under the leadership of Rev. Dr. George S. Chadbourne, presiding elder of the North Boston district. Their first pastor was Rev. Eliot Hansen, who was installed in 1889.[19] Their second pastor, J.P. Andersen, presided over the construction of their own church building on the corner of Thoreau Street and Thoreau Court, which was dedicated on 8 October 1893. In 1894 they had forty members and listed twelve baptisms of children. However, by 1897 their membership had already slipped to thirty.[20] They struggled along with dwindling membership, especially during the War years when immigration slowed to a trickle. Eventually the Great Depression forced them to close their doors in the middle of the 1930s. During the entire time of their existence, they maintained warm relations with their brethren at Trinitarian and in the Evangelical Free Church, and often met together for celebrations and common outreach events.[21]

Those who remained behind and had not joined the Methodist-Episcopal church were discouraged, but continued their meetings at Wright Tavern with Ole Thorpe as their leader.

Concord, October 14. An alarm was rung in at 7.30 A.M. for fire in the boot and shoe store occupied by Mr. Ole O. Thorpe, situated on Main Street, the building being owned by Mr. George B. Davis. The fire was located in the back shop, where Mr. Thorpe carries on repairing. It was confined to this room, as the department was quickly on hand and cut off what might have been quite a fire if it had had a good start. The front room was somewhat damaged by water. The fire was caused by carelessness.

— *Annual Reports of the Town Officers of Concord, Mass. for the Year Ending March 12, 1888,* (Boston: Thomas Todd, Printer, 1 Somerset Street, 1888), p72.

Shortly after this, the women of the Society formed a local chapter of the Women's Missionary Society (WMS). These ladies did much to help hold the Wright Tavern group together.[22] And so the work continued for a few more years.

In October 1889, Rev. Gustav A. Dahl began serving at the Boston (Roxbury) Free Church with support from the Massachusetts Home Missionary Society.[23] Shortly after he arrived in Boston, he reached out to the Concord brethren, and began to conduct evangelistic meetings in the vestry of the Trinitarian Congregational Church, at which all were encouraged and some were saved.

At a regular meeting on 11 February 1890, the Standing Committee of the Trinitarian Congregational Church took note of the Norwegian meetings being held in the vestry:

> 11 Feb'y 1890: Regular meeting of Standing Committee. William T. Farrar and the clerk were appointed a committee to investigate the character of the services held by the Norwegian Lutherans at occasional intervals in our vestry.[24]

At the annual congregational meeting in September 1890, the treasurer reported that the Norwegians had paid $20.00 for use of the vestry that year.[25]

On 6 September 1890, the Eastern Norwegian-Danish Association was formed and met for the first time at North Church Chapel in Bridgeport, CT. This was the first meeting of like-minded Norwegian free churches in the United States. Rev. Ellingsen, who had served for a short time in Boston, was elected secretary for one year.

In the fall of 1890, Gustav Dahl left for Jersey City, NJ, where he conducted evangelistic meetings in December, resulting in the formation of the Jersey City Evangelical Free Church in January 1891. He continued as pastor there until 1897, after their first building was dedicated. That year Rev. Dahl founded another new Free Church in Brooklyn.[26] The Jersey City and Brooklyn churches would be sources of blessing to the Concord church in the future.

Gustav A. Dahl.

In October 1890, Rev. S.K. Didriksen, freshly ordained by Chicago Theological Seminary, returned to fill the open position in Boston, where he served as pastor for four years. In addition to advancing the work in Roxbury and the Boston area, he took an interest in the Concord brethren, and by the fall of

Rev. Severin K. Didriksen.

1891 had begun meeting with the group every other week in the vestry at Trinitarian Congregational. He also took Ole O. Thorpe under his wing and encouraged him as leader of the group. In March 1892, Mr. Thorpe was invited to speak at the Boston church's annual missions conference. He became a regular speaker in Boston thereafter, preaching at special occasions and in the absence of their pastor.[27]

In their 1892 annual report, the deacons of Trinitarian commented on the Scandinavian work in their midst:

> Bro. Ole O. Thorpe has held meetings in the vestry one a week where fifty or more of our Norwegian friends have come to gather to engage in prayer and sacred songs. We think this is a good work and worthy of the support of the church. Let us encourage our brother in his labor of love. The pastor has met with these brethren at different times and given them a word of encouragement.

Although the federal census records for 1890 are unavailable, it is clear that Norwegian immigration had accelerated during the 1880s. Trinitarian records indicate that the total Scandinavian constituency in

Concord had grown to a little over 300,[28] indicating an ample opportunity for outreach.

On 26-28 September 1891 the Norwegian-Danish Association met in Boston, and reorganized itself as the Eastern Evangelical Free Church Association. The Concord group was represented at this meeting, although it had not yet been fully organized. At that conference S.K. Didriksen from Boston was elected to a three-year term as Secretary, and Ole O. Thorpe was elected chairman, a position to which he was annually reelected for five years, and again in 1897 after a one-year hiatus. Ludvig Ellingsen served as vice chairman that year, and Gustav Dahl delivered the annual sermon. Ole Thorpe delivered the sermon the following year when the conference was held in Providence, RI.[29]

The September 1893 annual meeting at Trinitarian was a significant "reunion" observance, which included celebrating various facets of church life. Among them:

> "Our Norwegian Friends." An inscription on a Norwegian coin is "Whatever is of truth, honor, and of good report, leave among the hills of Norway." We rejoice that our Norwegian friends, while leaving these qualities, bring them with them. Responded to by Deacon Ole O. Thorpe.[30]

Prof. R. A. Jernberg of the Chicago Theological Seminary will preach for the Scandinavian society at the vestry of the Congregational church, Wednesday, Aug 12 at 8 p.m.
—*Concord Enterprise*, Friday, 7 August 1891, p1.

With the encouragement and support of Rev. S.K. Didriksen from Boston, on 16 November 1893, the Society formally reorganized as the *Skandinaviske Trefaldigheds Menighed* (Scandinavian Trinitarian Congregational) Church, and united with the Trinitarian Congregational Church as its Scandinavian Branch. Mr. Ole O. Thorpe, who was still a deacon and clerk of Trinitarian, was invited to be their first pastor.

In later years, both the Scandinavian M.E. Church and the Evangelical Free Church would claim the Scandinavian Mission Society as their common roots, and Ole Thorpe as the man who helped establish them. Both churches maintained warm relations until the SME church closed its doors in the late 1930s.

Chapter 2:
Skandinaviske Trefaldigheds Menighed

The Scandinavian Branch of Trinitarian Congregational Church
(1893-1919)

Trinitarian Congregational Church, Concord Mass, 1898. Courtesy Trinitarian Congregational Church.

Trinitarian Congregational Church

In the early nineteenth century, many of the congregational churches in towns across Massachusetts were drifting toward Unitarianism. In 1826, when the First Parish Church in Concord had officially embraced it, a group of people, desiring to reaffirm their belief in the historical Christian faith, split off to form the Second Congregational Church of Concord (later renamed the Trinitarian Congregational Church). One of their most enduring and beloved pastors was the Reverend George A. Tewksbury (1891-1921). By the providence of God, his ministry coincided almost exactly with that of the Scandinavian Branch, which he actively supported and nurtured. This close relationship continued for twenty-seven years.

Trinitarian provided free access to the vestry on Sunday and Wednesday evenings and taught the Norwegian children in the American Sunday Schools. Members of the Scandinavian Branch were members of Trinitarian itself, and often served Trinitarian as deacons or members of the standing committee. Scandinavian pastors were installed as associate pastors of Trinitarian. Progress was reported at least annually to the congregation either by the deacons, senior pastor or the pastor of the Branch.

While the long years since they have gone separate ways may have allowed a certain amnesia to set in, the historical bonds that tie these two churches together can never ultimately be broken. Their welcoming love, service, and generosity to the Scandinavian community will never be forgotten.

The Scandinavian Branch

Skandinaviske Trefaldigheds Menighed, or the Scandinavian Trinitarian Congregational Church, was organized on 16 November 1893[1], and immediately united with the Trinitarian Congregational Church as its Scandinavian Branch. There had been a desire to form an independent church, but the people lacked the resources, experience and confidence to strike out on their own. Trinitarian Congregational was familiar, friendly, and like-minded in faith and practice. Most of the people who belonged to the Scandinavian group (including its leaders) were already members of Trinitarian. The American church welcomed the new group with open arms.

Because of his longtime leadership and support, they wasted no time in extending a call to Mr. Ole O. Thorpe to be their first pastor. The records at Trinitarian, quoted here in their entirety[2], illuminate the process of the ordination and installation, and the interactions between various congregations within the Congregational conference, and also shows that the Scandinavian Branch was considered a distinct, albeit dependent, church.

11 Feb 1894:

A meeting of the committee of the church after Sunday evening service Feb 11 to see what recommendations the committee would make on calling an Ecclesiastical Council to ordain and install Mr. Ole O. Thorpe. Voted to recommend by the above.

Ole O. Thorpe, clerk.

16 Feb 1894:

At a regular Church meeting Febr 16 1894 the following business was transacted: To see what action, if any, the church will take in regard to the invitation extended by the Scandinavian Brothers to our Bro. Ole O. Thorpe to become their pastor, and accepted by him—also in regard to Bro. Thorpe's request that a council of churches be called to ordain and install him in due form. On motion of Deacon Hopkins the church voted to endorse the invitation of the Scandinavians to Bro. Thorpe.

On motion of Dea. Todd the church voted to accede to Bro. Thorpe's request for a council, the same to be held in the church Thursday, March 1st 1894, for the purpose of ordaining and installing Mr. Ole O. Thorpe as pastor of the Scandinavians connected with our church.

On motion of Dea. Todd the church voted to give the authority to the church committee in conjunction with a committee from the Scandinavians, to call said council.

Geo. W. Hopkins clerk pro-tem, Ole O. Thorpe, clerk.

On 21 Feb 1894 the following letter was sent to area congregational churches, inviting them to send pastors and/or delegates to the ordination council for Mr. Thorpe:

The Trinitarian Cong'l Church in Concord Mass
Sendeth Greeting

The Scandinavian members of this church—organized as a branch of this church—having united in the choice of Ole O. Thorpe to be their Pastor and Teacher, the church has endorsed this action. Mr. Thorpe has accepted their call and desires to be duly ordained and installed. We therefore affectionately request your attendance, by your pastor or a delegate, in an Ecclesiastical Council, at our meeting house Thursday, March 1st 1894 at three o'clock in the afternoon to review our proceedings to examine the candidate and, if deemed expedient, to assist in the ordaining and installing service.

Wishing you grace, mercy and peace, we are yours in the Lord,

Geo. A. Tewksbury, pastor
Thomas Todd, deacon
Ole O. Thorpe, deacon and clerk
Geo. H. Hopkins, deacon
Benjamin Moody
Walter F. Baker

Committee of the church

The churches and individuals invited to this council are:

Acton, South Acton, Bedford, Blackstone, Milleville (Norwegian), Boston (Norwegian), Concord Junction Union Church, Fitchburg (Swedish), South Framingham, Lexington, Lincoln, Maynard, Worcester (Norwegian) and Rev. Joshua Coit, Rev. Calvin Keyser

1 March 1894: An Ecclesiastical Council called by the Trinitarian Cong'l Church in Concord, met in their house of worship on Thursday the first day of March 1894 at three o'clock P.M. Was called to order by Rev. Joshua Coit. Rev. Edwin Smith of Bedford was chosen Moderator and Rev. W. W. Campbell of West Concord scribe. The moderator led in prayer.

The churches represented were as follows:

Acton Cong'l	John Fletcher	Delegate
South Acton Cong'l	Joel Gelchell	Delegate
Bedford Cong'l	Rev. Edwin Smith	Pastor

Millville Norwegian Cong'l	Rev. D. M. Didriksen	Pastor
Boston Norwegian Cong'l	Rev. S. K. Didriksen	Pastor
Concord Junc Union Church	Rev. W. W. Campbell	Pastor
	Rev. W. J. Batt	Delegate
South Framingham Cong'l	Rev. F. E. Emrich	Pastor
Lexington Cong'l	E. C. Whitney	Delegate
Lincoln Cong'l	J. H. Farrar	Delegate
Worcester Norwegian Cong'l	Rev. N. C. Barrie	Pastor
	Rev. Joshua Coit	
	Rev. Calvin Keyser	

The clerk of the Scandinavian Branch of the Trinitarian Cong'l Church in Concord read the record of the action of the Branch in calling Mr. Thorpe to be their pastor, and the letter of Mr. Thorpe accepting the call.

The record of the Trinitarian Cong'l Church endorsing the call was also read. It was voted that the papers presented be deemed satisfactory. Mr. Thorpe read a statement of his religious history and of his theological belief. It was voted that these statements are satisfactory. The council then voted to be by themselves.

In private session it was unanimously voted to proceed with the ordination and installation service and the scribe, Rev. S.K. Didriksen and the candidate were appointed a committee to arrange for the order of service in the evening.

They submitted the following program:
1. Organ voluntary
2. Statement by Moderator
3. Reading of Record of Council
4. Invocation - Rev D.M. Didriksen
5. Reading of scripture - Rev N.C. Barrie
6. Solo - Miss Jenny L. Hatch

7. Sermon - Rev. F.E. Emerick
8. Hymn
9. Ordaining and Installing Prayer - Rev Joshua Coit
10. Right Hand of Fellowship - Rev Edw. E. Bradley
11. Charge to the Pastor - Rev Edwin Smith
12. Address to the People - Rev. S.K. Didriksen
13. Quartet
14. Concluding Prayer - Rev Calvin Keyser
15. Hymn
16. Benediction by the Pastor

It was voted to dissolve at the end of the evening service.

Voted to take a recess until 7 o'clock.

The service as arranged was followed and Mr. Thorpe was ordained and installed Pastor of the Branch Scandinavian Trinitarian Church of Concord Mass.

Rev Edwin Smith, Moderator

Rev. W.W. Campbell, Scribe

The now Reverend Thorpe was installed as an associate pastor of Trinitarian with primary responsibilities for the Scandinavian work. His salary was $600 (approximately $16,300 in 2017 dollars) per year, paid mainly by the Scandinavians, although part of his salary was covered by a yearly donation from the Massachusetts Home Missionary Society, as well as occasional gifts from the Scandinavian Alliance Mission (founded by Fredrik Franson, later renamed The Evangelical Alliance Mission, or TEAM). Meanwhile, Rev. Thorpe continued to work at his shoe store and also served in his various official positions at Trinitarian (deacon and clerk). He served as the Scandinavian Branch pastor from 1894-1901, again from 1906-1913, and

Rev. Ole O. Thorpe
(1894-1901, 1906-1913, 1914)

also for a short time as interim pastor during 1914. His heart was never far from the work even when he wasn't serving in an official capacity, and his efforts were blessed by God. He also faithfully supported the Branch financially even when he was not the pastor.

Rev. Thorpe was also active in the Free Church movement through at least part of his time in ministry. As described earlier, from 1891 through 1895 he served as chairman of the Eastern Norwegian-Danish Evangelical Free Church Association. He was elected again in 1897, after which he was succeeded by Severin Didriksen, who by this time was serving in New Haven, CT, the host church of the annual conference that year.[3] He also continued to preach occasionally (two or three times per year) at the Boston (Roxbury) church for their annual missions conference and other times as needed.[4]

The Scandinavian Branch held Norwegian worship services in the vestry every Sunday and Wednesday evening, plus frequent Thursday evening prayer services in homes. On Sunday mornings some of the adults attended the American worship services, and the children attended the American Sunday School classes. Members of the Branch were actually members of the Trinitarian Church, and some of them (Lars and Rudolph Petersen and Ole Thorpe, for example) served in high offices at Trinitarian such as deacon, clerk, and members of the standing committee. The Branch kept its own financial records, but reported them in the Trinitarian annual reports.

In the 1899 Trinitarian annual report, we read:

> The same is to be said of the Scandinavian Department of our work, under the efficient and devoted care of our brother, Rev. Ole O. Thorpe. We feel that he is deserving of greatest encouragement in his endeavors, and that his work reacts most favorably upon our general church life. His services Sunday and Wednesday evenings have been well attended, the average during the year 1898 having been, respectively, 39 and 37, and still continuing good. A Thursday evening prayer meeting is also maintained at private houses, and is a helpful spiritual agency. Our prayer is that God may constantly bless this work, and that many through it may be saved in Christ.[5]

In the 1900 annual report, it appears that much of the preaching for the Norwegian services was provided by Rev. L. J. Pedersen from the Boston EFC, and from Nikolai Berg (N.B.) Ursin as resident pastor. Ursin was a recent immigrant from Norway, and also probably a student.

On 3 February 1900, Rev. Thorpe conducted the ceremony for the marriage of Anton and Pauline (Christiansen) Hoff. Sometime shortly afterward, the Hoffs began hosting a newly-formed *Norske Ungdoms Forening* (Norwegian Young People's Society) in their home on Union Street in Concord.[6] Many of the young people in this group (including John Swen) went on to become charter members and leaders in the church.

On 1 March 1901, Rev. Thorpe wrote the following letter of resignation to his flock:

> To the Trinitarian Cong'l Church, Concord Mass.
>
> Dear Brethren,
>
> Early in the spring of 1894 I had the honor of receiving a unanimous call to be your pastor and teacher, a call which I accepted as a call from God. The success of our labors together, and the many tokens of love and esteem by which you have shown your appreciation, have further strengthened my belief that I did not misunderstand the will of God.
>
> The only thing I regret, in looking back upon these years is, that I feel that I have not fully realized that which I so fondly expected as a fruit of our labor, namely: To enlist the cooperation of the majority of the Scandinavian population of our town in the interest of the church. To foster a stronger sense for religious and spiritual things, and to lead the people up to a higher life both morally and spiritually. This has been my great aim, and the highest ideal of my life, during my Pastoral work among you.
>
> Some of the reasons why I have not been able to bring about these results are in my mind, <u>First</u>: My own inability to fill the position as your spiritual leader, and <u>Secondly</u>: The lack of interest shown by a great number of the people, by reason of which I failed to secure a sufficient support to carry on the work.
>
> This convinces me that the time has come, when a change in the pastoral office may prove beneficial and be the means of promoting a greater interest for the work of Christ in this office.
>
> Therefore: after prayerful consideration, I herewith tender the resignation of my office and return to you the

charge entrusted to me seven and one half years ago, the resignation to take effect on 31st day of May, 1901, and I ask you to unite with me at your earliest convenience in calling a council to dissolve the now existing relation between pastor and people.

Affectionately

Ole O. Thorpe

Concord March 1st 1901.[7]

THE OPEN AIR SERVICE

The open air service was largely attended Sunday afternoon. All seats were occupied with a good sprinkling on terra firma. The music was furnished by Joseph Dominico with accordion. The preacher was Rev Ole O. Thorpe, the well known Norwegian minister of Concord. With commanding presence and a fine delivery Mr. Thorpe held the attention of the audience to the finish. Mr. Porter of Concord accompanied Mr. Thorpe and added much to the interest of the service.

—Concord Enterprise, 9 July 1902. The service was held in Maynard.

According to the tradition of the Congregational churches, the covenant between pastor and congregation is not taken lightly, and to dissolve this covenant, either through resignation or dismissal, required an ecclesiastical council similar to one for a call or ordination. It was therefore a strong signal of their recognition of the Scandinavian Branch as a distinct church that a council was called for this purpose. This council was convened on 29 May 1901, and included delegates and pastors from the Lincoln and Acton churches, plus the West Union Congregational church, and the Norwegian church from Boston (Rev. L. J. Pedersen) attended. There were also three other individuals from Boston, including Rev. Morten Olsen, Rev. Carl. M. Jacobsen, and Rev. D.M. Didriksen (one of the founders of the Boston church).[8]

On the evening of 31 May, the congregation unanimously adopted the following statement of support for Rev. Thorpe:

In giving our endorsement to the acceptance of the resignation of Rev. Ole O. Thorpe by the Scandinavian Branch of this church, we desire to place on record our sense of the ability and faithfulness of Mr. Thorpe in caring for this

department of our work. We yield with reluctance and
regret to his own sense of duty in deciding that he cannot
longer continue it. He has our highest confidence and
esteem. We recommend him heartily to the confidence of
the churches of Christ and of his brethren in the ministry.
He has repeatedly occupied our pulpit and always
acceptably. We wish for him the largest measure of success
in whatever service the Lord may appoint for him in his
Kingdom.

Voted that a copy of this minute be sent to Rev. Ole O.
Thorpe.

Yours in Christian Fellowship, Benj. Moody, Clerk pro-
tem[9]

After Rev. Thorpe's resignation, Rev. Sigvert Andersen from Chicago
Theological Seminary arrived in August to carry on the work.[10] His
ministry evidently did not last long, as he is not mentioned in the 1902
annual report, nor in any of the official Trinitarian records. We know
he served in Concord for at least a few months, because he preached at
the Roxbury church on 25 August 1901.[11] What became of him after that
is unknown, for he does not appear in any list of Free Church pastors
after this time. After he left Concord, the preaching ministry was filled
by various preachers and lay people. Rev. Tewksbury also gladly helped
when he was able. In the 1904 annual report, we read:

The Sunday evening Scandinavian has been continued,
with preaching by clergymen from Boston or elsewhere,
and occasionally by Mr. Thorpe. That of Wednesday
evening has been suspended since March, in consequence,
mainly, of the difficulty of securing preachers both for this
and Sunday evening.

We trust that for their own greater good, and that of
their children, our Scandinavian friends may be more and
more inclined to connect themselves with our English
services of worship; to which they are always most
welcome.[12]

In the annual report of the Eastern Evangelical Free Church Association
of 1903, Concord did not send a delegate, but Rudolph Petersen sent a
written report on their status:

As you know, we have no preacher here, but the meetings
have been well maintained and have been well attended.

Many have throughout the year sought the Lord, so we have the belief that the meetings have not been held in vain. We hope that God will send us his blessing in greater measure hereafter. Pray for us, friends, that God may further bless us in the future.

On behalf of the congregation, your little brother in the Lord, R. Petersen.[13]

For a couple of years, from the end of 1906 until November 1908, Rev. N.B. Ursin, by now a graduate of Chicago Theological Seminary, again served as resident pastor.[14],[15] While in Concord this time, he married Olava Larsen. The wedding took place on 18 March 1908, conducted by Rev. L.J. Pedersen from the Boston/Roxbury church. Shortly after his marriage, Rev. Ursin and his wife left for Waupaca, Wisconsin to take on a new pastorate. He went on to pastor numerous Norwegian Lutheran churches in Michigan and Wisconsin. In November 1908, Rev. Ole O. Thorpe resumed his ministry as pastor. However, no council was convened to reinstall him.

Nikolai Berg (N.B.) Ursin (1906-1908)

Although they were formally a part of Trinitarian Congregational, the Branch continued to maintain close ties with other Norwegian Evangelical Free Churches through the Eastern EFC Association, and especially the young work in Boston. The Boston church often shared special services with the Scandinavian Branch, providing pulpit supply when needed. There was clearly a close bond between the two churches. During the Branch's pastoral vacancy from 1901 to 1907, the Boston church often provided much of the pulpit supply, mainly from their pastor, Rev. L.J. Pederson. Rev. Thorpe continued to help as well with occasional preaching, and the senior pastor of Trinitarian, Rev. Tewksbury, also gladly helped when he was able. [16]

During this time the Norwegian-Danish Evangelical Free Church Association was becoming stronger and more formalized. In 1910, Rev. L.J. Pedersen from the Boston church resigned to take on the leadership of a new Bible Institute and Academy of the Norwegian Free

Churches of North America in Rushford, MN. This school provided undergraduate-level theological training for free church pastors for many years. Also, the Eastern and Western Evangelical Free Church Associations were becoming more closely knit. In 1910, they began publishing their annual reports together and sent delegates to a national conference. In 1912, the national Norwegian-Danish Evangelical Free Church Association was incorporated in the state of Minnesota. The Scandinavian Branch maintained close ties and membership in the national and eastern Evangelical Free Church Associations, and often sent delegates to the national and eastern conferences when they were able.

In 1912, Rev. Thorpe again felt he could no longer continue to bear the responsibility of pastoring the church, so he tendered his resignation, but continued to preach until June 1913, after which Theodor Jensen from the Norwegian Evangelical Free Church of Brooklyn, NY, and a recent graduate from Chicago Theological Seminary, arrived to take his place. On 28 January 1914 an ecclesiastical council was con-

Young People's Society, picture given to Pauline and Anton Hoff, 22 October 1905. Back row L-R: Oleanna Christiansen, Christian Olsen, John Swen, Unknown, Unknown, Gena Lundaleus. Middle: Unknown, Martha Gundersen, Anders Overgaard, Unknown, Unknown. Seated: Unknown, Unknown. Courtesy of the Hoff/Olsen family.

vened for his ordination and installation over the Scandinavian Branch.[17] But he served only until the beginning of September 1914, after which Rev. Thorpe again assumed interim duties for about four months.

During this interim time, there arose a question about the viability of the Branch, as it appeared the work might be running out of steam. On 16 November 1914, a meeting was held in Pastor Tewksbury's study:

> Monday, November 16, 1914
>
> At the request of Dr. F.E. Emrich, Secretary of the Massachusetts Home Missionary Society, a joint meeting of the Church and of the Standing Committees, of which meeting all the members of the committees had been notified by the clerk, was held in the pastor's study, this evening.
>
> There were present of the Church Committee: Dea. Thomas Todd, Dea. Lars Peterson, Dea. Benjamin Moody, Charles R. Borland, the pastor and the clerk, and of the Standing Committee: Thomas Todd, Jr., and Charles H. Towle. Also, there were present, Dr. Emrich and Rev. John J. Walker, treasurer of the above named Society.
>
> The clerk was informed that Mr. Ole O. Thorpe of the Standing Committee was confined at home, by illness.
>
> Dr. Emrich stated that his object in asking for the meeting was to learn the judgment of the committees as to continuing the former annual appropriation of $240 hitherto made by the Society, toward the maintenance of the work of the "Scandinavian Branch" of the church.
>
> After full and free exchange of opinion by all members of the committees, it appeared to be the sense of the meeting, with no non-concurring voice, that the appropriation should be continued.
>
> The meeting was informal. The importance of the Scandinavian work, as a department of the church, was recognized, and the friendliest feeling for it was indicated by all. [18]

Frederick E. Emrich, who years before had been a driving force behind the formation of the Western Association of the Norwegian-Danish Free Church, was now secretary of the Massachusetts Home Mission Society. From at least 1913 he had taken an active interest in the Scandinavian Branch, and the warm affection the worshipers had for him was evident in the annual reports of the Trinitarian Church for at least six years. He did a great deal to keep the work alive and encourage the group to press on.[19]

Rev. Adolph O. Huseby assumed the pastoral duties of the Branch around Christmas 1914. Rev. Huseby, also a graduate of Chicago Theological Seminary, served until 1919.[20]

A renewed application for aid was made by the Branch to the Massachusetts Home Missionary Society the following November.[21] This request was granted.

The Branch did not seem to operate on a budget, but simply accounted for contributions and expenses as they came in. The annual report for the year 1913 (a particularly good year) was as follows (as reported by treasurer Emil O. Thorpe, younger brother of Ole O. Thorpe):[22]

Income:

Balance on hand 1 January 1913	51.71
Collections for the year	273.39
Monthly contribution	174.00
Home Mission	210.00
Bazaar	72.15
Basket Party	18.82
17 May festival (Norwegian Independence Day)	18.50
4 July	16.00
Christmas celebration	13.29
Mrs. Trask	3.00
Totals	850.86

Expenses:

Pastor's Salary	630.00
Pianist	15.00
Communion	2.50
Contribution to Home Missions	25.80
Mrs. Andersen India (missionary)	14.28
Pastor Pedersen Rushford (special speaker)	14.00
Balance, 1 January 1914	149.28

While Rev. Ole O. Thorpe owned his own home on Hubbard Street, the other pastors were expected to acquire their own lodging. For example,

Rev. Huseby was a boarder at 31 Stow Road (just down Hubbard Street from the church) during his ministry.

During the years of Rev. Huseby's ministry the Branch struggled to maintain momentum. Much of this can be attributed to the fact that the War in Europe had essentially shut down immigration from Europe. As Rev. Huseby reported in 1918:

**Adolph O. Huseby
(1914-1919)**

> ...The average attendance has been: Sunday evenings, 39; Wednesday evenings, 15. Had the times been as before the war, the attendance would surely have been much larger. Since the war broke out in Europe, we haven't had a single new-comer among our church people. And besides that, some of our old "churchgoers" have moved away, and still others have died. Thus, after all, we are satisfied with the numbers we have had.[23]

In 1919, Rev. Huseby resigned and left in discouragement. Committed membership (i.e., those who regularly contributed to the work) had dropped precipitously, and the work was in disarray. In the final annual report submitted by the Branch, Anton Hoff wrote:

> Rev. Adolph O. Huseby, who, coming from Wisconsin, began his work with the Branch at the beginning of 1915, continued in its charge until the spring of 1919. His preaching was thoroughly evangelical, marked by sincere belief, and a strong desire to advance the work. While here, he made 1,248 calls, baptized 20 children, and received 11 members into the church.[24]

Arlo Odegaard, in his book *With Singleness of Heart*, was less complimentary about the ministry of Rev. Huseby while at Concord. He states:

> This choice was most unfortunate, as the church suffered considerably under his pastorate of almost four years' duration, and he left the work in a poor and run-down condition. He spoke out strongly against the Free Church, and we find his name was stricken from the list of clergymen of the Free Church in 1927.[25]

Regardless of who or what was to blame, the attendance and health of the Branch in 1919 was of great concern and would require intervention. There was discussion of discontinuing it altogether.

During the entire twenty-six years of the Scandinavian Branch, services were held in the vestry of the church, which they were granted free of charge. The congregation always considered themselves a welcome part of the Trinitarian congregation.

But as the Branch struggled, pressure increased to give up and merge with the American church. This was evident even in the annual reports, for example, from 1904:

> ... We trust that for their own greater good, and that of their children, our Scandinavian friends may be more and more inclined to connect themselves with our English services of worship; to which they are always most welcome.[26]

The feelings of the mother church grew more intense, as seen in 1911:

> The feeling grows that those of Scandinavian birth, who have come to understand English as well practically as native Americans, should for their own sake as well as for their children identify themselves more largely with our American Lord's Day and weekly services, in which they would be cordially welcomed both for their presence and sustaining help. We have but one church. Those in the Norwegian section are members of the American church as much as others; they are counted on its roll. The wheel within the wheel is not to revolve by itself, but to move with the larger circle, as a part of the whole. So will the best results come to each, even those of largest divine blessing upon both.[27]

These sentiments were repeated again in 1914.

Why didn't the Norwegian church simply assimilate into the larger congregation? They do not appear to have been motivated simply by a

---

SOCIAL TIME

Wednesday evening the Norwegian branch of the Trinitarian church held a very successful entertainment and social hour in the church vestry, in memory of the 10th complete independence of Norway. The entertainment consisted of a musical program followed by interesting addresses, after which coffee, cake and sandwiches were served.
—*Concord Enterprise*, 12 June

desire to maintain a separate immigrant community. Like most immigrant families, they sought to become Americanized as soon as possible after arrival in their new country. Their children were expected to learn English, and Norwegian was seldom spoken in the home, at least not in front of the children. The members of the Branch spoke fluent English, even if they enjoyed hearing their native tongue in the church services. The strongest argument in support of language not being a factor is this: a mere three years after the founding of the church at Lang Street, services were being held in both Norwegian and English.

Young People's Society. Standing, L-R: Martin Knutsen, Gena Lundaleus, Matilda Jörgensen, Pauline Knutsen, John Swen. Seated, L-R: Christian Olsen, Julia Swen Johnson, Chris Carlson, Martha Gundersen, Thora Jörgensen. Courtesy of the Hoff/Olsen family.

But other forces were at work. The small congregation in Concord was part of the Free Church movement, encouraged by the people who had brought it to Boston and who supported it from Chicago. Through all their years, they continued to be an active part in the new Norwegian-Danish Evangelical Free Church Association even though they belonged to the Congregational church.

As David Gustafson summarizes:

> a new identity emerged among these Danes and Norwegians that centered in evangelical ecumenicalism–cooperation among evangelicals as taught and demonstrated by Moody. Furthermore, this new identity included preaching the free grace of God, calling inquirers to personal faith, and holding to the premillennial return of Christ's Second Coming. This new identity was no doubt the reason why the Norwegian-Danish Evangelical Free Church remained distinct from the American Congregationalists, and eventually dissolved their affiliation with them. There was a closer identity, for instance, with Moody and his view of Christ's return, and Franson and the Scandinavian Alliance Mission. As the name indicates, the Evangelical Free viewed themselves neither as Lutherans, nor Baptists, nor Congregationalists, nor Methodists, but as free Evangelicals, and they cherished their freedom.[28]

And so even after twenty-six years had gone by, the hope of having their own house of worship was never forgotten, nor did it ever die. But in the interim, international tensions, a raging world war and growing resistance to immigration began to sap the strength of the immigrant community. Time was running short.

It must be stated that throughout this time the Women's Missionary Society also continued to do its part to help keep the dream alive, setting aside their monthly dues for a building fund.[29] After World War I, they raised their dues to twenty-five cents, enabling them to help with other church expenses and the pastor's salary.

Chapter 3:
A Place to Call Home

The Norwegian Zion Evangelical Free Church
(1919-1921)

Norwegian Zion Evangelical Free Church, 1920.

The catalyst for change was the resignation of Rev. Huseby in the spring of 1919. The group was already declining, due mainly to a dearth of immigration before and during the War. They could no longer count on a natural infusion of new blood from recent immigrants. They had no pastor, and limited resources to pay for a new one. The small group was discouraged, and at a crossroads. The way forward seemed impossible.

**Rev. E.M. Andersen
(1919-1921)**

In other words, God had them right where He wanted them.

God had already been at work. As early as 1917, Mr. and Mrs. Oscar Levine, leaders in the Roxbury church and members of the Free Church Home Missionary Society, had argued for hiring a traveling field missionary to bolster the outreach works in rural Massachusetts such as in Lowell, Worcester, Fall River, and Concord. But there was no money to pay for such a mission. At the 1917 meeting of the Home Missionary Society, held in conjunction with the Eastern Free Church annual meeting in Portland ME, they had agreed that the best approach to home missions was to pool their resources and merge with the Eastern Free Church Association.[1] Now the whole Eastern Association had a home mission department. It was just a matter of time to percolate the vision through the larger group.

At the May 1919 meeting of the Eastern Free Church Association held in Boston, Mr. and Mrs. Levine saw their dream come true. One of the main topics of discussion was the feasibility of expanding their home mission work to buy some tents for revival meetings, and employ a full-time field evangelist. As reported in the Norwegian Evangelical Free Churches Newsletter for the Brooklyn and Jersey City churches:

> "Of the provisions adopted, the Internal Mission was of particular importance. A brother was chosen to travel around our field, and especially then to visit the more neglected places, if possible to help the cause of God. It was also the idea to get a tent, set it up in a city, here or there,

to proclaim the gospel. Let us advance this cause and the spread of the kingdom of God, and support it by our means."[2]

Support it they did.

The excitement was so intense that four people who attended the meeting immediately pledged $250 toward the estimated $1500 that would be needed for the tents and other expenses.[3] E.M. Andersen, a young man who was serving in his first full-time

> E. M. Andersen announces in a letter from Concord that they are having a wonderful time in Concord with the meetings in the tent. Not a few have sought the Lord, and it is a great revival for the faithful. May the good work continue.
>
> —De Norske Ev. Frimenigheders Blad, August 1919, p2.

pastorate at the Norwegian Evangelical Free Church of Jersey City, N.J. ("The Vroom Street Church"), was extended a call by the association to become a full-time field evangelist, which he accepted on a temporary basis, taking a leave of absence from his position in Jersey City.

Rev. O.M. Jonswold, who had pastored in Boston until 1918, was now serving the 52nd Street Free Church in Brooklyn. He attended the Boston conference, also taking the opportunity to visit and encourage the brethren in Concord during their Wednesday evening service. He also undoubtedly discussed the situation in Concord with John Swen who was the delegate from Concord to the Boston conference.

Concord was the logical place to begin the new mission work. Plans were drawn up to hold four weeks of tent meetings in August at the vacant lot on Lang Street owned by Olaf Westby, a member of the Scandinavian Branch. They were fruitful meetings:

> ...revival fires began; new interest in the work was evident; souls were saved and others restored in the faith.[4]

The excitement of seeing souls won for Christ greatly encouraged the group. On 12 September 1919, meeting in the tent that had housed the evangelistic meetings, the small congregation agreed by consensus that it was time to build. Translated from the Norwegian minutes:

> There was a congregation meeting on September 12, 1919 in the tent, where we met to discuss the future and to try to build a house of God as a house of our own for the sake of God's Word.

Pastor Andersen read from the Word of God and prayed the Lord's blessing. He was elected chairman of the meeting, and Mr. Hoff as secretary.

There, a solemn case was presented to the friends whether we should, with God's blessing, be allowed to build our own house so that we could gather together around God's Word.

All attendants were invited to express their opinion in this matter. All those present expressed a longing for their own home, and it was therefore decided then and there that a house would be built. This is not something that has sprung up in a hurry, but has been a desire for almost 30 years, since we on November 16, 1893 were united with the Americans and stood under them, praying with them while we lacked strength enough to launch out into the deep. My [Mr. Hoff's] prayer is that it will be possible to lead it forward to completion without encountering many hindrances.[5]

Six men were charged with overseeing the project of acquiring the land and erecting a building: John Swen, Anton Hoff, John Andersen, Christian Monsen, Lars Petersen, and Rudolph Petersen.

Pastor Andersen, encouraged by the Spirit's work through the tent meetings, decided to accept the Eastern Association's call as permanent field missionary. He committed to see the construction of the Concord church to completion, also volunteering to help raise money for the project. But first he had to make a three-month trip home to make arrangements and complete his service in Jersey City. During that period, Rev. B.A. Jonassen, pastor of the free church in Tottenville (Staten Island) NY, was asked to serve as interim preacher until Pastor Andersen could return.

Within a week an agreement was reached with the owner of the vacant lot, Olaf Westby, to purchase it for a sum of $300. The lot

Sunday the 4th of January the congregation in Jersey City held a farewell party for Pastor Andersen and his family. After a little trip to his sister in Canada, Brother Andersen will travel to Concord for a few months. Brother Eikland is in the congregation in Jersey for a time until he and family come to South America. The congregation has called Prof. L. J. Pedersen.

— *De Norske Ev. Frimenigheders Blad*, January 1920, p3.

was worth twice as much, but Mr. Westby contributed half the price of the lot to the new Church. Since the church was not yet a legal entity, the lot was deeded to the three men who were acting as trustees at the time: Lars Petersen, Christian Monsen, and Christian Martinsen.

Excitement among the small group was palpable, although it was not shared by everyone in town. Understandably, there were many from within Trinitarian Congregational Church who were saddened by the impending departure of so many from within the Norwegian community. But there was also discouragement from the community at large, as seen in a letter to the editor of the *Concord Enterprise*, dated 8 October 1919:

Another Norwegian Church

Editor of the Enterprise:

It is reported that the Scandinavian branch of the Trinitarian Church has about decided to build a church for itself on Lang st[sic], where, it is said, a plot of ground has been offered for such a structure. The branch has been in existence for about 25 years, worshiping in the chapel of the Trinitarian Church and having the advantages of a church home without the heavy responsibilities of maintaining a church building. Its pastor has been, in effect, an associate pastor with that of the larger organization, and while the older members have enjoyed the privilege of hearing preaching in the dear familiar language of the home country, the children have come into the Sunday school of the church and become an increasing and important factor in the life of the church.

Now it is proposed to terminate the arrangement which has been of great advantage to the Scandinavian people and has imposed no heavy burden on them, and to erect a church building and assume the responsibility of keeping up the activities of the organization, unaided. To many this seems a large undertaking for a company not too numerous, and especially so at this time of very high-cost building, and high prices for fuel and other, necessary furnishings.

It would seem to many to be a most unfortunate and ill-advised move, not only as affecting the Scandinavian element themselves, but also the general well-being of the religious life of the community. It is a move entirely contrary to the trend of the times, which is toward church union rather than increase in the number of organizations. Also — and this is perhaps most important — it is a step away from the ideal of Americanization, which is a dominant thought today. Under the plan hitherto followed, the children came into the older and larger church as equal sharers in the instruction and ideals of democratic America. They blended in the most ready and complete fashion with the people of the English-speaking stock. To carry out the proposition of a new church body would cut off the youth from these obvious advantages and tend to restrict them in narrower lines.

The Scandinavian element in our population is highly regarded and their relations with the community are most cordial. In trade and in employment, their interests are linked closely with those of the others, and it would seem most deplorable to diminish the cordiality and closeness of these relations by any division among the people. As one who is not a member of the Trinitarian Church in this town, but who is keenly interested in its welfare and in that of the Scandinavian element, the writer sincerely hopes that the leaders of this new project will reflect carefully before committing themselves to the enterprise, which would entail great burdens on themselves and would mean a distinct loss to their children.

Yours truly, A CITIZEN.[6]

In an indication that the Norwegian group was not going to be so easily discouraged this time, a response was published the following week:

To The Public

In regard to the article entitled "Another Norwegian Church," printed in the Concord Enterprise of Oct 8, 1919, would like to inform the writer and the public of a few points concerning the Scandinavian branch of the Trinitarian Congregational church.

1. The fact is true that the Scandinavian people are making plans for their house of worship, but this idea has been in the minds of the Scandinavian people for many years.

2. Although they have had the advantages of a church home, they have had the responsibility of paying their own

expenses and, also, having the added expense of helping to support the Trinitarian church. The pastor, always called the associate pastor with that of the larger association, has been supported by the Scandinavian branch itself.

The children, of course, have been attending the Sunday school of the church, and this has been appreciated by the parents. However, the intention was and is to maintain the Sunday school in the new church in the English-speaking language, which they realize is an important factor in the life of the church and for Americanization as well.

Why should the children be restricted to narrow lines, when they will no doubt get as much instruction in religion as before, and the parents and others who have been born and brought up across in the Scandinavian countries have a thorough knowledge of the Bible as religion was one of the most important studies in the public schools.

Why should the closeness of the relations of these people diminish so quickly when their work will be carried on practically on the same basis as before with the one exception that they wish a house of their own?

They do realize as the writer states that this is a large undertaking, but if all those who profess and seem to be so interested in the Scandinavian element, would help towards this enterprise, if not more than with a kind word, would be greatly appreciated by "these people."

ANOTHER CITIZEN.[7]

This time, their hope would not be thwarted or delayed.

In 1918 and 1919 Trinitarian advertised the Scandinavian services in the Concord Enterprise newspaper less regularly than in the past. The last time Trinitarian advertised Scandinavian services in the Concord Enterprise was the 7 May 1919 issue. Odegaard, in his description of the Scandinavian Branch, stated that the church became inactive after the resignation of Rev. Huseby,[8] but clearly some people continued to gather regularly after this time. Whether they continued to meet in the vestry at Trinitarian or elsewhere (perhaps in homes) is unclear. The following year, while construction progressed, morning and evening services continued under the leadership of Rev. E.M. Andersen, but the advertisements do not indicate where they met. Most significantly, they started to refer to themselves as the Norwegian

Evangelical Free Church instead of the Scandinavian Branch of Trinitarian Congregational Church:

NORWEGIAN EVANGELICAL FREE CHURCH
Sunday School at 10 o'clock.
Morning service at 11 o'clock.
Young People's meeting at 5.
Rev. Mr. O. Thorpe will deliver a message to the young people at 5. Refreshments will be served and everybody is welcome to the services.
The Dorcas sewing circle meets Thursday afternoon at 4 o'clock, and Captain and Mrs Gabriel, Salvation Army workers will speak. All Scandinavian women are invited in the afternoon at 4. The captain will also speak in the evening in Norwegian.
Evening services on Sunday are at 8 o'clock. Everybody welcome.

—*Concord Weekly Enterprise*, 30 March 1920, p3.

Building plans and preparations proceeded quickly, with many people donating their money and time. They prepared to lay the cornerstone at 3:00 p.m. on the first Sunday in May 1920. Pastor Andersen opened the meeting and brother John Swen read God's Word and prayed. It

---

CORNERSTONE LAID
Exercises Took Place Sunday Afternoon — Church Will Be Beautiful When Completed
The cornerstone of the Norwegian Evangelical Free Church on Lang St was laid on Sunday afternoon at 3:30.
A large crowd assembled for the occasion, which was marked by two very inspiring talks by Rev. I. Loe of Boston and Rev. E. Bonnevie Kluver, pastor of the local Methodist Episcopal church. The cornerstone was laid by the pastor, Rev. E.M. Anderson.
A chorus from the Boston Free church sang at both the afternoon and evening services. Their singing was greatly enjoyed by all.
The church on Lang st.[sic] is a modern structure and when finished will be a beautiful building. It will have a complete basement and a large auditorium.
The Norwegian people of Concord and vicinity are looking forward great anticipation to the completion of their new home, for which they have longed many years.

— *Concord Weekly Enterprise*, 12 May 1920, p6.

was a moving ceremony at which Oscar
Levine read Scripture and gave the
invocation, Pastor Ingvald J. Loe from
the Boston Free Church and Rev. E.
Bonnevie   Kluver   from   the
Scandinavian   Methodist   Episcopal
Church of Concord preached, the choir
from the Boston Free Church sang, and
Pastor Andersen laid the cornerstone.

The building was mostly completed by mid-October, and on Friday
evening, 29 October 1920, the first official congregational meeting was
held in the church building. Pastor Andersen was chosen as the
moderator for the meeting, and Rudolph Petersen was appointed
secretary. Twenty-nine people rose to become charter members, of
which twenty-one belonged to the Trinitarian Congregational Church.
A letter was written to Trinitarian requesting that their names be
removed from the rolls:

Concord, Mass.
Nov. 8, 1920
The Trinitarian Church of Concord, Mass.

Dear Fellow Workers:

The Norwegian Evangelical Free Church of Concord, Mass.
is now completed and we wish to take this opportunity to
thank the fellow members of this church for all the privileges we have enjoyed as members and fellow workers.

Before we withdraw our names we wish to acknowledge
the kindness of letting us have the church at any time and
the janitor service, light, and use of the church parlors, for
all these privileges, we extend a most heartfelt gratitude,
and assure you all of the silent tribute which shall always
remain in the hearts of the Norwegian people for all these
kindnesses.

Though we, the undersigned, withdraw our names from
this Trinitarian Church, we'll never forget all these benefits
bestowed upon us.

Likewise a personal gratitude to Rev. Mr. Tewksbury,
who has been and always will be a most welcome guest
among us.

Mr. and Mrs. John Anderson

Mr. and Mrs. Christian Martinson
Mr. and Mrs. Christian Monson [Monsen]
Mr. and Mrs. Alof Stansby [Olaf Stensby]
Mr. and Mrs. Thore Johnson
Mrs. A. Kristafferson [Christoffersen]
Mrs. Samuel Lee
Mrs. Johanne Anderson[Joanna Andersen]
Miss Pauline Knudsen
Miss Karen Olsen
Miss Matilda Jorgensen
Miss Thora Jorgensen
Mr. John Sven [Swen]
Mr. Edward Anderson
Mr. Martin O. Helsher [Martinus Helsjier]
Mr. Anton Hoff[9]

The first constitution[10] was read and adopted, and 300 copies were printed for distribution. Brief biographies of each of the charter members and friends of the church may be found in Appendix A.

The full statement of faith from the original constitution (translated from the Norwegian) follows:

1. We believe in a personal God, Father, Son and Holy Spirit—John 1:14; 14:26.

2. We believe in the verbal inspiration of the Bible—2 Tim 3:16; 2 Pet 1:21.

3. We believe that man was created in the image of God, and that he fell—and through his fall all have become sinners before God—Gen 1:27; Rom 3:23.

4. We believe that through the obedience and sufferings of Christ, and through His blood, redemption was wrought for all that would receive and believe—John 3:16; 1 Pet 1:18-19; Heb 9:36.

5. We believe that without regeneration by the Holy Spirit man is forever shut away from God—John 3:3; Mat 18:2-3.

6. We believe in the resurrection from the dead, and that both the just and the unjust shall give an account to God for their works—2 Cor 5:10; John 5:28-29.

7. We believe that Christ has a visible Church on earth, and that He is the head of the same—and every one that is born of the Spirit belongs to the Church—Mat 16:18; Eph 2:19-22; Acts 2:42.

8. We believe in baptism in the name of the Father and of the Son and of the Holy Spirit. As to age and method we give conscious liberty—Mat 28:19.

9. In that we confess these words to be the teaching of the Bible we declare ourselves willing to cooperate with all that have participated in the same faith, and with same will we work together in grace for the advancement of His kingdom.

One can easily see the influence of Moody and Franson in the statement, with strong statements about the inspiration of Scripture, the key points of personal salvation, the universal church, liberty about things which normally divide denominations, and willingness to partner with other churches (believers only but all believers). Interestingly, it says almost nothing about eschatology other than what would be familiar from the Apostles' Creed. This by no means implies that they weren't interested in the imminent return of Christ, but rather mirrors Dwight Moody's own feelings that disagreement about such things should not divide true believers. The fact that Rev. Andersen was an alumnus of Moody's own school would cause one to expect that his ministry would emphasize this.

Another insight to be gleaned from this statement of faith is the relationship of the individual free churches to the Norwegian Evangelical Free Church Association. Since 1912, the association had a twelve-point statement of faith (see Appendix D), which was a much more specific and complete synopsis of the fundamentals of the faith than the one adopted by the Concord church. It is interesting that the NEFCA statement of faith was not used by the new church. Rather, the Concord creed is remarkably similar to the one used by the Vroom Street Free Church in Jersey City where E.M. Andersen served before coming to Concord.[11] In any event, the relationship of the individual churches with the Free Church Association did not require them to adopt a common creed. This was in keeping with the spirit of the Free Churches.

Conspicuously missing from the list of charter members were Lars and Rudolph Petersen, Olaf Westby and Ole O. Thorpe. Lars (68), Rudolph (52) and Ole (62) were older now, and were deeply entrenched in the ministry at Trinitarian. Between them they had been members of Trinitarian for a total of 100 years! They held numerous important elected offices and were deeply committed to the welfare of Trinitarian, which had ministered to them for so long. Nevertheless, they committed time and resources to the new endeavor. Lars served as trustee for the new church and held the deed for the land until the new church was officially incorporated and ownership of the land could be transferred. Rudolph acted as church secretary until the church was incorporated. All three of them attended Sunday evening services for several years, while continuing to attend morning services at Trinitarian. Rudolph shows up as a regular giver to the Free Church as late as 1929. Olaf Westby's wife's health may have prevented his participation in the new endeavor. She passed away in 1923, and a few years later he moved to Littleton, MA. Similarly, Ole Thorpe's wife Pauline's health may have been a factor, as she died of a stroke less than two years after the dedication of the Lang Street building.

The building was formally dedicated to the glory of the Lord on 14 November 1920, and a four-day Bible conference followed, with

DEDICATION SERVICE

The Norwegian Zion Evening[sic] Free Church of Concord, Mass., will be dedicated on Sunday, November 14th. Three big meetings will be held at 10:30 a.m., 3:30 p.m. and 7:30 in the evening.

Speakers from New York, New Jersey and other places will participate in all the services. A special program of music has been arranged for all the services.

Refreshments will be served between the afternoon and evening services. The afternoon meeting will be conducted chiefly in the English and Rev. N.W. Nelson from Brooklyn, NY will be the chief speaker.

A hearty invitation is extended to all.

—*Concord Weekly Enterprise*, 10 November 1920, p4.

preaching by Rev. N.W. Nelsen from Brooklyn, NY, the chairman of the national Norwegian-Danish Evangelical Free Church Association. For the congregation, the day was bittersweet. They knew they would soon have to say farewell to Pastor Andersen, who planned to return to New Jersey, having completed his job of establishing the church. They sent him off with prayer and gratitude, and on 29 November, they agreed to call Rev. Olaf Thompsen from the Salem Evangelical Free Church in West New Brighton, Staten Island, NY to replace him, starting on 1 February 1921. His salary was set at $125 per month, plus vegetables and wood. Rev. Thompsen became the third consecutive pastor to arrive from the greater New York City area free churches to serve in Concord.

John Swen was chosen as the church's first elder, with John Andersen and Christian Martinsen as deacons. The secretary was Rudolph Petersen, and Anton Hoff was selected as treasurer (he had served for years in that capacity at the Scandinavian Branch). The first trustees were John Andersen, Edward Andersen, Christian Monsen, John Swen and Olaf Stensby. Auditors were Edward Andersen and Karen Olsen.

As a side note, these events occurred contemporaneously with the ratification of the Nineteenth Amendment to the US Constitution granting women the right to vote. Many congregational churches at that time did not allow women the right to vote at church meetings. Yet there is no discussion whatsoever in the church records about whether the new constitution should permit women to vote in congregational meetings. It was just assumed. Indeed, Trinitarian had granted women the right to vote at congregational meetings back in 1868, more than twenty-five years before the Scandinavian Branch was even formed, so the issue had long since been settled. The Evangelical Free Church has never limited the vote of women members and has accepted women delegates to the national and district conferences, although the Free Church takes the position that women should not be pastors, elders, or deacons who function as elders.

In fact, the ladies of the Women's Missionary Society (WMS) had long been supporting the fledgling community. For many years the society spent so much in aid to the local church, that their foreign missions focus began to slacken. So in 1923, the Rebecca Sewing Circle was formed under the leadership of Mrs. John Andersen, and pledged support for a missionary with the Scandinavian Alliance Mission. The Circle continued until 1962, when it became the White Cross branch of the Women's Missionary Society.[12]

The church record book provides much detail about the various people who sacrificed time, money, and talents to finish the work. In all $9,931.07 was pledged or loaned, and total expenses for the land and the building were $9,748.61, for a net balance of $187.46.

One notable gift from the townsfolk at the time: a bell that used to hang in the tower of the Lang Street church, and is now on display in the foyer of Faith EFC in Acton. It is a beautiful cast brass ship's bell engraved with "Britannia 1862." This bell was donated by Miss Alicia M. Keyes and Mrs. Annie S. (Keyes) Emerson, both daughters of John Shepard Keyes. Alicia was a prominent artist and art teacher/lecturer in Concord. Her sister Annie was the wife of Edward Waldo Emerson, son of Ralph Waldo Emerson; their brother was Judge

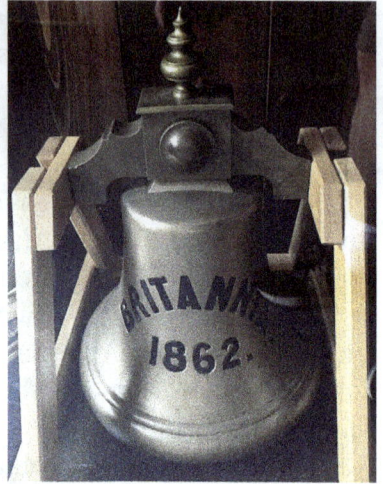

Church Bell.

Prescott Keyes, a notable district judge in Concord at the time. They were all members of First Parish (Unitarian) Church in Concord.

The bell itself came from the Steamship *Britannia*, an iron-hulled, side-wheel steamship built in Leith, Scotland, designed to run the Union Navy's blockade of the Confederate coast during the US Civil War. She was captured on 25 June 1863 and sent to Boston, where she was re-commissioned the *USS Britannia* in the Union Navy to enforce the blockade. After the war, which included several naval battles with mixed results, she was decommissioned at Philadelphia on 28 June 1865, re-documented as the *SS Britannia*, and sailed under the US flag as a merchantman ship until she was sold at auction in 1886.[13]

How the bell came into the possession of Miss Keyes is equally interesting because of its intersection with another significant piece of American history. It is said that on 19 April 1775, after the battle at the old North Bridge in Concord, a retreating British soldier took a shot at local blacksmith Elisha Jones, who was standing in the doorway of his shed. The bullet hole is still visible, earning the house the nickname "The Bullet Hole House." In time John Shepard Keyes and his wife Martha L. (Prescott) Keyes bought the house from a descendant of Elisha Jones, and in 1863 they deeded the property over to their daughter, Alicia M. Keyes.

John Shepard Keyes was a US Marshall for the district of Massachusetts (Boston) during the Civil War. In this role, he was responsible for the processing of contraband cargo and "war prize" ships that were seized from the Confederacy. Many of the ships and most of the cargo were sold at auction. The *Britannia* came under his jurisdiction before it was taken by the US Navy. Somehow, he acquired the bell when the ship was refitted for the Navy, and placed it on top of the barn of the Bullet Hole House.

Judge Prescott Keyes, Alicia's brother, described the bell and weathervane on the barn in his book, *Houses in Concord in 1885*:

> The bell on the barn was from the English blockade runner Britannia brought in and condemned in Boston [in the Civil War], and the points of the compass under the vane are the sword and oar, the badges of the Marshall's office out of the income of which it was repaired and refitted.
>
> In the spring of 1865 work was begun renovating the old house...[14]

The bell remained in the possession of Alicia until she donated it to the new church on Lang Street.

Medlemmernes Navne.

1	Mr	Anthon Hoff	Concord
2	Mr. Mrs.	John Mikkelsen	Concord
	Mrs	Kristoffersen *joined Nov. 8 – 1924*	Concord Junction
	Mr. Mrs.	Martin O Helsjer *Westford Rd.*	Concord
	Mr. Mrs.	Thora Johnsen *Lowell Rd.*	Concord
	Mr. Mrs.	Kristian Mansin	Concord Junction
	Mr. Mrs.	John Andersen	Concord Junction
	Mrs.	Samuel Lee *Grove St*	Concord Junction
	Mrs.	Mabel Hansen *Holm.*	Concord Junction
1	Miss	Thora Jörgensen *% Philip Dain*	Concord
1	Miss	Matilde Jorgensen *% H. Edmund*	Concord
	Mrs	Johanne Andersen *died June 25. 1924.*	Concord Jct.
	Mr. Mrs.	Kristian Martinsen	Concord Mass
1	Miss	Karen Olsen *Main St.*	Concord Mass
	Mr. Mrs.	Olaf Stensby *joined Nov. 8 – 1921*	Concord Mass
2	Mr. Mrs.	John Swen	Concord Mass
	Mr. Mrs.	H. Hansen	Concord Mass
1	Mrs.	Olive Andersen	Concord Junction
1	Mrs.	Pauline Knudsen *Ewen* *% E. For*	Concord.
	Mrs	Edvald Andersen	Concord Junction
	Mr. Mrs.	J. M. Hay *Died ind January 9 – 1921*	Concord
1		Ella Christoffersen joined Nov. 9. 1924.	Concord Jct.
		Annie Olsen " " "	
		Olga Hoff. " " "	nath Acton
		Alice Hoff " " "	nath Acton.
1		Inga Cahill. " " "	Concord Jct.

List of Charter Members from original church record book.

Chapter 4:
The Norwegian Evangelical Free Church

(1921-1954)

The most important source of new congregants to an ethnic church is immigration. Until the outbreak of World War I, there was a steady and healthy stream of new Norwegian blood entering the country. But during the War, immigration slowed to a trickle. After the War, the US Immigration Acts of 1921 and 1924 set quotas which effectively ended mass migration to America from most countries. Popular progressive ideologies in vogue at the time would also drive those who did make the trip to the New World to quickly assimilate into American culture. The lack of new Norwegian blood would eventually force the new little church in Concord to start reaching out to the non-Norwegian community around them.

The Early Years

Immediately after the dedication of the new building, the work prospered. Olaf Thompsen took over as pastor on 1 February 1921. Interestingly, E.M. Andersen had served as interim pastor at the Staten Island church before they called Rev. Thompsen in 1917.[1] Now he was following Andersen to Concord.

As in the Scandinavian Branch, the main worship service was held in Norwegian on Sunday evenings. English-language Sunday School classes were held on Sunday mornings.

Thanks to the help of Ole M. Dahl, an attorney from Boston who attended the Roxbury Evangelical Free Church, on 27 April 1921 the church was formally incorporated with the Commonwealth of Massachusetts as the

Rev. Olaf Thompsen and family (1921-1922)

Norwegian Evangelical Free Church of Concord. It is not clear why the word "Zion" was dropped from the name.

As mentioned earlier, the church was not a legal entity when the church property was originally purchased, so the property had been deeded to the trustees of the unincorporated society (Lars Petersen, Christian Monsen and Christian Martinsen). Trustees were elected yearly at that time, so in October 1921 the trustee board consisted of John Andersen, Edward Andersen, Christian Monsen (re-elected) and John Swen. On 28 Jan 1922, the original trustees formally deeded the property to the church in the care of the new trustees.[2]

On 21 February 1922, the Sons of Norway Tordenskjold Lodge 184 donated a beautiful clock to the church in appreciation for hosting their lodge meetings. The clock, which hangs in the current church office, still keeps good time when it is wound!

Pastor Thompsen served the flock for a little over a year before stepping down in April 1922. That December he returned to Norway, where he continued to be involved in Gospel ministry.

Rev. Thompsen's departure left the church without a regular pastor for over a year, which proved to be quite a hardship for such a young work, especially for those working among the young people. A call was extended to Pastor Robert Anders from Tottenville (Staten Island), but he declined. While the search proceeded, the ministry was maintained with help from many traveling preachers.

Finally, in April 1923 the church called Olaf M. Johnsen from Brooklyn, NY at a salary of $100 per month. After the vote, "coffee and

cake were served," as usual! Johnsen began his ministry in the latter part of May 1923, and served until August 1935, making him the longest-serving pastor until Rev. Doug Welch (1989-2005). During this time the church enjoyed growth and stability, and continued their warm relationship with the friends and brethren at the Boston (Roxbury) Free Church. The Roxbury brethren would visit the Concord church—they helped celebrate anniversaries of the Lang Street dedication, for example—and members of the Concord church would likewise attend Roxbury's special services.

Rev. Olaf Johnsen
(1923-1935)

Shortly after being called to Concord, in October 1923 Pastor Johnsen was ordained by his home church in Brooklyn. John Swen was sent to Brooklyn to represent the Concord brethren at the ordination ceremony.

Rev. Johnsen had the pleasure on 5 November 1923 of officiating at the first wedding in the new building: Mabel Monsen, daughter of Christian Monsen and Olava (Andersen) Monsen, married Ludvig Holm, son of John and Marie (Mikkelsen) Holm. Mabel was a charter member of the church. Their daughter, Marion Christiansen, currently attends the church when she is able.

On 12 August 1927, Ole O. Thorpe died. A September memorial service was held in his honor at the Trinitarian Congregational Church, at which members of the Lang Street church joined to honor the man who pastored them so faithfully in the Scandinavian Branch. Pastor Johnsen gave the opening prayer and a warm tribute to Rev. Thorpe's devoted service to the Norwegian people.

Also during Rev. Johnsen's ministry, the church began work on a new parsonage. Up to this point the pastors were responsible for their own housing. In 1925 Pastor Johnsen's address was listed as 130 Commonwealth Avenue, and in 1929 he lived at 12 Assabet Road (near the Concord Rotary today). At the 1926 annual meeting, John Swen, Anton Hoff and John Andersen were tasked to search for a possible

Marriage of Ludvig and Mabel (Monsen) Holm. Courtesy Marion Christiansen.

future home for the minister, or a suitable lot to build on at an affordable price.

In September, they came back to the congregation, suggesting that the trustees approach Lars Petersen about purchasing a vacant lot he owned on Lang Street, just down the road and across the street from the church. Lars was willing, and John Andersen, John Swen and Anders Christoffersen purchased the lot and gave it to the church, a gift that was received with gratitude.[3] In April 1928, a fund was created to finance construction of a parsonage on the lot, but contributions came in too slowly; so in November 1933 the building committee was authorized to borrow up to $3,800. Later that month, they secured a loan from the Congregational Church Building Society for $3,500, to be paid off in thirteen years, and construction began.

The Great Depression?

During the 1930s the entire country was engulfed in the Great Depression, and Massachusetts was not spared from its effects. In fact, the state had already been experiencing economic troubles due to the exodus of two of its major industries: textiles and shoe-making. Interestingly, the church did not seem to be adversely affected, judging from the minutes of the business meetings. Perhaps this was due to the type of jobs that many of the members held. There were still farmers and retailers among the congregation. The reputation of being "the servants' church" was well-earned. It is also possible that these immigrants were just frugal and better prepared for economic

IMPRESSIVE MEMORIAL SERVICE

An impressive and inspiring memorial service in honor of the late Rev. Ole O. Thorpe was held in the chapel of the Trinitarian Congregational Church Sunday evening, when grateful recognition was given to the long period of faithful service he had rendered his church and his community and the high place he held in the esteem in which he was held.

The chapel was crowded to the doors. The members of the Norwegian Evangelical Free church, descendent of the Norwegian Branch of the Trinitarian Congregational Church of which Rev. Mr. Thorpe had been pastor for 14 years, joined in the tribute.

The services opened with the singing of some of the favorite hymns of Rev. Mr. Thorpe, with Mr. Leslie R. Moore at the piano.

Rev. Olaf M. Johnson, pastor of the Evangelical Free Church offered the opening prayer. Mr. Charles H. Towle, clerk of the Trinitarian Congregational church, spoke of the long official relationship Mr. Thorpe had maintained with the Church as member of the Standing Committee, member of the Church committee, and deacon since 1924. He had been ordained minister in 1894.

Deacon Lars Peterson, who met Mr. Thorpe at the railroad station when he first came to Concord, and had been a close friend ever since, spoke of Rev. Mr. Thorpe's early life and service here. Rev. Mr. Johnson gave a feeling tribute to his devoted service to the Norwegian people; and Rev. Dr. Gail Cleland, pastor of the church, read a letter from Rev. D.F.E. Emrich, one of the senior ministers of the New England Conference of Congregational ministers, who preached the ordination sermon for Mr. Thorpe, and had been very close to him, in which he paid high tribute to Mr. Thorpe's character and service.

Deacon Benjamin Moody followed in a thoughtful estimation of Mr. Thorpe's invaluable service as a churchman and citizen. in the congregation expressed their appreciation of Mr. Thorpe's life and paid high tribute to his character.

Rev. Dr. Cleland, as pastor, spoke of the fine spirit of cooperation displayed by Mr. Thorpe toward his pastor and of the help he had given. It was he who received Dr. Cleland and extended the right hand of fellowship when he joined the Concord church; and he had held up his pastor's hands.

Dr. Cleland pronounced the benediction and the service concluded with the singing of another of Mr. Thorpe's favorite hymns.

The crowded house the earnest words, the spirit of gratitude were a striking testimony to the permanence of Rev. Mr. Thorpe's influence.

— Memorial Service for Rev. Ole O. Thorpe, *Concord Enterprise*, 21 September 1927, p15.

downturns than most. Or perhaps the town of Concord was more insulated from the ups and downs of the economy.

In any event, it was during the early years of the Depression (1932) that the church took out a loan to build out the cellar, and the very next year voted to take out a mortgage for the new parsonage.

Many of the congregational meetings included discussions of how to help the national and eastern Free Church Associations and the school or additional missionaries. The amounts pledged tended to be small (tens of dollars), but people always seemed to be able to give something. Given that many of the free churches were struggling at the time, this is remarkable. Of course, the Concord church would have its dry spells later.

Norwegian to English

After the new Norwegian church was founded, it did not take long before the congregants realized they needed to think about conducting services in English.

During the Scandinavian Branch years, Norwegian preaching services were always held on Sunday evenings, with a mid-week Norwegian service on Wednesday evenings. A Thursday evening prayer meeting was held in homes, and all children attended the English Sunday School program at Trinitarian. It is not clear whether holding Sunday meetings in the evening was simply due to the logistics of building usage, or if that time was considered best for the rural, farming community. What we do know is that once they began meeting on their own at Lang Street, the brethren continued the tradition of Sunday evening worship and Sunday morning Sunday School for many years. All of these worship services were in Norwegian, but Sunday School for the youth was in English.

Nonetheless, most Norwegian immigrants, wishing to be fully accepted as Americans, learned English quickly, and their children were native English speakers. In many Norwegian homes only English was spoken in front of the children who were often not taught the Norwegian language.[4] So it was apparent to everyone that the best way to reach the next generation, as well as the community at large, was to

Original Parsonage, 1932

hold English services. As with any such major change, this was accomplished over a period of years, mainly during the ministry of Rev. Olaf Johnsen.

At a special meeting on 12 July 1923, the church voted to hold Sunday evening meetings in English on the second and fourth Sundays of each month. On the other weeks, services would still be conducted in Norwegian. This was announced in the Concord Enterprise newspaper on 8 August 1923:

Evangelical Free Church!

Lang Street, Olaf M. Johnsen, Pastor. Beginning next Sunday, Aug 12, English services will be held on the second and fourth Sundays of each month. On the other Sundays in Norwegian. Meeting time, 8 P.M. Thursday 8 P.M. Bible study and prayer.[5]

Although English was sometimes used in recording official meeting minutes, most records prior to 1923 were in Norwegian. However, by the second half of 1923, all official records were in English.

It was not until fall 1929 that the church began to hold communion in English on alternate months. At the annual meeting of 1930, it was agreed to ask E.M. Andersen (the church's first pastor) to come for two weeks in February. If he agreed, the services would be in English. We also read the first recorded suggestion that the church "consider the possibility of having Sunday Morning meetings. This matter to be taken up some Sunday night at the close of a Norwegian service."[6] Sunday morning services would have to wait another two decades.

The congregation continued to have warm relations with the Norwegian Methodist Episcopal church, as is seen in the following entry dated 31 December 1930:

> The Sewing Circle Mission had its Christmas Tree Wednesday Night Dec 31, 1930. The program was singing and the String Band played and Mrs. Webber spoke for that meeting and a watch night service was held by which the Methodist friends joined in with us. The pastor of that church spoke for that meeting, which ended in that year in closing with prayer. With thanks to God—John Andersen, Sec.[7]

In March 1933 the church voted not to change the remaining Norwegian meetings to English; however they did agree to change the fifth Sunday of the month to English.

But the final change to English was inevitable. In the fall of 1933 English became the official language for the general conference of the Norwegian-Danish Evangelical Free Church Association. Within another year the words "Norwegian-Danish" had been dropped from the official name of the Association.

Finally, in November 1933, the Norwegian services which had been held on the first and third Sunday evenings of each month, were moved to four o'clock in the afternoon on the same days. Further, all Sunday evening services would now be in English. To reinforce the goal of reaching the next generation for Christ, the Young People's Society (youth group) was also asked to hold their services every Sunday (presumably they had only been meeting on English Sundays).

The String Band

In 1927 a String Band, the church's first "worship team," was formed under the leadership of Inga Cahill, daughter of Samuel and Karen Lee. Over the years, this unique group provided music at regular church services and on special occasions, and also visited area churches, nursing homes, hospitals, etc. The band was active for about twenty years. In the Heritage Room of the church today rests a 63-string zither that was played by John Swen in the String Band. These zithers consisted of seven chords of nine strings each, designed to be strummed with a pick. Unfortunately, the zither is no longer usable due to its poor condition, but it still bears silent testimony to an important ministry of the church which delighted audiences for many years.

The String Band, 1945. Standing L-R: John Swen, Alfred W. Davis, Jr., Harry P. Odland. Sitting L-R: Mrs. Esther Davis, Mrs. Dorothy Swen, Mrs. Ella Johnson, Miss Annie J. Olsen, Mrs. Inga Cahill

Farewell to Pastor Olaf Johnsen

In July 1935 Pastor Johnsen read his letter of resignation. The congregation unanimously asked him to reconsider, but he felt that God was calling him to leave. In August a large *fest* was held in his honor at which Rev. L.J. Pedersen from the Roxbury church spoke.

On 1 September 1935, Mr. Otto Rafos and his family arrived from Brooklyn, NY to begin his ministry in Concord. A special welcome festival was held in November with help from the friends from the Roxbury Church. Pastor Pedersen from Boston conducted the service. Later that month, the fifteenth annual celebration of the dedication of the Concord church building was held with the participation of Rev. Pedersen and the Boston church choir. The Boston church continued to support and nurture the Lang Street church as an older sister.

Rev. Otto Rafos
(1935-1940)

Rev. Rafos was known as a gifted soloist:

> Seldom has the Free Church had the privilege of being served by a pastor so wonderfully gifted as a soloist as Pastor Rafos. His messages in song as well as in his sermons endeared him to the hearts of his listeners. To those who knew him, he was known as "Otto, the Singer." We feel privileged to have tapes of that rich, full bass voice, now stilled forever. The messages he portrayed will live on for years to come.[8]

On 24 June 1936, Mr. Rafos became the first pastor ordained in the Concord church.[9] His ordination examination, conducted by a Congregational Ecclesiastical Council, was attended by pastors and delegates from area churches including Lancaster, Ayer, Acton, Portland (Maine), Boston, and others, and all participated in the ordination service that evening. Interestingly, shortly prior to his ordination, Mr. Rafos became the first pastor of the church to be accepted as a member of the church, and the only member-pastor the church had until the 1950s. For the first thirty years of the church, the pastor was just an employee of the church, a non-member of the congregation and a non-voting member of the various committees of the church.

In April 1939, Pastor Rafos reported that thought was being given to the potential union of the national Swedish and Norwegian-Danish

Free Church associations. The congregation instructed Rev. Rafos to report to the national meeting that our opinion was "neither yes [n]or no." Neither denomination was ready at the time, and it would take another decade for the merger to be completed.

At the January 1941 annual meeting of the congregation,

> A letter from Rev. Arnold Olsen regarding special meetings to be held in Boston, Portland, & Concord was read.
>
> These meetings were in connection with the 50th Jubilee of the Eastern Assoc. of the Free Church and we had a blessed time together with Rev. Arnold Olsen, Rev. Emanuel Carlson and Rev. N.L. Larson.[10]

At the time, Rev. Olson was pastor of the Salem Evangelical Free Church of Staten Island, NY. But the following year, he would be elected president of the Norwegian-Danish Evangelical Free Church Association. He went on to chair the committee to orchestrate the merger of the Norwegian-Danish and Swedish Free Churches into the Evangelical Free Church of America, and subsequently acted as the EFCA's longest-serving president from 1952-1976.

Church picnic, 1935. Pastor Rafos is toward the back on the right.

The War Years

Pastor Rafos resigned in June 1940 effective 1 September, and moved to Somerville, MA, but continued to fellowship with the church, often preaching when the pastor was absent. Desiring to serve his country, Rev. Rafos entered the Armed Forces as a Navy Chaplain. Later during the war, brothers March and Richard (Rit) Purinton met Chaplain Rafos while on Naval duty in Hawaii.

After Rev. Rafos stepped down, the church debated whether to call a new pastor immediately or acquire interim help while a search was made.[11] It was decided to send a request to Gordon College and the New England Fellowship to see if someone could conduct Sunday School and Sunday evening services. By July they had decided on a young single man, Mr. Harry P. Odland, for a three-month interim position starting as soon after 1 September 1940 as possible. His work impressed everyone enough that in November he was invited to remain full-time at a salary of $1,000/year.

Pastor Odland became the second pastor to be ordained in the church, this time by the Eastern Evangelical Free Church Association. The Ordination examination was conducted during the annual anniversary celebration *fest* on 14 November 1941, with Rev. Arnold T. Olsen presiding, and representation of free churches from Boston, Bridgeport, Hartford, Portland, and Staten Island. Former pastor Rev. Otto Rafos also attended, as did Rev. Gunnar Gundersen (who would eventually become pastor at

**Rev. Harry Odland
(1940-1947)**

Lang Street after Rev. Odland). Pastors of the other local churches in Concord and Carlisle attended the evening celebration service.

The year 1942 brought home to everyone the reality of war, especially so because many young men of the church were serving in the armed forces. The war reinforced in the minds of all that our confidence is not in the world, but in God alone. To help keep the servicemen always present in the prayers of the church, the ladies of the Rebekah Sewing Circle gave the church a Service Roll with the names of those serving overseas inscribed. They also contributed to the American Bible Society that provided New Testaments and Bibles to soldiers and sailors across the world. The various church departments also took turns writing to each serviceman throughout the years:

> As to the correspondence with our men in service, it was requested this be a continuous service for this year: Each

sec. of the various branches of the Church activities and Church Sec. should as their turn is recorded and notified by the Church Sec., send their communications forth, that they may hear what we are doing and know we are also including them in our thoughts.[12]

During 1943 even more young men left for the service. Despite the chaos of war, fourteen new members were added to the rolls on confession of faith in the same year.

To the great relief of everyone, 1945 brought the end of the war. This was a time of special gratitude for answered prayer by the church—every one of its servicemen returned whole and in good health. This added to the sense of joy and praise as the church celebrated its twenty-fifth anniversary that year.

Church Board, 1945. Standing, L-R: John Andersen, Deacon; Christian Lee, Trustee; Thomas Thoresen, Deacon. Sitting L-R: Inga Cahill, Financial Secretary; Alfred W. Davis Jr., Treasurer; John Swen, Elder; Harry P. Odland, Pastor; Andres Christoffersen, Trustee; Ethel Bacon, Secretary. Not shown: Anton Hoff, Trustee; Alfred Madsen, Deacon.

During the war years, the finances of the church had been tight, as they tried to balance the cost of the parsonage, taxes on the parsonage, insurance costs, and needed repairs to the church building. At the beginning of 1941, the balance on hand in the General Fund was $24.61. By the end of the year, it was $286. The General Fund giving rose from a little over $1,800 in 1941 to over $3,700 in 1943. As in the past, the Women's Missionary Society helped pay for many improvements and new items for the church. Of the $1,800 received in 1941, $276 came from the WMS—over 15% of the church's total general budget! The Lord blessed the commitment of the people, and by 1945 a brand new Hammond Electric Organ costing $1,686 was purchased in full.

As an interesting side note, the pastor was given three weeks of vacation each year, and Rev. Rafos sometimes filled in for Pastor Odland while he was out of the pulpit. The payment for pulpit supply for each service was $5.00; this became the standard gift in payment for pulpit supply for some time.

As of the 1943 annual report, the church had forty-three members, and was supporting six missionaries, in addition to Trinity Seminary, the Eastern Free Church Association, and its own general expenses.

Congregation in 1945 (25th anniversary celebration).

After The War

The end of the war brought optimism and opportunity to everyone, and the church was no exception. The church grew in attendance, and opportunities for ministry abounded. In 1946, the church made the final payment on its parsonage — the entire church property was now debt free. At the same time, the parsonage interior was completely redecorated, just in time for Pastor Odland's marriage to Alice Nelson of Brooklyn!

Pastor Odland left in the fall of 1947, and the church called Rev. Gunnar Gunderson to fill the vacancy. Rev. Gunderson was well known to the church, having been involved in many special services. Moreover, the String Band had played several times at churches in New Hampshire which he pastored. Now, fresh from a tour of duty in the Army, he accepted the call and began his ministry on 18 January 1948. That same year, the congregation mourned the death of Rev. E.M. Andersen, who had been so important in bringing the church to birth in 1920.

At the Eastern Free Church Association annual conference, Pastor Gunderson, who had always been actively involved with the eastern Free Churches, was appointed secretary for a term of three years.

The post-war years saw explosive growth in the church, in part because of a general spiritual awakening in the country, but also thanks to the beginning of the "baby boom." In 1949 the church had seen such growth, especially among children and youth, that people were beginning to talk about the possibility of starting a building fund and a committee to consider how they could expand. By the end of 1950, the church had seventy-two members, and numerous weddings and births had been reported.

In June 1950, the Norwegian-Danish and Swedish Free Churches merged to form the Evangelical Free Church of America (EFCA). The Concord church registered their vote in favor of the merger, twenty-one to four. Dr. E.A. Halleen, who had been president of the Swedish association, was elected as the EFCA's first president, and served for one year. In 1951, Arnold T. Olsen, who had been president of the Norwegian-Danish association for eight years, and served as chairman of the merger committee, was elected as EFCA's second president, serving in that capacity until 1976.

Rev. Gunnar Gunderson (1948-1952)

In the fall of 1950, under the leadership of Pastor Gunderson, the church added a Sunday morning worship service on a trial basis. This

REV. ODLAND
TAKES BRIDE
IN BROOKLYN

Married To Alice E. Nelson In Pretty Ceremony;
To Live Here

Concord—Miss Alice Evelyn Nelson, daughter of Mr. and Mrs. John R. Nelson of Croton-On-Hudson, New York, was married recently to the Rev. Harry P. Odland, pastor of the Evangelical Free Church in a ceremony performed by the Rev. N. W. Nelson at the Norwegian Evangelical Free Church, Brooklyn, New York.

The bride was given in marriage by her father and wore a silk chiffon gown with a train and long net veil. White gardenias, carnations, and bouvardia formed her bouquet.

Mrs. Ray Nelson was the matron of honor and she wore a blue organdy gown with a head dress of blue flowers. Blue delphiniums and pink carnations formed her bouquet. The brides maids were the Misses Grace Nelson and Nonie Alcorn and were dressed in peach marquisette gowns with headdresses of peach flowers. Their bouquets were pink carnations and snapdragons.

Miss Doris Nelson was the junior bridesmaid and was dressed in blue marqukette, also with blue flowers in her hair. She carried a bouquet of blue delphiniums and pink carnations. Muriel Peltzer was the flower girl.

Rev Selmer Jacobson of Williams Bay, Wisconsin, was the best man at the ceremony and the ushers were Rev. Albert Anderson of Hartford, Connecticut, and John Nelson, a brother of the bride.

A reception followed at Ridge Colony Restaurant, Brooklyn, and after a wedding trip the couple will reside in Concord.

— *Concord Enterprise*, 4 July 1946, p5

was a way of recognizing that, although the Sunday School was drawing in many children, the adult Bible school class was not drawing in many parents. It was hoped that this change would draw more parents in to hear God's Word. The Sunday School time was changed to 10:30-11:15, after which the older children would join their parents for the "unified worship service" (children under eight attended a junior church service). The morning service ended in the spring at the close of the Sunday School year, but resumed the following fall with minor timing adjustments, and attendance steadily increased. This pattern continued until 1956, when the morning service was permanently held year-round.

Also during Rev. Gunderson's tenure, the church began to form new fellowship groups to meet the targeted needs of various segments of the church, such as, a junior Free Church Youth Fellowship (FCYF) and a young married couples group. The couples group turned out to be particularly effective, as it drew in young married couples from outside the church.

In October 1951, the Concord church hosted the Eastern District conference at which the pastor, Rev. Gunderson, was called to take up the roles of field representative and superintendent for the Eastern District Association, beginning in March 1952. A special farewell service was held on 26 February. Professor Paul Jewett was the first to serve as interim pastor from March through May; many other pastors from local churches and Free Churches around the country also preached while the church searched for a new pastor. There was definite interest in the possibility of calling Rev. Robert Westa, since he was well known to the congregation, but he was not available at the time. After considering various other candidates, the church settled on Rev. Hyland T. Richmond, who began his pulpit ministry in late fall of 1952.

Earlier in 1952, another resignation had occurred. According to church records, "we [the church] were sorry to accept Mr. John Swen's resignation in the middle of the year after 47 years of faithful service to the church as elder."[13] He had been the church elder since its Scandinavian Branch days, and had served the church in just about every capacity until age and ill health made it impossible to continue.

Ninety members and friends threw a special testimonial dinner in his honor on 29 January 1953, and named him a board member emeritus. He died 27 April that year. John Andersen, also a charter member, became elder in his place.

Ordinary People, Extraordinary Impact:
John Swen and John Andersen

John Swen and John Andersen were both on the steering committee to build the church. John Swen was a carpenter by trade, and he contributed time, materials and money to the effort. John Andersen, a farmer, was generous with his money. But it was not just their involvement in founding the church that made a difference.

John Swen served as elder of the church from the day it was organized until shortly before his death in 1953. He also served as trustee, deacon, chairman, song leader, choir director and janitor—sometimes concurrently! In addition to his normal generous contributions, he frequently gave extra to pay for specific needs that the church could not afford. For many years he could be found at the church keeping the church clean. This was not a paid position—he did it because he wanted to help. He also involved in the purchase of the property for the original parsonage and building the house thereon. If the church was open, he was there.

Marion Purinton fondly remembers that during the cold winters John would go to the church early on Sundays to stoke the fire, come back to pick up neighborhood children for Sunday school, providing them blankets to keep warm in his unheated car. Periodically during the service he would get up and re-load the furnace to keep everyone warm.

John Andersen was elected as a deacon and trustee when the church was organized and served variously in those and other positions until the death of John Swen in 1953, when he replaced him as elder. Most notable was his generosity to the church, often donating or loaning large sums of money to pay for necessities, including (multiple times) the pastor's salary.

Between the two of them, these men invested over one hundred years of service for the benefit of the church. If their various concurrent offices were counted separately, it would be much more. They lived out their love for God's church and were faithful to the end.

World War II Honor Roll

Name	Service	Rank	Date Entered Service	Months of Foreign Service	Theater
Theodore L. Olsen	Army	PFC	1/16/1941	33	Asia-Pacific
Edward H. Monsen	Army	PFC	1/16/1941	47	Asia-Pacific
Charles J. Carson	Air Corps	S/Sgt	3/25/1941	12	Asia-Pacific
Malcolm C. Carson	Marines	S/Sgt	1/14/1942	26	Asia-Pacific
Ralph G. Burstad	Army	T/Sgt	2/24/1942	27	Asia-Pacific
Walter A. Anderson	Army	T/Sgt	6/17/1942	33	Europe
Pastor Otto T. Rafos	Navy	Chaplain/ LtC	12/27/1942	19	Asia-Pacific
James M. Anderson	Air Corps	S/Sgt	3/1/1943	8	Europe
March G. Purinton, Jr	Navy	RM 2/c	3/1/1943	18	Asia-Pacific
William A. Thoresen	Navy	F 1/c	10/8/1943	15	Asia-Pacific
Richard N. Purinton	Navy	RM 2/c	12/6/1943	13	Asia-Pacific
Mildred E. Holm	US Cadet	Nurse	1/4/1944		

Chapter 5:
The Evangelical Free Church of Concord

(1954-1974)

Years of Building and Growth

Rev. Hyland T. Richmond was welcomed to Concord on 2 November 1952, serving as pastor until 6 September 1959.

During the 1950s, the activity of the church reached a crescendo. Sunday School enrollment exploded to a high of over 120 in 1958. Pioneer Girls, Christian Service Brigade, and Daily Vacation Bible School ministries thrived, drawing many children from non-Christian homes. In 1954,

Rev. Hyland T. Richmond (1952-1959)

seventeen of the forty girls in Pioneer Girls professed faith in Christ, and there were numerous conversions recorded from Vacation Bible School. The nursery and cradle rolls were bursting at the seams. New ministries were started, such as a Men's Brotherhood, and a co-ed Sunday School class for ages fifteen to thirty.

Also during the early 1950s, the Korean conflict and the Cold War began to impact church life. Bob and Paul Thoresen were in everyone's prayers during their years of service, especially as Bob served in Korea.

In 1954, the congregation began putting together its comprehensive set of youth programs, including Pioneer Girls and Christian Service Brigade. A committee was formed to oversee these ministries.

Also that year, in response to a need for greater ethnic diversity of the EFCA nationally and a desire to appeal to more people locally, the official name of the church was changed to the Evangelical Free Church of Concord. The constitution was amended to specify that in the case of dissolution of the church, the property would belong to the Evangelical Free Church of America (previously it was listed as the Norwegian-Danish Evangelical Free Church Association of America). Pastor Richmond and his wife were granted full voting membership in the church—only the second time this had happened since the church was founded in 1920. All future pastors and their wives would be granted membership as part of their call.

Around the same time, the property next door to the church was put up for sale, and the church wasted no time in purchasing it. Plans were developed for a new 30 x 50 foot addition for Sunday School rooms, as well as a complete renovation of the sanctuary, which improved its aesthetics but actually reduced seating capacity to 120 from about 140. Finances were tight, so the congregants decided to do the work themselves rather than contract it out. The new Sunday School rooms were pressed into service in the spring of 1958, and in February 1959 a dedication service was held for the "completely reconstructed sanctuary and new building."

It is interesting to note that, since most of the work on the building was done by people in the church, a lot of the church board and congregation meeting times were taken up with discussions about renovation and construction details. This probably only worked because congregation meetings were usually attended by fewer than twenty members.

During the 1950s, many of the older, first-generation immigrant members began to pass away, leaving vacancies where they had served faithfully for so many years. These vacancies were being filled by the next generation—most of them the children of older members and their spouses. The many non-Norwegian names showed that the children of the old guard were thoroughly Americanized by this time. The Concord

Original sanctuary interior, 1920-1959

Free Church was becoming an American church, although the vast majority still claimed Norwegian descent, and Concord townsfolk still thought of it as the Norwegian servants' church.

It could be said that during this time the congregation began to turn its attention inward, perhaps exacerbated by the long, hard effort expended on renovations. The church was beginning to lose sight of its primary mission, although this was not yet obvious to leadership. All outward signs indicated a healthy, vibrant church; after all, the new youth programs (Pioneer Girls, Brigade, and Vacation Bible School) were reaping significant spiritual harvest throughout the late 1950s. In the spring of 1958 the congregation sponsored a Christian youth rally with Jack Wyrtzen in the Concord High School. Over 600 attended, and over one hundred decisions for Christ were recorded.[1] Many evangelical churches in the surrounding area supported the rally.

The difference was in the focus of church leadership on the building project, ignoring the signs that the church was becoming irrelevant to the people of the town. Worse, the townspeople were beginning to oppose evangelical activity in Concord. They actively fought against the use of the school for the Jack Wyrtzen rally, although they eventually allowed it to proceed.[2]

Renovated sanctuary interior, 1959

Amid plentiful harvest, the congregation was not planning how to spread new seed among increasingly hard and infertile soil in the town. The problem would become apparent during the next season of harvest, not the current one. Unfortunately, by that time other stresses would be commanding everyone's attention.

At the quarterly business meeting on 21 April 1958, the pastor, elders, and deacons proposed a motion to move communion services to the first Wednesday of each month, and only permit church members of protestant churches to partake. After much discussion, the church voted not to change the rules regarding who could receive communion. To this day, the church practices an open communion of believers only, but all believers.

Decline

During the summer of 1959, Pastor Richmond resigned to accept a call elsewhere. The transition was a difficult one for the church and was not handled well. Its negative impact lasted through many years and affected multiple pastors. The particular circumstances surrounding this challenging time are discussed in more detail in Part Three.

On 28 September 1959, leadership convened a special business meeting to consider calling a new pastor. Only twenty members attended (out of a possible seventy-six). A first vote to answer the question, "Do you feel we are ready to vote for a pastor?" was carried fourteen to three. A ballot was then presented with three names in addition to "No Call," and a vote was taken: Donald Barnes (14), Rev. Samuel Kostreva (1), Rev. John Hobson (0), and "No Call" (4).

"Mr. Barnes having received more than the 2/3 vote necessary will be extended a call to become pastor."[3]

At the 13 October quarterly business meeting, it was reported that there was insufficient cash in the mission fund to meet commitments. It was voted that only one-half of Rev. Barnes' expenses to move to Concord would be paid to him. Financial distress was causing the congregation to pull back on their commitment to adequately pay the pastor. Once the pastor arrived, there was apparently no announcement or article in the local paper. Leadership was too distracted to think about putting out a press release.

Rev. Donald Barnes
(1959-1961)

A major focus in 1960 was to completely update the church's constitution and bylaws which had not been significantly revised since the church's inception in 1920. This undertaking allowed the congregation to reorganize their committee structure to align better with the ministry needs of the church. The work began in May and involved four long congregational meetings from July through early September to review and approve each article. The new document was given final approval on 6 September 1960.[4] Elections for the new committee structure occurred in October. While this effort was important and long overdue, it consumed a great deal of attention of the leadership and congregation as a whole, which might have been better spent dealing with addressing the issues that had emerged at the end of Pastor Richmond's service.

Leading up to the work on the new constitution, Pastor Barnes conducted a church membership class, attended mainly by young people and new attenders who had previously expressed interest. During Rev. Richmond's pastorate many of the young people had grown to adulthood and married, and new people had begun to attend. But there had been little emphasis on such things as formal membership, so the membership roll was mainly unchanged during the late 1950s. Therefore the church clerk was also instructed to send letters to the current membership asking each member to indicate his or her "desire of re-evaluation of membership on our Church Roll." In April 1960 twenty-one new members were welcomed, and seven were removed, for a net increase of thirteen.

This batch of new members included children grown to adulthood, such as Linda Thoresen (who would later marry Bob Specht), new spouses of many members, such as Clough Vettrus, Jack Stuart, Barb Thoresen, and Marion Purinton, plus new families such as Cyril and Frances Perkin (Carolyn Light's parents), Joe and Ernest Tavilla and their families (Joe married Pauline Olsen, grand-daughter of Anton and Pauline Hoff), and the Wentworths. All of these new members would be important in the future ministry of the church.

> **Reminiscences**
>
> Every year we would have a Children's Day and one year there were geraniums nicely wrapped in foil lining the stage. My son, David, and his friend knocked some of the plants off the stage during the service. All the children received a geranium, but Uncle Ted Thoresen pulled the boys aside and after speaking to them, gave each of them a flower with no blossoms. They learned their lesson and never did that again!
>
> Marion Purinton

These new members definitely provided a shot in the arm, but brought only temporary relief, as attendance generally continued to decline throughout the early 1960s, putting more pressure on finances.

At the annual meeting in January 1961 leadership first asked the congregation to consider the possibility of looking for a new location, which would be necessary if the church were to continue to grow. The property on Lang Street had limited room for expansion, parking was tight, and there were continuing repair needs and upgrades. The congregation authorized the executive committee to create a "building site committee" to look into options. In April the committee, which included the pastor, March Purinton Jr., Bob Thoresen, and others, reported on the availability of "some land located on Route #2 in Acton." After considering the numerous repair needs in the current building, the congregation voted to ask the committee to continue their research, and to begin raising funds toward the purchase of new land. But in July, the Macone property on Lang Street next door to the church was put up for sale, and the committee was asked to investigate that instead. It turned out to be too expensive to pursue at the time, but the momentum for a move had been lost. Contributions to the building fund trickled slowly in over the next few years.

Interestingly, during this time Malcolm Dunn and his sister Judith were attending the Concord Free Church.[5] Together they owned and managed over 200 acres of land along Taylor Street in Acton, on which they managed a dairy farm and apple orchard. They also owned other land in Acton and Littleton. At this time the Dunns were beginning to divest themselves of portions of their land. Some of their property had been taken by eminent domain for Route 2 expansion, but Malcolm had begun subdividing the land to sell for homes (and two churches!).[6] But there is no indication that the church or the Dunns showed any interest in a mutual agreement. The congregation was not yet ready for the move to Acton.

In April 1961 the EFCA Eastern District began the search for a district camp site. With outreach to youth being such an integral part of the church's vision for ministry, it was only natural that the congregation would want to be involved. Deacon Gardner Benson was nominated as representative from Concord, with Bob Thoresen as alternate. This was the beginning of the church's long involvement with what eventually became Camp Spofford, near Keene, NH.

On 27 August 1961 Rev. Barnes submitted his resignation, resulting once again in the church being without a pastor. Plans for a "kick-off" banquet for the new Land and Building Fund were put on hold. Initially it was decided not to call an interim pastor during the search, but to rely instead on guest speakers, including numerous evangelists, pastors, missionaries and laymen. Of special note was a visit by Rev. Gordon

**Dr. Charles Pfeiffer
(interim)
(1961-1962)**

Andersen, the son of Rev. E.M. Andersen who helped found the church! However, after the first candidate withdrew and the second one was rejected, it became clear that the search process would take longer than hoped. Dr. Charles Pfeiffer from Gordon Divinity School was asked to assume the role of interim preacher while the search continued. He served from the end of 1961 until Rev. Westa arrived in August 1962. One of Dr. Pfeiffer's last duties as interim pastor was to unite Janet Andersen and John (Jack) Stuart in matrimony in a ceremony at Trinitarian Congregational Church.

At a special meeting on 21 March 1962 the congregation cast a "very near unanimous vote" to call Rev. Robert S. Westa as pastor. He accepted the call on 29 April, and formally began his ministry on 1 September 1962, although he had preached for the three prior Sundays. Interestingly, he attributed his conversion to Christ to the faithful tent preaching of E.M. Andersen, the evangelist/pastor who helped bring the Concord Free Church into existence.

During this period, the church continued to experience a season of malaise. Although membership stabilized, it did not rebound. At the October 1962 business meeting, nominations for boards and committees were difficult to come by, as many people declined their nominations from the floor.[7]

**Rev. Robert Westa
(1962-1964)**

In the summer of 1963, in an attempt to consolidate the oversight of giving to missionaries, a new Missionary Committee was formed. This committee was not, however, a separately elected board. The members of the committee consisted of representatives from each of the organizations that had been contributing annually to missions: the church treasurer (March

Purinton Sr.), the financial secretary (Alfred Davis), the WMS representative (Esther Davis), the Sunday School representative (Esther Davis), and the youth director (Bob Thoresen).

During August 1963 the church held joint summer services with Carlisle Congregational Church. Carlisle and the Concord church shared a number of family connections, and they sometimes combined their choirs for special musical performances such as cantatas. But these joint services were particularly welcomed during the "summer doldrums" when attendance was so light.

At this point, Pastor Westa was struggling to lift the church out of its listlessness and weariness. After working under the new constitution for a few years, Pastor Westa, in what was probably the longest pastor's report in the history of the church (seven full typewritten pages), detailed what he thought would be a more efficient organization. He envisioned a church which would operate more like a business with the Pastor as chief executive and an executive board with representation of all the committees. It is not clear what became of the proposal, although his report was well received: "We all truly received a blessing from this report. Alice Thoresen made a motion we accept it as read with heartfelt thanks. George Hodgeson seconded it and it was so voted."[8]

Also in his report, the Pastor hinted at one of the biggest challenges the church faced:

> An advertising campaign was launched to acquaint the surrounding community with our church. The response to date has been nil. This leads me to believe that the best method is Acts 20:20, "from house to house." This plan will soon be set up beginning with a training session for visitors. Again I would like to coordinate our church with reference to our "outlying" districts with some sort of "cottage prayer meeting" activity.[9]

A large part of the problem the church faced was the townspeople's impression of the church as an ethnic congregation, and a "servants' church," that is, the church that was founded and attended by the domestic servants of the elite. Visitation proved ineffective in changing minds. The church's future in Concord was becoming bleak. But neither Westa nor leadership were yet ready to move out of Concord.

Instead they chose what seemed to be the safer route. At a special business meeting on 11 September 1963 with forty members (about

50%) in attendance, Pastor Westa made a case for purchasing the Macone property next door to the church, upon which rested a large duplex house. He had already sent a letter to the Macones requesting first choice to purchase if they should decide to sell, which the Macones granted. After a "lengthy discussion," a motion was made to give the trustees authority to negotiate and purchase the property at a price not to exceed $40,000. That motion failed after discussion from the floor. Another motion authorizing the trustees to purchase the property at a maximum price of $35,000 was also defeated. Finally, a motion to purchase the property (with no price limit) was carried by "the majority present." The clear implication is that this was by no means a unanimous vote. A couple of weeks later another special meeting was called to decide whether $40,000 was an appropriate price to pay. The twenty-nine members present deemed it too high, and by secret ballot they asked the committee to offer $35,000, and leave the result in the Lord's hands. The Macones accepted the offer, the new property was purchased, and the old parsonage sold for $21,000—all of this was completed by April 1964. With the acquisition of the Macone property, the church now had a new parsonage, office space, and some additional land for potential expansion.

In November 1963, the nation was rocked by the news that President Kennedy had been assassinated. The church joined the nation in mourning, and the following entry was placed in the official record:

November 22, 1963

Our nation was deeply saddened on this day as the news traveled via Radio and TV from state to state, "President John F. Kennedy was assassinated in Dallas, Texas!" The accused: Lee Oswald. President Kennedy was born May 29, 1917. He was a married man with two small children.

A "memorial service" was conducted Sunday AM, Nov 24, with Rev. R. Westa officiating. our church was full. (The president was buried in Arlington National Cemetery on Nov 25).

As the darkness of a Monday night engulfed our nation, we pause to pay a silent tribute to this man who led our nation from 1961 to late in 1963.

We pay tribute and pray, but we also dedicate ourselves anew to make this nation a better one, under God, even as we witness for Christ.

"A soul departs—a town grieves—a flag dips"
"But they that wait upon the Lord shall renew their strength; they shall mount up with wings as eagles; they shall run and not be weary; they shall walk and not faint..." (Is 40:31, KJV)[10]

For 1964, the general budget for the year was approximately $9,000 (a little over $71,000 in 2017 dollars), and the Missions budget was approximately $2,000 (about $15,800 in 2017).

In April 1964 Gardner Benson resigned as church moderator and deacon, and his wife, Emma, resigned as Sunday School superintendent. Others who had recently left the church included George and Ruth Andersen, Christine and Ron Jackson, Ernie and Ginny Tavilla, and Joe and Pauline Tavilla, all to attend elsewhere. During this time the young work at Grace Chapel in Lexington was undergoing a growth spurt and building program, drawing many families away. For Pauline and Joe Tavilla, the draw was especially strong since they lived in Lexington, and Joe's relatives had been one of the founding families. Pauline's sister-in-law Tina had led the youth program for years, injecting tremendous excitement and life into it. But upon her departure from Concord the youth program imploded. Similarly, Ernest Tavilla had been Sunday School superintendent, another position of importance to the youth ministry. These hits to the youth ministry would cause others to consider leaving as well.

Around this same time, Malcolm Dunn and his sister Judith decided the time had come for them to liquidate the dairy business and the rest of their property and move to Maine. Over the years they had acquired land along Whitney and Hogan Ponds near Oxford, Maine, on which they established the Dunn's Camps, Christian campgrounds dedicated for refreshment, recreation, and rest for ministers and missionaries, as well as retreats for church and youth groups. In addition to subdividing some of their Acton property for homes, they sold a large block of land bordering Taylor Road and Minot Avenue to the Town of Acton. In 1971 the town built the Luther Conant Elementary School on this property.[11]

In November 1964, Rev. Westa resigned to become Deputation Secretary of Christ's Mission in Hackensack, NJ. He ended his ministry 1 January 1965. On 14 December a special business meeting was called to consider Rev. Arnold H. Olsen as candidate for pastor. After a

Macone property, purchased 1964

lengthy discussion a vote was taken, in which the church decided against a call. Rev. Olsen went on to become pastor at the Waltham and Westwood free churches for many years.

During the search for a new pastor, Dr. Roger Nicole, then a professor at Gordon Divinity School, served as a guest preacher beginning in January 1965. In addition to enthralling the congregation with his French accent, he also provided suggestions for pastoral candidates. One of these, Mr. Gordon Condit, a recent graduate of Gordon Divinity School, accepted the call to come to Concord, and began his ministry 1 August 1965.

**Gordon Condit
(1965-1972)**

It was a daunting task to assume the mantle of leadership of a church, but Pastor Condit, fresh out of seminary, jumped in with both feet. He and his wife Jo-Ann were of a similar age with many of the young couples who were just beginning to assume leadership responsibilities, and they learned together under the watchful eye of the older generation.

Inexperience did not prevent Pastor Condit from seeing specific areas to be addressed, however. In his first pastor's annual report, after only a few months in the saddle, he gave the following assessment:

> The welcome we received was warm and sincere. You have been a great encouragement and help to us in this, our first full-time pastorate. We appreciate your understanding and your patience—all of these kindnesses make us ever thankful for this opportunity to minister in Concord.
>
> We've seen a substantial interest in our morning worship, although we know there are many more who could and should be worshipping with us. Our evening services have varied both in content and in attendance. We've tried in a small measure to stimulate interest without falling into the snare of having mere Christian entertainment.
>
> What can we say about our prayer meetings or the prayer life of the church? Is it the times in which we live or is it always like this? The prayer meeting is not well attended. Spiritually we are guilty of the sin of prayerlessness, we are not a praying church. The spiritual life of our church in this regard is at a low ebb. There is, however, a faithful nucleus who are very responsive in our Bible study and prayer. These have a heart's concern for the work of the Lord and His Church and for these we are thankful. May God by His Spirit lay it upon the hearts of others to join us in prayer.[12]

In addition to his normal pastoral duties, Pastor Condit became involved in the Daily Vacation Bible School. During the summer of 1966, the children were delighted with the puppeteering work of Caroll Spinney, the person behind those characters who would later become famous as Big Bird and Oscar the Grouch. Spinney, a graduate of Acton High School (later known as Acton-Boxborough Regional High School), was a friend of someone in the congregation, who convinced him to perform. All of this was before Big Bird became famous on Sesame Street, of course! In the fall of 1966, Pastor Condit joined Barbara and Joe McGuerty as sponsors for the Young People's Society.

Another significant change initiated by Pastor Condit was in the area of baptism. Up to this point, all of the pastors of the Concord Free Church had practiced infant baptism as well as adult believer's baptism. In both cases, the ordinance was not considered to confer saving grace.

True salvation has always been understood as being the result of "saving faith" through the regenerating power of the Holy Spirit. Confirmation classes were held frequently for young people, with the intent and expectation that they would profess and confirm their faith in Christ at that time or thereafter. Pastor Condit was the first pastor to perform only believer's baptism on those old enough to understand and profess faith in Christ. In place of infant baptism he would hold ceremonies in which the parents would dedicate their children to the Lord and commit to raise their children in the nurture and admonition of the Lord.

Around this time the trustees removed the baptistry and floored it over, because it had become unsafe. Subsequently, until the new church was built in Acton, baptisms were typically performed in the lake at Camp Spofford, or Immanuel Baptist Church in Bedford.

Also in the spring of 1966 the congregation began to discuss the possibility of deaconesses, who would have the same duties and authority as a deacon. Reasons for and against the proposal were voiced from the floor, but no motion was put forward at that time.

That year seventeen new members joined the rolls, including the Condits. These included surnames like Putnam, Korhonen, McGuerty and Goodemote.

Youth Director
David and Susan McBride
1967-1970

In October 1967 the Board of Education hired David McBride, a student at Gordon Divinity School, as Youth Director for $10.00/week. He continued successfully in this capacity until his graduation in spring 1970.

On 4 May 1969 Gordon Condit became the third pastor to be ordained while serving in the church.

The church hosted a Family "Crusade" 23-26 October 1969, during which nineteen young people made decisions for Christ. This event was so successful that plans immediately began for a 1970 crusade with a wider audience in view.

Attendance was up. A preaching series on stewardship had a positive effect on church finances. Outlook was positive.

The church still struggled, however, with its reputation as an ethnic congregation, and the townsfolk no longer seemed interested in the little "servants' church" on Lang Street. The increasingly secular culture made it even more difficult to attract new people from the town to an evangelical church. But commitment to the Scriptures and salvation by faith alone in Christ alone was never open for negotiation.

Reminiscences

For three years March and I, along with two other couples, went up to Camp Spofford with the youth group to cook for them. Each night we had to wait for the youth group to finish what they were doing in the big room downstairs so that we could go to sleep. We had to sleep on the couches. While trying to sleep we could hear the water running in the pipes, toilets flushing, people walking around, etc. So you can say we did not sleep well at all. So, for years 2 and 3 they made arrangements for us to stay at the hotel down the street so we could get some sleep! It was fun to cook for the kids. After those trips, Pastor Condit who was there, gave us the 3 monkeys: Hear No Evil, See No Evil, and Speak No Evil. I still have at least one of them. What happens in Spofford stays in Spofford!

Marion Purinton

Time to Move?

Improvements to the financial health of the church probably emboldened the leadership to restart discussions about potential relocation of the church, which culminated in a special board meeting in April 1970:

> April 16, 1970 special board meeting.
>
> A small unorganized group had previously met to discuss the future of the church and a possible need for relocation. Some of the reasons for this move were:
>
> 1.   Increased space for larger congregation
>
> 2.   Economies in operating a modern, properly designed building

3. More convenient location for majority of the church members

4. More prominent location to attract community at large

5. Disassociation with Ethnic Stigma among townspeople

6. Architecture of present building not acceptable to historical image of the town.

This group previously met with Rev. Arnold Hansen, Supt. of the Eastern District of the Evang. Free Church of America. Rev Hansen had related experiences of going through a similar relocation at Orange, NJ.

Asking for creation of an ad hoc "Site Committee" for the sole purpose of "the searching for, and investigation of potential sites for the relocation of the Concord Free Church." The board unanimously approved. Committee members nominated by the board were: Dean Comeau, George Thoresen, March Purinton, Sr., Olga Purinton.[13]

There had been much turnover in the church by this time; many older people had died, and others moved or attended elsewhere. In June 1970 Pastor Condit and the church secretary were asked to get together to go over the membership list checking for "delinquency, etc."

In the fall of 1970 the church celebrated the fiftieth anniversary of its founding. The president of the Evangelical Free Church of America, Rev. Arnold T. Olsen, delivered the message.

At the following annual meeting on 19 January 1971, the board recommended creation of another ad hoc committee to evaluate and make recommendations concerning the administration and the constitution of the church.

In the summer of 1971 events unfolded quickly:

July 22, 1971 Special Board Meeting

The official Board held a "special" meeting in the lower auditorium of the church. Eleven members were present.

Moderator Purinton opened the meeting with prayer at 7:30 pm.

The purpose of the meeting was to discuss a specified parcel of property owned by a Mr. Joyce in Acton, off Route

**Fiftieth Anniversary celebration with EFCA
president Rev. Arnold T. Olsen.**

#2 and Hosmer St—with the possibilities of selling or renting our property and relocating at said place.

Jim Goodemote produced a drawn plan showing the approximate location etc. The Joyce property consists of 4 1/4 acres of land, a large house about 35 years old, and a barn. The house is in good condition and could be used for a parsonage. The only repairs needed is in modernizing the kitchen. The church could be built on a knoll in the background. The overall price of this property is $42,500.

After a lengthy discussion on need for church growth, plus location, finances, taxes, assessment, and interest charges, Jim Goodemote made a motion: "we pursue the possibilities of purchasing the Joyce property by looking into every detail." (Jim has accepted this responsibility). Max Laurence seconded his motion and it so carried. Another special board meeting will be called, at which time Jim will give us his report on the property.

In September (after vacation) a church business meeting will be called and each member will have his chance to voice his opinion and vote. The meeting was over at 9:45 pm and Pastor Condit closed in prayer.

Respectfully submitted,
Marjorie E. Andersen, Secretary[14]

During the summer, the committee investigated the property and reported back to the board:

August 26, 1971 Special Board Meeting

A special meeting of the official board was held on Thursday evening at 7:30. The main purpose for the meeting was to discuss further progress on a parcel of land for relocation off Route #2 on Hosmer Street, Acton, by the "Land and Site Committee."

Jim Goodemote has been doing some extensive work, evaluating the location, etc. As compared to Concord and her surrounding towns, Acton showed the most positive growth within the past 5 years. This parcel of land measures 4 1/3 acres. A large farm house, barn and garage are included. The price quoted is $42,500. Charts, maps and monographs were on display for our edification. The Board also visited the property in question.

A lengthy discussion of sincere mixed feelings were aired. All were aware of a <u>definite</u> need to progress. Spiritual growth is needed. It was agreed we should not stand still — but act, as the Lord opened doors. Our present property is presently worth approximately $80,000. Here we have assets which should be used for the Lord.

Trustee George Thoresen suggested ways we could purchase the Acton property without feeling a financial burden through remortgaging and renting the parsonage.

It was finally decided, we must create spiritual enthusiasm instead of apathy. In so doing, the Board voted affirmatively on the following (motion by Jim G.): On Sat Sept 11 the Church Board shall sponsor an open-house meeting from 2-4 pm. All interested persons and members shall visit said property at Acton and afterward report to the church for discussion....

A second motion, also made by Jim, followed: "A special business meeting of church members shall be held on Wednesday, Sept 15, following the prayer meeting for the sole purpose of voting on the Acton property....

Trustee George Thoresen agreed to get in touch with trustee Dean Comeau for an estimate on cost for the needed improvements on present parsonage (for rental purposes) plus estimating cost of needed improvements on the house at Acton (for future parsonage)....[15]

The church secretary's report for 1971 provides additional insight:

> On September 11 we held a very important meeting in the form of "Open House." As our special speaker, we had Rev. Arne Hansen. This meeting was held to discuss possibilities of re-locating. A site committee was previously organized with trustee James Goodemote as chairman...
>
> September and October were very important months for our Church. Special Board and business meetings were held for the purpose of relocating. The site committee busily checked on property for sale in Concord and Acton. A piece of land in Acton, near the Concord line, appeared to be the best buy. This land is off Route #2 on Hosmer Street. There appeared to be some disagreement as to location, etc. It was, therefore, decided to have an open session of prayer before casting our votes, to seek God's will in this matter. Finally, with all votes cast, the majority vote was to purchase the property. Thus, the site committee, with the Board of Trustees, handled all legal transactions, and the new Church will be erected in Acton. The new parsonage is on the property and is being made ready for our Pastor. It was decided we rent the old parsonage in Concord.[16]

Executive Council, 1970. Standing, L-R: deacons Roger Soule, Maxwell Lawrence, Clough Vettrus, March Purinton, Jr. Seated, L-R: John Andersen, elder; Gordon Condit, pastor; Marjorie Andersen, secretary; Thomas Thoresen, elder.

The actual minutes of the special business meeting report that there were thirty-eight members and four adherents present for the vote. There was a great deal of prayer and discussion, and the secret vote results were twenty-three in favor, thirteen opposed, and two blank ballots. It was clearly an emotional and heart-wrenching time for the congregation, both young and old. Probably not since the church had been founded were the members asked to make such a difficult decision. Although the vote was well over the majority required to pass, the number of 'no' votes was a foreshadowing of trouble to come, because of the intensity of feelings on both sides.

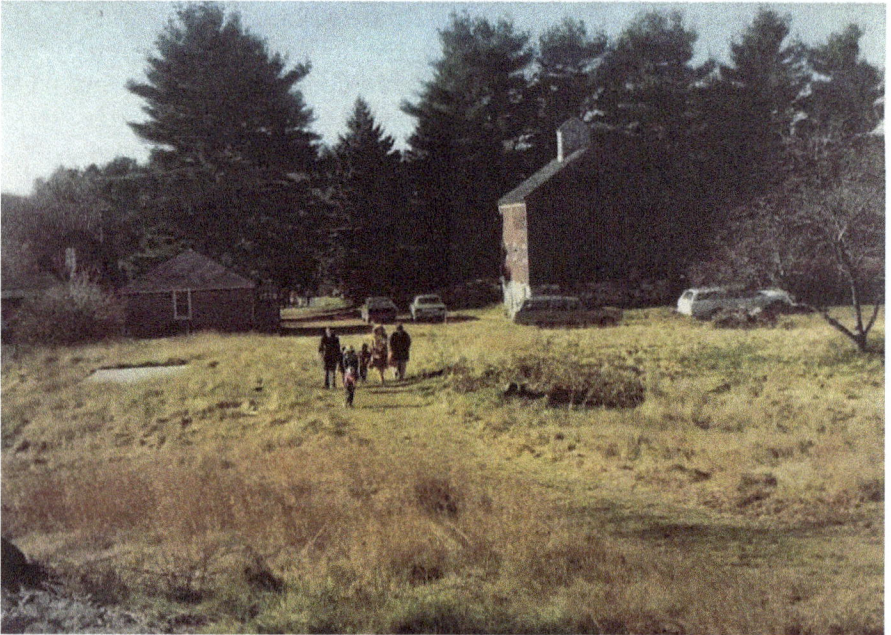

Hosmer Street property, showing the barn (right) and garage (left). The parsonage is out of the picture to the right. Picture taken from what would become the front entrance to the church.

The spiritual work of the church was not interrupted by all these events. That fall in November 1971, the church sponsored a special Youth and Family Conference at Acton-Boxborough Regional High School featuring John DeBrine, (founder and host of the Songtime radio program that was popular across New England at the time), during which twenty-eight decisions for Christ were recorded.

By the end of 1971, the Acton property had been financed and the purchase was completed. Work immediately began on making the new parsonage ready for occupancy, and turning the existing parsonage back into a duplex in preparation for renting it out.

Any time the people of God embark on a new work of faith, the evil one fights back, and this was no exception. A prominent family in the congregation was split apart by moral failure, which was not properly addressed. Eventually most of the extended family left to attend elsewhere. In 1972, the family of George Thoresen was rocked by the death of their daughter Catherine, who went into a coma after receiving

Reminiscences

I came with my parents from the Free Church in Roxbury, so I attended the Free Church since I was a child. It was a very integral part for my life even at a very early age. It will be memories that I will always remember, the strawberry shortcake socials we had and the singing around the Christmas tree. Along with the memories comes the remembrance of the very special people that attended the church. We were a family. Not all of us were related (LOL). We didn't always see eye to eye on things at business meetings, but when opinions got a little steamy we would always stop and have prayer and if needed we would dismiss the meeting and have it the following week.

When the move was in the talking stage a committee was formed, which Bob was a part of, and they met every Saturday for two years to pray for the Lord's leading and what He wanted for the church. They then pursued a new location for the church. When it was time to vote, and this was very hard for me to leave Concord, I still remember the older people not wanting to leave but knew it was God's leading to do so. They also realized that the church would close if we didn't. It was an emotional time. The Lord was so faithful and we just kept trusting in all of it. Also, even though the numbers were down and it got very concerning for us financially, we remained faithful to the Lord and He always provided and we were never unable to take care of our responsibilities.

Linda Specht

anesthesia to have her wisdom teeth pulled. The congregation had surrounded the family in prayer, but she did not survive. George and Eleanor, who had been primary motivators for the move to Acton, withdrew from leadership to mourn and recover.

Others began to express their opposition to the move by resigning their membership and leaving the church. When it was learned that all of the trustees would be required to co-sign the mortgage on the new property, the chairman of the trustee board resigned and quit the church, forcing another to take his place.[17] One can only imagine the emotions that would arise at being asked to put one's financial security on the line for a purchase of such magnitude that one had counseled against, and that one believed was a mistake and doomed to fail!

In such a short time, the whole congregation was shaken to its core. Construction plans for the new location were put on hold, but, of course, the land had already been purchased and work on the parsonages had to continue.

Pastor Condit moved into the new parsonage in March 1972. Once the old parsonage was empty, work to convert the building back into a

Parsonage at 54 Hosmer St, since 1972

two-family house began. One side was rented out by 1 April, while the other side, which needed a new kitchen, was rented by 1 May.

The congregation planned to hold outdoor evangelistic services at the Hosmer Street property in summer 1972. They also started to formulate plans for a church building to be erected on the new site. The first step was to conduct a site/land survey.

At the spring business meeting that year, the congregation was asked to consider new names for the church when it moved to Acton. Some of the names suggested were:[18]

- Community Bible Church

- Evangelical Free Church of Acton

- Faith Evangelical Free Church

- Hope Evangelical Free Church

No consensus on a new name was reached at this time.

At the same meeting, people began to speak openly of the way the church was hemorrhaging people, and the resulting financial drain on the church.

By May 1972, the financial condition of the church had deteriorated again to the point where there were no funds to pay salaries and other bills.[19] Money was reallocated from other accounts to make up the difference. Although support for individual missionaries on the field was maintained, support for institutions such as Trinity Evangelical Divinity School was temporarily curtailed.

Sunday School and church attendance and membership declined precipitously. Between 1970 and 1975, forty-five members were removed from the active rolls. Of these, four were deceased, thirteen had been members since before 1960, and the rest had become members during the 1960s. Twenty-four of those who left (about 30% of the total active membership) left between 1972 and 1974. As attendance declined, fewer people were available to maintain ministry, and many of the youth ministries (Pioneer Girls, Christian Service Brigade, etc.) were halted, which put a further drain on attendance, because, as one member put it, "people wanted more for their children." At the same time, Grace Chapel in nearby Lexington was growing quickly, partly because of its dynamic youth program. Once it became clear that the church was going to move eventually, it seemed to many like a good time to cast around and see what else was available. Others left because they were not up to the challenge of reinventing the church and starting over.

That summer, letters began to circulate about a "vote of confidence"

Reminiscences

I was born into this church family, the daughter of March and Marion Purinton. When I recall my years growing up in church, I think of service to our Lord and the family bond it created. My parents served, and my brothers and I were happy to help. Dad was treasurer for the Sunday School offering, while his dad, March Purinton, Sr., was church treasurer. At that time, during the Sunday School hour, all the classes met together during the first 15 min. An offering was taken, and people celebrating a recent birthday were invited to come forward to put a penny per year of their age into a birthday bank that looked like a birthday cake. We then recited a birthday wish, "Many happy returns on the day of your birth, may sunshine and gladness be given, and may the dear Lord prepare you on earth for a beautiful birthday in Heaven." These coins were designated for the missions budget. As a young child, I enjoyed seeing my dad carry the gray drawstring money bag into the house along with his Bible. I knew the card table would be opened in the living room and we would be helping count the offering by opening the offering envelopes and stacking the coins into neat $1.00 stacks.

Later, as an adult, the stacks of coins turned into currency and checks as I now serve on the finance committee as the church financial secretary. I have served for many years, through all our campaigns for the building projects, and ups and downs of our church budget, asking at business meetings, "Can we do this or that?" It has been a joy to see how the Lord works through, and blesses, those who trust in Him. I look forward to seeing how the Lord carries us through our current challenge to give Him a 100th anniversary gift of paying down our mortgage.

Karen Hanson

in the direction of the church.[20] So on 12 September the executive board called a special congregational meeting to discuss the situation. Members and friends of the church were invited. With forty-three members and friends present, the moderator opened the discussion by describing the four main reasons why people were leaving the church:[21]

- Looking for a bigger, healthier church, rather than one that seemed to be shrinking
- Looking for a church with better programs
- Looking for a healthy, vibrant young people's group
- Concerns about the move and purchase of the property

At the meeting, Pastor Condit also spoke, and after describing some of the events of the past year, tendered his resignation, effective after sixty days as required by the constitution. At a later special business meeting on 26 September 1972, Pastor Condit, with approval from the board, asked to have his resignation made effective on 30 September[22] so he could assume a position at a church in Greeley, Colorado. This inaugurated a period of almost a year without a pastor.

During the ensuing year, the executive board had charge of finding qualified candidates for pastor. Their main criteria were "the ability and burden to move to Acton." The church considered a number of pastoral candidates, of which two were brought in and received call votes, but both declined to come. An attempt was also made to restart a youth program with an intern from Gordon College, but that only lasted a few months. In the meantime, people continued to leave the church. One of the special meetings to call a pastor drew only fifteen members. When it became clear that the search would be lengthy, Rev. Edson Fast was invited to become interim pastor starting 26 November 1972.

The church had reached a nadir and was in mortal danger. So many had left that Sunday attendance often numbered in the twenties. The people were so discouraged that serious consideration was given to either holding a re-vote on the decision to move or even closing altogether:

> A discussion then followed concerning the future of our church. Moderator March Purinton gave a few points on why we should move to Acton and our seeking a new pastor. In both of these important decisions we should seek the Lord's will and not our own... [23]

But discouragement gave way to faith. The members decided to give it one more try and continue to seek another pastor.[24]

Rev. Fast remained in the role of interim pastor until finally the church settled on candidate Rev. Kenneth Spence, a youth pastor from Cresskill, NJ, whom Bob Thoresen had met at Camp Spofford, and recommended as a candidate. At a meeting with twenty-one members present, plus three absentee ballots, the vote to extend a call to Ken was unanimous. He accepted the call and began his ministry on 15 July 1973.

When asked why he accepted the call to lead a church in such dire straits, Rev. Spence responded that he knew that he was a young pastor with no experience and the stakes were high, but he had found a number of leaders who were committed to do whatever it would take to rebuild and reinvent the church—among them Jim Goodemote, Jack

Ordinary People, Extraordinary Impact:
March Purinton, Jr.

March and his brother Richard (Rit) served together in WWII, returning to join their father, March Sr., as faithful servants in the church, starting as ushers. From the middle of the 1960s through 1975, some of the most tumultuous years of the church, March served as a deacon and church moderator.

Perhaps most significantly, when the congregation began to have second thoughts about the move to Acton, and was considering closing down, he passionately addressed the congregation as moderator, reminding everyone why they had embarked on this path and giving reasons why they should stay the course and keep going.

Stuart, and Bob Thoresen. By this time almost the only people remaining were the most dedicated, ready to do whatever it would take to continue the work in Acton. They were unified in their vision and mission. [25]

With the arrival of Rev. Spence, the fall of 1973 saw the beginnings of a turnaround as the "old guard" was replaced with a new leadership team. But the expense of maintaining the old property as well as the new, along with issues associated with renting out the old parsonage, would continue to drain resources and divert attention. The time to act had come.

Chapter 6:
Faith Evangelical Chapel

(1974-1993)

Faith Evangelical Chapel, 1976.

A New Church Comes to Acton

The annual meeting on 22 January 1974 was decisive for the life of the church. At this meeting, the congregation voted (twenty-five to two with two abstentions) to:

1. Move all church Sunday services to the Conant School, Acton, starting on Palm Sunday, 7 April 1974.
2. Put all Lang Street church property up for sale immediately.
3. Change the name of the church to "Faith Evangelical Chapel."[1]

**Rev. Kenneth Spence
(1973-1979)**

The name change was noteworthy in itself, for a number of reasons. First of all, it created a clean "break" from the ethnic history of the Lang Street church. And although the church remained affiliated with the Evangelical Free Church of America, the new name minimized any denominational ties, a decision that was felt to be desirable at the time. Significantly, in the newspaper article announcing the move to Acton, no mention was made of the church's former name, Evangelical Free Church of Concord. Rather, emphasis was put on a "new beginning," and the "new church" that was coming "to Acton." The church was re-inventing itself.

The lever had been pulled, the move was on. The next two and a half months required all hands on deck to take care of paperwork for the name change, rent the school, update signs, stationery, newspaper articles, radio and TV ads, move furniture into storage, inventory items to be sold, and get the old property ready for sale. The furnishings of the Lang Street building were stored in the barn on the Acton property; the organ was sold to Lexington Christian Academy; and the old property was put up for sale. That spring on Palm Sunday, the church held its first services at the Conant School near the new property.

Although it was not remembered by most people, the Conant School resided on property that had been originally owned by Malcolm and Judith Dunn, who had attended the church between 1959 and 1964.[2]

Faith Evangelical Church Worship Services In Acton

ACTON — Faith Evangelical Chapel begins worship services in Acton on Palm Sunday. On April 7, 1974, a new church will come to Acton. The new group will begin meeting in the Luther Conant Grammar School on Taylor Road in Acton, just off Route 2, under the leadership of Rev. Kenneth F. Spence. The

congregation is made up of a good number of Acton residents and there is great enthusiasm concerning this new beginning.

The church will offer a full compliment of services with Sunday School at 9:45 a.m. and the morning worship hour at 11:00 a.m. In addition there will also be an evening Fellowship hour at 6:00 p.m. on Sunday, also meeting at the school. Tuesday night prayer service will be held at 54 Hosmer Street in Acton.

Long term plans are under consideration and property has been purchased in Acton on which the congregation hopes to erect their future church building. It is their hope that, with this beginning, many will be able to take advantage of the ministry of the word of God and also join together to worship Him. The church has as its main objective, a Bible-centered ministry and a family oriented church life.

Assabet Valley Beacon, 20 March 1974, p15. Courtesy GateHouse Media.

Of course, not everyone was happy. March Purinton Sr., longtime treasurer for the church, and his wife resigned and left the church in protest, and Inga Cahill, who had been financial secretary for decades, and led the church musically for many years, asked to have her name removed from membership.[3]

The next week, on Easter Sunday, a sunrise service was held on the new property at 6:00 a.m., followed by a family breakfast at a local restaurant.[4] And on 23 April 1974 the spring quarterly business meeting was held at the parsonage on Hosmer Street for the first time, with twenty-two members present.[5] At that meeting it was announced that there would be a baptism service at Immanuel Baptist Church in Bedford. The visitation program was well underway, making sure that everyone who visited the church received a follow-up visit soon thereafter.

The year 1974 was also the beginning of a sort of spiritual revival at the church. While the church met at Conant School, Martin and Joyce Cassity headed up a visitation program on Monday nights, encouraging people to try the new church, as well as reaching out to those who had already visited. In addition, Pastor Spence made it a personal goal to "touch everyone who touched us," and he personally visited as many visitors as possible. Although Pastor Spence did not give an altar call or invitation to trust Christ every week, he did make an effort to explain the plan of salvation as part of each message. As so often happens, a few people who are excited about their newfound faith in Christ will bring in their immediate family and circle of friends. Others who were already believers were attracted by the new church in the school and became excited to be a part of this new adventure.

As a result, sixteen new members were welcomed in, and most importantly, six baptisms took place as people publicly proclaimed faith in Christ. The youth program also ramped back up under the leadership of A. Raymond Randall Jr. as youth director. Raymond served as an intern from 1974 until his graduation from Gordon Conwell in 1977.

Almost symbolically, the church mourned the loss of both of its elders that same year. Charter member John Andersen and Thomas (Ted) Thoresen[6] were called home to glory within months of each other. John Andersen's will designated a $1000 gift to the church, which was placed in the new building fund as seed money. Esther Davis also asked that the memorial fund for her husband, Alfred Davis, be placed in the building fund.

Loss of both elders, who had been elected to lifetime posts, created an opportunity to change the bylaws to elect elders for three-year terms. At the fall 1974 business meeting Bob Thoresen, Jim Goodemote, and George Werber were the first elders elected for three-year terms. Also at that meeting two new committees were formed: a building committee that would oversee the details of design and construction of the new building, and a building finance committee that would be in charge of raising funds for the construction.

Groundbreaking for the new building in Acton occurred on 7 December 1975, and construction was soon underway. The Lang Street property was sold a few days later, on 11 December 1975 for $100,000, freeing the congregation from the heavy burden of maintaining the property and acting as landlord for the parsonage. The sale also provided much-needed funds for the new construction, estimated to cost approximately $250,000. A capital campaign called "Together We Build" was also underway.

Services at the school were well-attended, and Sunday School rooms, which held only a few students at the beginning of the year, were soon bursting at the seams. A vibrant music program, including a choir and many soloists, was in full swing under the leadership of Joy Green. Many new members were added to the rolls, and people were committing their lives to Christ.

The building was completed by the fall of 1976, in time for new ministry activities to begin in September. On 3 October 1976 the new building was dedicated to the glory of God. Eastern District Superintendent Arne Hansen preached at the service, and Rev. Gordon Andersen, son of Rev. E.M. Andersen, who helped found the church in

Groundbreaking. L-R: George Werber, Clough Vettrus, Bob Specht, Rev. Ken Spence, Bob Thoresen, Asst. Superintendent Byron Seashore. Courtesy Vettrus family.

New sanctuary interior - 1976

1920, was also present. The new sanctuary boasted a seating capacity of 225 on the main floor, plus room for another 75 in the balcony, as well as space for 100 more in the overflow room. There was also plenty of parking to accommodate everyone.

On 5 December 1976, Rev. Spence became the fourth pastor to be ordained to the gospel ministry while serving at the church.

The congregation began to experience some growing pains at this time, especially in the area of organization and committee structure. The old bylaws did not reflect how things were currently done, and revisions would have to be made. For example, as stated above, the position of elder, originally a lifetime appointment, became a board of at least three men, each elected for three-year terms. The elders concentrated on the spiritual leadership and overall ministry direction of the church, while the deacons made sure that needs of the people were being met and no one in need was neglected or overlooked. In 1976, the deacons began to divide up the list of families among themselves to ensure that each family was cared for—a practice that continues to this day. They also created a "Deacons' Fund" to be used for taking care of short-term financial necessities of anyone in need.

The fund was seeded with $200 from the general fund, and quickly grew as people donated generously for this purpose.

The pattern of growth and expansion continued through 1977. The annual meeting in January had fifty-two members in attendance, and over twenty new members had been added to the rolls in the previous year. Fifteen additional members were added in 1977, and ten people followed the Lord in believer's baptism. Rev. William Lupole from Staten Island arrived in June to become the first full-time Pastor of Youth and Education, marking the first time that the congregation had two full-time pastors. In August he married Susan, and the two settled in Concord. Under his ministry, the Sunday Schools, Christian Service Brigade, Pioneer Girls, and youth groups thrived.

By this time, it was already becoming evident that the new building had insufficient education space for the rapidly increasing Sunday

Ordinary People, Extraordinary Impact: Jim Goodemote

Jim joined the church in the sixties, and dug in quickly, acting for years as Sunday School superintendent, teacher, assistant treasurer, elder and serving on the missions committee. He was a prime mover on the "site committee" that found the current church property on Hosmer Street, and made the necessary arrangements and negotiations to allow the move to happen. His commitment to see it through helped the church persist during the crisis years of the early 1970s, and provided stability and leadership to the church in the early Acton years. The Goodemote's departure in 1982 to New York was a sad time for all, and many fondly remember his "sword drills" and song leading on Sunday evenings.

School classes. This would be an ongoing problem for years. It was also clear that the balcony would need to be put to use sooner than expected, so pews were installed. The rapid growth necessitated creation of new committees to oversee and coordinate various ministries that were starting up. Church expenses grew by over 100% over two years, but giving still exceeded expenditures.

Youth Pastor Rev. William and Susan Lupole (1977-1981)

As early as 1977 Pastor Spence was growing concerned that the church was beginning to rest on its laurels. The immediate vision and goal of moving to Acton had been accomplished. What would be next? At a board meeting in the spring of 1977 he called for a two-day retreat for the board members to join in prayer and set goals.

But by the end of 1978, Rev. Spence was worried that although the church appeared to be prospering, the huge influx of people was resulting in a dilution of the vision of the church. In the 1978 pastor's report, Rev. Spence sounded a note of caution, even while rejoicing that thirty people had formally joined the membership roll:

> In the wake of some of the enthusiasm from this growth, it is also evident that we have been affected by the loss of a number of faithful families, some of whom were with us for just a short time. These losses make it necessary for us to look carefully at the spiritual dynamic of the body as the year comes to a close.
>
> The challenge of Paul stands out so pointedly, that I would encourage our close attention. "Do not merely look out for your own personal interests but also for the interest of others (Phil 2:4). In a body of diversified interests this is difficult, but necessary. In conjunction with this attitude, I would lay out a goal for the New Year. That goal is that we make every effort to establish a richer fellowship which will draw the body together with greater interests and purpose.[7]

While perhaps not fully understanding its significance, the church was beginning to feel the effects of a phenomenon that was taking root in the culture around them. This was the early phase of the high-tech boom in the Greater Boston suburbs. All of the surrounding towns became much more transient as a constant flow of people moved in and out of the area. During the church's first fifty years in Concord, its membership had deep roots in the town, and was fairly stable (while growing slowly). The move to Acton drew in people who had no New England roots, who were following new technology jobs, and many of whom had little experience with church life. The volume of temporary attenders was much higher, even though the net change in attendance remained manageable. This also meant that a large percentage of the congregation had only a few years' experience in the inner workings of a church, and their roots and sense of loyalty did not run deep.

The 1970s were also years of economic "stagflation," where unemployment was growing at the same time as inflation was increasing. The number of two-income families was rapidly expanding at this time. In 1980, for the first time more families had both spouses working outside the home than those with only one income.[8] Families were becoming busier (and more tired), and had less time for volunteer work. It is hard to overestimate the influence that these cultural changes had on the American church in general, and on Faith Chapel in particular.

Despite signs that people were growing tired, the excitement of growth and ministry continued. Sunday School attendance was averaging 120, including three adult classes, and the youth ministries were continuing to grow, with many decisions for Christ being made by the teens. A new Bible quiz team was formed and competed successfully with other churches in the district.

Crisis came at the January 1979 annual meeting, when Rev. Spence unexpectedly read his resignation letter and stepped down as pastor to take on a new ministry in Allentown, PA. This was a very difficult pastoral transition for the church, partly because of Pastor Spence's popularity, but also because there were many new and young believers who had never experienced the process of pastoral change before.

During the interim period, fruitful ministry continued as before. But even with the rapid growth that Faith Chapel had been experiencing, there was a shortage of people who were ready to take up the mantle of leadership. Youth Pastor Bill Lupole helped provide much-needed stability and perspective, and the elders and deacons expanded their roles to fill the gap while the search committee looked for a new senior pastor. The deacons began an "associate deacon" program, in which each deacon became a mentor for another young man who could experience the ministry first-hand and consider a call to that ministry. The Christian Education Board, as it was then known, re-emerged to help coordinate leadership of the Sunday School and youth ministries.

In 1979 the church decided that it was time to do something about the barn on the property. Although the structure of the barn itself was sound, its fieldstone foundation was crumbling, and it would be far too expensive to bring it up to code for it to be available as extra space for any public use. It also obstructed the view of the church building from the driveway. The Acton Historical Society, which had recently acquired the old historic Hosmer House on Main Street, was interested in moving the barn to its property. But in the end, it was sold to a neighbor behind the church, who moved it to his own property. The barn is still visible through the trees from the north side of the church property, on private property at 48 Alcott Street.[9]

For the first seven months after Ken Spence left, the elders, deacons and Pastor Bill took care of preaching with help from guest speakers. But by fall it was clear that it would be a long process, so in September 1979, Dr. Royce Gruenler, a professor at Gordon Conwell, was hired to serve as interim pastor while the search continued.

Finally, in March 1980, the board presented Rev. David R. Fife as a candidate, and on 4 March a special business meeting was held to consider his call. Seventy-two members and four adherents were present, which represented a large percentage of the membership (unlike many pastoral call meetings in the past). The final vote was forty-six in favor, and twenty-five opposed, or a 65% affirmative vote. With the understanding that this was sufficient, the call was extended, Pastor Fife accepted, and began his ministry shortly afterward.

Rev. David Fife
(1980-1982)

Even before Pastor Fife was called, however, a minor exodus from the church had begun. Indeed, in 1979 and 1980, forty-five people left—some moved out of the area; others began to attend other local churches, particularly Grace Chapel, by now a very large church in nearby Lexington. On the other hand, during those same years twenty-nine new members were added. In fact, in 1979 there was a net gain in membership of seven people.

Like Pastor Spence, Pastor Fife recognized that there were significant issues to address, and some consolidation to be done. But he and many members of church leadership were unable to reach an agreement on the best approach. Pastor Fife believed the church needed to focus on relationships and body life, whereas some of the leadership wanted to concentrate on the organizational structure of the church, administration, and development of a vision to carry us forward. At a board meeting in September 1980, Pastor Fife expressed pleasure with the way the deacons were caring for their families, but dismay with the "negative spirit being shown by some people of the congregation." It was necessary that people love and pray for one another.

In spite of conflicting perspectives between pastor and leadership, effective ministry ensued. In 1980, under the leadership of the Missions Committee, many people in the congregation participated in creating beautiful hanging banners, one for each missionary supported by Faith Chapel. These banners are used even today to keep the work of each missionary in the minds and prayers of the congregation. At least two banners are on display every week. That same year, the Missions Committee presented the first "Faith Promise" challenge, with funds targeted to send Bibles to Poland. Response to the Faith Promise concept was so significant that by 1984 the entire missions budget was based on Faith Promises, and grew from $17,000 (18% of the total budget) in 1983 to over $41,000 (25%) for 1985! Children and youth ministries continued to flourish, and souls were converted to Christ, despite the loss of Rev. Bill Lupole, who left in the spring of 1981 to become a senior pastor in Illinois.

In 1980, a member of the church, Lois Anderson, painted a mural of a pastoral scene with Jesus caring for his sheep, and it was hung over the baptistry facing the sanctuary. The mural hung there until 1989, when it was replaced by a large wooden cross created by Bob Thoresen.

Baptistry mural donated by Lois Anderson in 1980.

Also during Pastor Fife's ministry, the church's constitution and bylaws were finally rewritten and adopted in the spring of 1981. One significant change enacted under the new bylaws was the change of the term of office for committee members to a September-to-August schedule. This new schedule better reflected the ministry year of the church. Previously, committee membership turned over in January, a potentially disruptive practice as it occurred in the middle of the most active part of the year. The new bylaws also codified many new boards and committees. The bylaws were written with a large congregation in mind, but boards and committees require people to populate them— alas, membership had begun to decline by this time. In ensuing years, the church would often struggle to fill all its vacancies. There were too few people to do all the work, and everyone was getting tired. Few were available to engage in new, outward-focused ministry.

During 1981, Bill James, a member of the church who had experience with the Navigators ministry, began a discipleship ministry based on the Navigators' Colossians 2:7 program. This initial group eventually went on to become the leadership for several 2:7 groups in the church in which many participated.

Meanwhile, Sue Bennett and Judy Kastelein had been praying for a women's Bible study in Acton. At the time, Joy Bible Study, an evangelical, interdenominational ministry at Grace Chapel, Lexington had a very fruitful ministry. God had laid it on the hearts of two women from Joy, Dorothy Brooks and Mrs. Chase, to start a satellite study in Acton. In 1981, God brought these four women together to pray about the possibilities. Over the course of the next year, the groundwork was laid for them to start a daughter Joy Bible Study, modeled on *Community Bible Study* in California, as an outreach in the greater Acton area. Joy would use the church's sanctuary, classrooms, kitchen, and nurseries on Wednesday mornings during the school year.

Joy Bible Study in Acton opened in September 1982, with studies in Jonah and Paul's letter to the Philippians. Since then it has met at the church every year, becoming the predominant women's Bible study in the area, drawing a large number of women from the community as well as the church.

After Bill Lupole left, an associate pastor search committee was formed to define the new responsibilities for the position. But Pastor Fife's resignation in late 1981 caused the church to set aside the search for an associate and form a different search committee to find a new senior pastor. In the meantime, elder Bob Thoresen took oversight of the youth ministry, which was buttressed by activities with the local Crossroads ministry. In 1982 Elliot and Lynda Cook from Crossroads arrived to lead the youth ministry until April 1983.

Pastor Fife's resignation was effective 14 February 1982, when he left to begin a long and successful ministry in Rockport, MA. Two weeks later Rev. Kenneth McCowan from Lexington Christian Academy arrived as interim pastor during the search process. Rev. McCowan was an excellent preacher, and he had a number of "groupies," people who followed him from church to church as he provided preaching ministry for various congregations. It was at his suggestion that the communion service was changed so that the deacons would serve the pastor after he served them (prior to that, the pastor would typically serve himself). His suggestion is still followed in the same manner to this day.

Even during the interim, the Colossians 2:7 program expanded, and an additional new evangelistic discipleship program called Agape Ministries (based on a program used by Grace Chapel in Lexington) was started. The church enthusiastically supported the Billy Graham Cru-

Ordinary People, Extraordinary Impact: Clough and Helen Vettrus

Ruth Helen Thoresen, was the eldest daughter of Elder Thomas (Ted) and Ruth Thoresen. Having grown up in the church, she was involved in just about every facet of church life, including the Young People's Society, and later the Women's Missionary Society and Sunday School. In 1952 she married Clough Vettrus, who shared a love for the Lord and His church. In their later years, Helen could be found every Sunday working in the nursery so that the young mothers could enjoy the worship services. She always had extra food in the oven on Sundays so they could invite visitors and newcomers over for dinner and make them feel welcome.

Clough served as an usher and deacon for many years. Even after retiring from formal service, he continued to regularly visit shut-ins and seniors, making sure they were never forgotten. He did this until his own health issues forced him into confinement himself. Helen died in 1983, and Clough in 1995. They modeled the kind of love of the brethren and servant spirit that healthy churches are built upon.

sade in Boston (held the week of 30 May to 6 June 1982), through prayer and by providing counselors for the meetings, as well as phone counselors for the televised programs. Buses were rented so that people from the congregation could bring their unsaved friends and relatives to hear the Gospel proclaimed by Dr. Graham. This all culminated in a "Discovery" Sunday School course to help establish new believers in their Christian life. Many decisions for Christ were reported.

That summer the missions committee sponsored two young women from the church, Kris DeCanio and Kim Brannon, as summer missionaries holding 5-Day Clubs based on Child Evangelism Fellowship's ministry of the same name. The program had a total enrollment of 146 children, only twenty-six of whom were from Faith Chapel. God's hand was at work, and forty-six decisions for Christ were recorded.

God taught the congregation a significant spiritual lesson about generosity during 1982.[10] The deacons received a letter from a local evangelical congregation (not a Free Church) asking for prayers, as they were going through hard times and were unable to meet some major financial commitments. They did not ask for financial help, but Faith Chapel's deacon board contacted their leadership to learn more. After talking and praying with them, a special congregational meeting was called after one of the morning worship services, for the specific purpose of raising money to help them pay their oil bill. The other congregation was overwhelmed by this show of concern and generosity. Later that year at the annual Thanksgiving praise service, elder Bob Thoresen gave praise to God, reminding the congregation that at the time of the gift, Faith Chapel's own finances were not healthy, but God had rewarded the church's generosity by blessing its own financial condition. Also some visitors in the congregation that day had observed the special meeting and were so moved by the process that they began attending regularly and became members of the church. This was a great learning lesson about the faithfulness of God, and the need to put Christ's Kingdom above one's own church or denomination.

During this time without a pastor, the church was also able to make the parsonage available free of charge to a family who needed a place to stay.

Rev. Martin Crain began his ministry at Faith Chapel on 12 September 1982. His "down home" style quickly endeared him to many in the congregation. He preferred to be called "Marty" rather than Pastor Crain. At a fall "Chuck Wagon" social, he donned a white cowboy hat and sang a rousing rendition of "Ya Done Stomped On My Heart." He also challenged the youth group to invite their friends to a fall kickoff social by promising to swallow a goldfish if there were over twenty in attendance. They did, and he did.

Rev. Dr. Marin and Lydia Crain, Scott and Allison (1982-1988)

But Marty was very serious about the ministry and spiritual life of the church. In light of the recent transition of leadership, and the need to establish a clear ministry focus, the search for a full-time associate pastor was again put on hold. Instead, in the fall of 1983, David Pattison joined as part-time youth director.

Next year, the Eastern District Association of the EFCA split into three smaller districts: the New England District (NEDA), the Ohio/Pennsylvania District (OhPen, eventually renamed the Allegheny District), and a smaller Eastern District (EDA) concentrated in New York, New Jersey, Delaware and Virginia. Faith Chapel hosted the first annual NEDA conference in March 1983, memorable in part because of a major snowstorm which caused a power outage.

Later that fall, after careful consideration, the Elders replaced Sunday evening services with home groups—each group met weekly and once a month in a "community" (church-wide) gathering. Further, to improve attendance at Sunday School, the Sunday morning schedule was changed: worship would now begin at 9:30 a.m., followed by a coffee fellowship time and Sunday School at 11:00 a.m. So for its first thirty years, the church held only evening worship services. The next thirty-four years there were services on Sunday mornings and evenings. But since 1984, evening services have typically not been held, except for special circumstances.

Dave and Jane Pattison
Youth Director (1983-1985)
Pastor of Youth and Young Adults (1985-1987)

The year 1985 proved to be a transitional one for the church, as many families involved in leadership moved away. This resulted in a turnover of almost 20% in church attendance. Many important boards and committees were understaffed, making it obvious that there were too many boards and committees for a church this size. Further, the church was struggling to assimilate newcomers effectively. Some people were overextended and growing weary, while others were not sufficiently involved. Plans to plant a church in a neighboring town were put on hold because no team was ready to put in the required effort. As had been true since the beginning, the youth ministry was always considered of prime importance, as many families were being reached through their teens. So a full-time position for Minister of Youth and Young Adults was created. Dave Pattison was given first consideration and called to fill the position.

During the mid-1980s, the church began to catch a new vision of home and foreign missions. In the beginning of 1985, Pastor Crain and his wife, Lydia, embarked on a three-week trip to visit missionaries Earl and Phyllis Blomberg in Venezuela, and Roger and Betty Dorris in Peru. They also took a side trip into the jungle to observe the work of other Free Church missionaries there. In February, Mike and Julie Miller went on a trip to join Bruce and Joy Fleming and teach at the Bangui Evangelical School of Theology (BEST), a seminary in Bangui, Central African Republic. The same year, Frank and Veronica DeCanio moved to Dallas to prepare for the full-time mission field.

The 1986 annual missions report summarizes:

> As we look back over the past few years, we have seen the missions budget go from about $17,000 in 1983 to over $46,000 in 1986. Our missionary families who we support have increased from eight to sixteen and for the first time this next year, we shall support one of our own young people who has gone into full-time missionary service.
>
> Some of our youth have gone as a group on two summer missionary projects, while others have gone out separately with TEEN missions to such countries as Egypt, Belgium, Alaska and Venezuela.
>
> Our pastor and his wife caught a new vision of missions from their trip to South America in January of 1985 to visit two of our missionary families there, as did two of our other couples who visited Africa and Europe that same year. Also, a mature couple from our midst began full-time seminary training this fall in preparation for the mission field.
>
> At present we see people from our congregation actively working in different spheres where the Lord has particu-

larly led them: 1) prison ministry, 2) foreign students, 3) Community Supper, 4) rescue missions, 5) Child Evangelism 5-Day Clubs, 6) home visitation, 7) inviting unsaved neighbors to Bible studies, and 8) prayer support. More people have taken the challenge to be prayer partners for particular missionaries than ever before.[11]

In 1986, in order to provide more room for Sunday School and nursery needs, moveable walls were installed downstairs in the fellowship hall. These walls provided better soundproofing and could be taken down for occasions that required the entire fellowship hall. Although they were intended for temporary use until the building could be expanded, the walls are still being used to this day, although they are no longer considered movable because of their condition.

The transience of the congregation continued, forcing leadership to concentrate on the basics of worship, prayer, Bible study, discipleship, outreach and fellowship. Additional ministry was pursued on a personal level, such as involvement with Joy Bible Study, Community Supper (sponsored by Acton Congregational Church), and the ministry at the Concord Prison farm.

In 1987, Pastor Crain was instrumental in forging a close relationship with the Korean Baptist Church, which began using Faith Chapel's facilities for all of their Sunday activities—an arrangement that has continued to this day. The Korean church eventually joined the EFCA.

Also that year, Pastor Crain became the Reverend Doctor Martin Crain when he completed his Doctor of Ministry degree at Trinity Evangelical Divinity School.

In April, the missions committee held a mini-conference whose theme was church planting. One of the guest speakers was Rev. Doug Welch from Waterville, ME.

After Dave Pattison's departure in June 1987, a new job description was created for an Associate Pastor of Youth and Family Life, and a search committee was formed. By the end of the year, the search had produced Rev. Brad Johnson as a candidate for the position.

This placed Pastor Crain in a difficult position. Around this same time, he had been approached to submit his name in nomination as a candidate to become Superintendent of the New England District Association of the EFCA. The election for superintendent would not occur until the district conference in March, but it would not be fair to the

Reminiscences

One of the first major undertakings for "Faith Chapel" after Pastor Crain joined us in 1982 was to host the annual conference for pastors and representatives from the newly formed New England District in March 1983. Somehow, I volunteered to find host homes for many of the attendees. All went well until we had a major snowstorm which caused us to lose power on the night of the banquet. Our feast turned into a wonderfully spiritual catacomb-like worship service in the old fellowship hall, with just cold food, after which we needed to house lots of additional people. God amazingly provided beds for those who could not get home through the generosity of His people here at Faith, showing me that His resources know no end. Fast forward a few years, just before Pastor Crain moved on to become the New England District Superintendent. The Korean Baptist Church began worshiping here in 1987. One of the ways we joined with them was to have one of their leaders join us for prayer at our BYE meetings. I remember that as we all prayed, either in English or Korean, I had the distinct sense that God was giving us a foretaste of heaven where there will be believers of every tongue and tribe. Even though I only understood the word for Jesus, I could feel the Spirit moving among us.

Sue Bennett

congregation or Brad to go through a candidating process without knowing that Marty might be leaving soon. Marty explained the situation to Brad and the elders prior to Brad's candidating weekend in January, and he announced his plans to the congregation before the vote to call Brad. At the special call meeting, the congregation agreed that the position needed to be filled whether or not Faith Chapel had a senior pastor, and committed to Brad that he would be given input into the search process to make sure he could work with the new pastor. There were no expectations that Brad would resign when the new senior pastor arrived. Based on that understanding, Brad accepted the call and began his ministry as Pastor of Youth and Family Life in February 1988.

While Brad and his family looked for a more permanent place to live, Wayside Evangelical Free Church, which a few years previously

Rev. Brad Johnson
Pastor of Youth and Family Life
(1988-2004)
Associate Pastor (2004-2006)

had moved from Hudson to Sudbury, offered them a place to stay in a barn on their property which had been converted into a livable space. The Johnson's remained there until they were able to purchase a home on Main Street in north Acton.

After Marty left for Keene, NH on 1 May, the preaching ministry was supplied by capable men within the congregation (Steve Hall, Mike Miller, and Jim Coster), as well as guest speakers, such as Rev. Donald Fisher. But the elders soon realized that the continuity of one interim pastor would most help the church. This need was filled by Don Fisher.

At a congregational meeting on 20 May 1989, Rev. Doug Welch was called as senior pastor. He began his ministry on 27 August 1989, coming to the church from Waterville, Maine. That summer, improvements were made to the parsonage to ready it for its new occupants. The church also committed to renovating the kitchen in the parsonage, but that would have to wait another year or so.

The years 1989-1991 brought breathtaking changes on the international stage, with the fall of the Berlin wall, reunification of Germany and the collapse of the Soviet Union. On top of all this, the United States built an international coalition to expel Iraq from Kuwait in the short and decisive Operation Desert Storm at the beginning of 1991. Taken together, these events greatly increased the confidence people had in the country and its place in the world, and eased the tensions that had accompanied the recent escalations of the Cold War.

A celebration with the Korean brethren took place in March 1990, as they joined the EFCA as the first Korean Evangelical Free Church in America.

That year, the church also began supporting Mike DeRosa in his efforts to plant a new Evangelical Free church in Shrewsbury, MA. In 1991, the Gluck family transferred their membership to worship and serve there.

In 1992, Pastor Doug reminded the congregation that the seventy-fifth anniversary of the church's founding was only a few years away. The anniversary had been celebrated every year in Concord, but since moving into the Acton facility in 1976, it was largely forgotten. Pastor Doug challenged the congregation to set a goal of offering the Lord a gift of seventy-five people led to Christ over the next three years. The Lord began to honor that goal almost immediately, as He drew twenty people to Himself over the first year, including four adults, ten teens and six children, who prayed with parents, friends, and through the public and private ministry of the church! Additionally, the youth group saw significant growth, an especially exciting fact as four of the ten teens who had accepted Christ that year were led to Christ by their teenage friends!

**Rev. Doug Welch
(1989-2005)**

That year, the congregation hired Harold Mims, a church member who was pursuing a degree in music, as part-time music director. During his nineteen months in the position, he helped the church see the potential of various styles of music as part of the fullness of worship.

Chapter 7:
Faith Evangelical Free Church

(1993-Present)

During the early 1990s, the congregation periodically amended the bylaws to adjust committee structures in an attempt to streamline where possible, and better align with the needs of the church as the ministry in Acton matured.

At the same time, the New England District (still headed by former pastor Marty Crain) encouraged all churches within the district to align themselves more explicitly with the Evangelical Free Church of America. By this time, the words "Evangelical Free" no longer carried any kind of ethnic connotation. To the contrary, the denomination was enjoying a good reputation as one of the fastest growing denominations in the country. The church was already trying to emphasize its EFCA connection by openly stating that it was affiliated with the Evangelical Free Church. Even so, the name "Faith Evangelical Chapel" was somewhat confusing, especially to those with a Free Church background. Pastor Brad was confronted with this fact when several people attending other churches told him they would have attended Faith had they known it was a Free Church.

So at the 30 September 1992 business meeting, a constitutional amendment was proposed to formally change the name to Faith Evangelical Free Church. As constitutional amendments required consideration at two consecutive meetings, the final vote did not occur until the January 1993 annual meeting. On 10 March 1993, the new name was officially registered with the Commonwealth of Massachusetts, effective 23 January 1993.

That year, Pastor Doug and FEFC member Jack MacLellan (a relatively new convert at the time) traveled on a mission trip to Africa to meet with Mike Ring and his family in Ethiopia, followed by visits with Tom and Julie Varno in Uganda, as well as Cindy Bennett at her college internship in Kenya—all missionaries the church supported at the time.

Another five adults, six teens, and two children prayed to receive Christ that year.

Although membership remained essentially flat during this period, the building was still overcrowded, due primarily to growing youth and children's programs. A building committee continued to look for options, but there was no doubt that expansion would be required. In 1993, the building committee researched alternatives, developed a conceptual plan for an addition, and presented initial recommendations for congregational feedback. The next step, requiring an investment of about $14,000 for architectural plans, was put on hold until that money could be raised.

Next year, another nine people were led to the Lord, and thirteen followed Him in believer's baptism. That brought the total number of people who had professed new faith in Christ since 1992 to forty-two. This marvelous news brought with it a discipleship challenge. There

---

Reminiscences

Who would have thought that a bible study could change your life? I went to Joy to get away from my two year old and be with adult women. I was curious about the Bible, and about Jesus. I grew up in a Presbyterian church, but had no clue about the gospel or being born again. After three weeks, I prayed to receive Jesus and my life was dramatically changed. I went from dark to light, chaos to order, lost to found. I couldn't get enough of the Bible. Soon I was leading bible study groups, teaching women's Sunday School, and directing Joy itself. What effect did Joy have on me? It changed everything: my identity, attitude, worldview, my roles as wife and mother. And I found a reason for loving and living. Degree of change: absolute.

Sally Abbott

continued to be significant transience within the congregation—45% turnover from 1989 to 1994! Although many families had moved on, other new faces arrived, many of whom were new or young believers.

In January 1995, on the occasion of the church's 75th anniversary celebrations, FEFC member Ed Bennett retrieved the original cornerstone dated "1920" from the Lang Street property, which by now was a residential building. Three different celebrations were held that year. The first, held in the spring and entitled "Days of Concord," reflected on the years at Lang Street. Pastor Ken Spence (1973-1979) reminded people that in past times of discouragement, serious thought had been given to closing down the church, but the Lord had moved and breathed new life into the congregation. As a result, many people had been saved and the church had revived.

At the fall "Harvest Supper," Pastor's David Fife (1980-1982) and Marty Crain (1982-1988) emphasized the faithful "Faith Chapel" years. And at the actual 18 November diamond anniversary dinner, testimonies were delivered by many of the over fifty new souls who had trusted in Christ over the past few years leading up to that time!

Also during the anniversary celebration year, the missions conference called attention to all of the missionaries the church had supported through the years. A letter written to each of the missionaries describes the scene:

> The sanctuary was decorated with a banner representing each of you, with a large banner hung in front depicting the world map. The large banner had our theme across the top and showed how we as a small body of believers can have a world-wide influence. Strung around the sanctuary was a two inch paper strip with every family name that has been supported in missions through our church over the past seventy-five years. There was close to ONE HUNDRED names! Praise God for His faithfulness over the years and the many souls that have come to know Him through our missions support here at FEFC.[1]

But 1995 was not all celebration. That spring, the church was forced to exercise discipline on one of the deacons for moral failure. When he was confronted, there was no fruit of repentance, so the membership committee was forced to remove him as deacon and revoke his membership. They unavoidably had to report that action to the congregation during a special business meeting called for that purpose. Pastor Doug helped the congregation through the process, leading them through the applicable scripture, reminding everyone that the verse, "let him be to you as a Gentile and a tax collector" (Matt 18:17), effectively called for them to treat him as they would any unbeliever, namely, that the congregants should refrain from fellowship, but pray for him and witness to him so that he might repent. For the next five years, a group prayed for him every Thursday evening at the weekly prayer meeting, and the elders prayed for him at every one of their meetings.

Meanwhile, God worked in his life to bring him to recognize his need, and in 2000, he repented, returned, and made himself accountable to an "angel team" who helped restore him to fellowship. Later that year, he was formally restored to full fellowship and membership before the congregation at a moving communion service to the glory of God. At the service the elders and deacons walked down the central aisle of the sanctuary surrounding the penitent sinner. On the platform he sat in a chair with the elders and deacons behind him and to either side. The pastor read Scripture about the Prodigal Son, as well as 2 Corinthians 2:5-11, after which the man stood and read Psalm 51 and sat back down. The pastor, elders and deacons then made a declaration of his restoration to fellowship and led a prayer of praise to God. An afghan/throw with spiritual words of praise was given to him as a reminder of the congregation's love for him, and then everyone participated in the Lord's Supper together.

This is reported here not to call attention to the sin or the sinner, but to give glory to God who forgives and restores the years that the locusts have eaten. Although the consequences of sin are real, and may not be relieved in this life, many learned first-hand that it is never too late to repent, and that God is in the business of forgiving.

Also in 1995, in recognition that Pastor Brad was already in his eighth year of ministry at Faith, and Pastor Doug was about to enter his seventh, the elders developed a sabbatical policy for pastoral staff. This policy was approved by the congregation at the annual meeting in January 1996. Pastor Brad took his first sabbatical that summer, and Pastor Doug took his the following summer.

For the ministry year 1996-1997, the elders designated Sunday evenings a time for church-wide home group studies of Henry Blackaby's *Experiencing God*. This was augmented by monthly "community" meetings at which the groups gathered together to share what they had learned. Blackaby's principles included:

1. God is always at work around us.

2. God pursues a continuing love relationship with us that is real and personal.

3. God invites us to become involved with Him in His work.

4. God speaks by the Holy Spirit through the Bible, prayer, circumstances, and the church to reveal Himself, His purposes, and His ways.

5. God's invitation for us to work with Him always leads us to a crisis of belief that requires faith and action.

6. We must make major adjustments in our lives to join God in what He is doing.

7. We come to know God by experience as we obey Him and He accomplishes His work through us.[2]

As the congregation considered these principles, many people were convicted that God was asking the church to step out in faith to expand the facilities. After much prayer and consideration, a special congregational meeting was held in June 1997. In recognition of the importance of consensus (based on Blackaby's fourth principle), the elders set a goal of an 85% affirmative vote before proceeding. When the result came in at 75%, the pastor discerned that

> This vote shows that we are not ready now but the need is there and we all see it — it may be timing is not now — 75% is affirmative vote we sense a leading but are not ready — cost is greater than we are ready to commit to now.[3]

At the 1998 annual meeting, the Board of Youth and Education proposed a presentation of a "live nativity" program for the community the following Christmas, based on a model seen at a church in Leominster, MA. Linda Beals volunteered to head the entire program. However, in the spring of 1998, tragedy struck as her beloved husband George, a highly respected leader and elder and a godly man, was diagnosed with terminal brain cancer, and died soon afterwards.

The years 1997 and 1998 were difficult financially for the church, partly because attendance was down, but mostly because expenses were higher than planned. In the summer of 1998, the general fund balance temporarily went in the red, causing much consternation—this meant that checks were being written against money that had been earmarked for other funds, such as missions. While this was not the first time such a thing had occurred in the church's history, the finance committee was understandably uncomfortable with such a scenario. So, in order to give the committee a policy for such circumstances, the church board and congregation formally authorized the finance committee to borrow against the other funds should the general fund balance ever dip below zero. The understanding was that the Church Board must be notified immediately afterward so that a special congregational meeting may be called to decide how to proceed further. Through it all, the Lord was faithful, and His people were responsive; the general fund ended up in the black, albeit by a much narrower margin than preferred!

With this as a backdrop, the building committee continued its activity, and a consensus was growing that ministry was being hampered by a shortage of space. So, at the 1999 annual meeting, the building committee presented a proposal for a two-phase building program: Phase one would consist of major repairs and renovations to the existing building to bring it up to code where necessary and enhance disability access. Phase two would focus on the construction of the actual addition. Three motions were presented in the form of questions:

1. Should we proceed with the two-phase plan?
2. Should we start now (i.e., do we begin fundraising)?
3. Should we hire Resource Services, Inc. (RSI) to help with fundraising?

Because of the continuing importance of consensus on such a major undertaking, the building committee again asked for an 85% affirmative vote on the first two motions, rather than the normal simple majority. This was an even higher bar than the requirement for calling a new pastor (75%)! With fifty-four members present, the vote on the first motion was forty-seven in favor and six against, with one abstention. Before the vote the congregation was informed that an abstaining vote would count as a "No." This meant that the vote was 83.3% affirmative, falling just short of the required 85%. "This was a disappointment to many, but Pastor Doug stated that the Lord has spoken, and for now it will be put on hold.[4]"

However, not only was the vote extremely close, there was also the question of how the abstention vote should be counted. Consequently, the Church Board called a special business meeting on 27 February, to reconsider the vote. This time, there were seventy-three members present. Motions one and two both carried by over 85%. The motion to hire RSI was tabled until the regular May meeting to give everyone more time to learn more about RSI and to discuss options. At the May meeting, the motion to retain RSI was carried by a wide margin.

Preparation for the building program was officially underway. Under the leadership of RSI, a stewardship campaign steering committee was formed, and the "Act on Faith" campaign began. The campaign drew pledges of about $450,000 to be paid over three years and planning for phase one accelerated.

Two months later the wind was taken out of everyone's sails when, on 20 April 1999, two students entered the high school in Columbine, Jefferson County, Colorado, and began a shooting spree that would claim the lives of ten students and a teacher, plus wounding twenty-one others, before they took their own lives. This was the deadliest high school shooting in US history at that time. Suddenly, schools no longer seemed safe. As often occurs in times of crisis, church attendance increased by about twenty for the next three Sundays, before settling back to normal. But it also solidified the resolve of parents and youth to reach out in the schools. Student-led prayer groups were formed at local junior and senior high schools, and "See You at the Pole" became a popular day of prayer in which students led prayer for their schools around the flagpole. Parents supported their children and towns in prayer around flag poles at their respective town halls. And the resolve of everyone to expand the building for youth ministry was amplified.

In 2000, Pastor Brad graduated from Seminary of the East with his Master of Divinity, augmenting his previous Master of Counseling degree from Grace Theological Seminary.

That fall, Acton Community Chorus, a choir that draws members from many MetroWest communities, requested the use of the sanctuary on Monday evenings for their practices. Recognizing the opportunity to increase visibility of the church to the surrounding towns, the church invited them in free of charge. They have continued to use the church every year to the present day.

Reminiscences

I'll never forget the day Pastor Doug asked me to join the 2001 Venezuela mission trip: What was holding me back? Well, frankly, my fear of dying from some nasty disease or getting sick from the water or being kidnapped. Strangely, I heard my mouth tell Pastor "yes, I'll go." A few months later, our team of twelve landed at the Caracus airport at 3 a.m. There to greet us were the goats (really), new smells, and, God bless them, the Venezuelan folks charged with getting us safely to our hotel that night. The next two weeks we threaded pipe, cut rebar, poured cement, and moved countless bricks to build new homes (and a church) for those who had lost everything in the devastating mudslides just months before. While that work was important and pleasing to God, equally memorable and significant were other moments. Moments we played with kids who were so poor they had barely enough to eat or wear. Moments we worshipped in Spanish alongside these devoted, beautiful Christians. Moments we ate lunch with the locals during the long, hot days, cracking jokes as we worked together. Don't ask me how we understood each other...we just did. I wept bitter tears when it was time to say good-bye. God had done a marvelous work. He showed me His people are everywhere, His Kingdom is real...and it's better to trust Him and obey. I'm so glad I did!

Karen Mullane

In 2001, the elders desired to shift Pastor Brad's ministry to focus on adult ministry. Since youth ministry continued to be a priority as well, a search was initiated for a part-time youth director who could off-load Brad's youth responsibilities. That search finally reached fruition in 2002 with the recognition of a member of the church who was already ministering as a youth sponsor. Unfortunately, the next year he was required to resign as youth director due to a moral failure. Unlike the case in 1995, this man was repentant and confessed, and although he was required to step down as youth director, after his restoration he was reinstated as a youth sponsor. However, these events required Pastor

Brad to postpone the change in his duties and continue as Pastor of Youth and Family Life.

As the plans for the first phase of expansion solidified, construction began in 2001. This included accessibility improvements, new sanctuary lighting, and some major repairs. New carpeting was installed in the sanctuary, as well as a chair lift to provide access to the platform. A new architectural firm was secured for phase two planning, since the original architect/builder had retired during the long delay.

On 11 September 2001, the nation was again rocked when four airliners were hijacked by al-Qaeda terrorists, crashing into the two World Trade towers and the Pentagon. People around the country opened their homes to those who had been stranded after all aircraft were grounded. Families in Acton were directly affected by the loss of life. And in describing the events of that day, many people found they could not avoid using a word that had fallen into disuse in recent years: "evil." The following Sunday, Faith EFC and other churches found their worship services swelled by over 30% as people sought comfort and answers to help make sense of what had happened.

In 2002, the congregation approved commencement of a second stewardship campaign, this time without the help of RSI. This campaign culminated in a banquet in January 2003, reaping pledges of about $390,000. In addition, the original mortgage on the old building was retired.

Most significantly from a community outreach standpoint, in the fall of 2002 the church presented the first "Journey to Bethlehem," a Living Nativity based on a script given to the church by Windham Bible Chapel in New Hampshire. Under the capable leadership of Jeri Welch and a large leadership team, the script was customized for Faith Evangelical Free Church, and the indoor play was expanded significantly. Almost every family in the church participated in some way, whether by building the stations, preparing the property, indoor or outdoor acting, lighting, prayer, evangelism, publicity, ushering, hospitality, parking, and baking thousands of homemade cookies. This first year even included a live camel, as well as sheep, goats, and a donkey. Beginning in 2004, the program would also include a live baby at the outdoor stable, (always a huge hit with children and adults alike). The response from the community to this three-night event has been overwhelming, and Journey to Bethlehem (JtB) has become a tradition of the church every year since 2002. People from Acton and the surrounding communities look forward to it every year. Many have been attracted to the church and become regular attenders, and many have expressed renewed interest in spiritual things or asked for prayer.

However, in the early 2000s the Catholic Church sexual abuse scandal caused many churches to re-examine their policies and procedures with respect to children's programs. As a result, the Board of Youth and Education (BYE) began instituting guidelines, resulting in changes to the classrooms (windows in every door) and policies for teachers, including requiring at least two teachers in each classroom. Background checks were also instituted for everyone who worked with children in any capacity. Sally Abbott, the point person on BYE for this initiative, was also the director of Joy Bible Study at that time. Joy had already been using the church for its meetings for over twenty years, and they had an active children's ministry to which women in the study could bring their children. Recognizing that the same security issues would apply to Joy's children's program, Sally and the other leaders of Joy approached the elders about building a closer relationship with the church so that it could be protected under the church's policies and insurance. The key to such a relationship would be to somehow maintain the independent nature of Joy so that women from all walks of life would be willing to attend.

An agreement was reached which allowed Joy to remain independent and interdenominational, while still being sponsored by the church with close communication between the directors and the elders. Most importantly, they would also adopt the church's policies and procedures regarding child care workers, allowing them to fall under the church's liability protection. This arrangement has proven to be mutually beneficial, as Joy has had a great outreach to women in the community, resulting in many coming to Christ, growing in their relationship with Him, and some choosing to attend Faith EFC.

In 2003, new lighting for the sanctuary was installed, which greatly enhanced the worship experience. However, much of the rest of the work was held up for another year because the State Handicap Access Board in Boston ruled that the baptistry must be accessible so that those with disabilities could be baptized by immersion, even though in the past, baptisms by pouring had been conducted on the main platform for those in wheelchairs. This ruling was clearly an interference by the state in church practices. The church was therefore forced to file an appeal in Superior Court, which overturned the ruling. But the ruling and subsequent appeal delayed approval of local building permits.

Journey to Bethlehem

The fall of 2003 marked the beginning of a difficult time for Pastor Doug and his family, which necessitated his taking time away from the ministry of the church to care for his family:

> This has ... been a very difficult year for Pastor Doug and his family, with the long-term care of Jeri's mother, and the death of both her parents within two months of each other, followed by the need to care for their daughter as she wrestles with clinical depression. So while Pastor Doug had

planned to come back from his sabbatical to apply his energies toward the next phase of his ministry among us, he found that his emotional and spiritual energy was required at home. So the elders released Pastor Doug from his daily and preaching duties for a time while he cares for his family.

Through all of this, we have seen God's provision and love. God has given us a godly pastor who not only faithfully serves us, but has also modeled for us how to be a good husband, son, and father. And God has provided the financial and leadership depth to the church so that we can trust Him and function effectively in the absence of a key leader. Pastor Brad has selflessly stepped back into the pulpit during the months of November and December, actually doing the job of two people, to stand in the gap for Pastor Doug. He took on additional counseling load, helped with the Nativity, and "fought fires," plus preaching, all while keeping the youth ministry and building program on track. We also want to thank the youth sponsors for stepping up and doing extra work to help Pastor Brad while his attention was elsewhere. In addition, many people stepped up and relieved Jeri by taking on her leadership duties for the Living Nativity. We would like to especially thank Karen Hanson and Mary Shaw for their doubled efforts. The elders want to thank the whole congregation for their patience, understanding, and expressions of love to the pastors and their families during this difficult time...[5]

For the first part of 2004, Pastor Brad continued to stand in for Pastor Doug while he ministered to his family. In March 2004, the pastors and elders hosted Ted Brewer for a one-day seminar on resolving conflict in a biblical and God-honoring manner. The time seemed ideal to hold this seminar, because there were no raging conflicts that threatened the church. It seemed best to discuss such things during times of relative calm.

Later in 2004, Pastor Doug returned to full-time ministry.

In August, the church hired Dan Kasey as part-time youth director. At the time, Dan was also working full-time for the Salvation Army. The addition of Dan freed Pastor Brad to concentrate on his duties as associate pastor with more emphasis on adult ministry. Dan became the primary youth leader, while Brad gave oversight and mentored Dan.

Phase one construction finally kicked into high gear and was completed in 2004. Renovations of the old building were completed, as well as the first part of the new addition, including a new entryway, an indoor lift, new entrance, new upstairs and downstairs bathrooms, a mechanical room (housing, among other things, the sprinkler system), as well as a beautiful "sunroom" where the old entryway used to be, with a new classroom on the lower level below the sunroom.

The third annual Journey to Bethlehem, led by Jeri Welch, included the volunteer work of more than three-fourths of the church community. Over 1,700 people from the surrounding towns and beyond passed through during the three-day presentation. Many expressed a desire to know more about Christ, and have a personal relationship with Him!

However, there were signs that the church still had work to do.

Periodically it is important to take a step back and look closely at the health of the church, its body life, and its various ongoing ministries. During the fall of 2004 and the first half of 2005, the elders and staff began that process, including a one-day offsite retreat with the deacons in January 2005, using the EFCA's "Ten Indicators of a Healthy Church." Discussion topics included areas in which the church excelled, and those where it fell short. Planning began for improving effectiveness. Of particular concern were the continuing general sense of malaise in the congregation, and a loss of a sense of purpose and vision, even during the business of new construction. Major areas of weakness included church planting and evangelism, personal discipleship, and effective, Spirit-filled worship. This was especially concerning as they were the very emphases and focal points for the church's ministry! Making matters worse, the congregation was aging—the nursery had few babies, and while the youth group was thriving, there was little representation among college and career or young families.

At the same time, finances were beginning to show signs of weakness as the church was still getting used to paying salaries for three staff members (senior pastor, associate pastor, and part-time youth director).

While leadership was working through these issues, Pastor Doug, after a great deal of soul-searching and prayer, came to the conclusion that the church could best go forward with new leadership. So in July

2005, he submitted his resignation as senior pastor, effective 18 September. Saying goodbye to Pastor Doug was especially hard as he had served at Faith for sixteen years, making him the longest-serving senior pastor in the church's history. Many people in the church had never known another pastor there, and everyone had become close to him and his family. For many, this was the first pastoral transition they had experienced. For others, it brought back bad memories of past involvement in churches that had experienced conflict or failure in the transition from one pastor to another. It was an unsettling time.

**Ordinary People,
Extraordinary Impact:
Faith Brayden**

Faith joined the church in the early days at Acton, and quickly threw herself into service. She loved to relate the stories behind favorite hymns, and often she would recite poems she had written. She considered the church library an important resource, and worked tirelessly to acquire, organize, and catalog books. But she was best known for her faithfulness and fervency in prayer. At the Concord prison farm, where she spent countless hours volunteering, she was known and loved by the inmates as Sister Faith. The men there looked forward to her frequent visits, and they knew she was always praying for them. When her own health failed and she became a shut-in herself, they were equally faithful in praying for her, and they joined the church in mourning her death in 2006.

Pastor Brad, who had just moved into his new duties as Associate Pastor, agreed to become the interim pastor while the search for Doug's replacement proceeded. The search committee began meeting in October, and, based on input from the congregation, and the qualifications defined in the bylaws and Scripture, developed a comprehensive pastoral profile which represented the church's collective vision of what characteristics the Holy Spirit would have them seek in their next pastor. Based on this profile, Pastor Brad formally asked that he be considered as a candidate, so the committee examined him first.

Meanwhile, Dan Kasey, though only part-time, took complete ownership of the youth program. But the church's contract with Dan was due to expire in 2006, and he wished to go into full-time ministry at Faith or elsewhere. So, although the Senior Pastor position was still technically open, a new position of Pastor of Youth and Family Life was created by congregational vote, and a second search committee was formed to determine the necessary qualifications and find a candidate. In a second vote, the congregation instructed the search committee to consider Dan Kasey for the position before looking outside the church. This process followed the precedent set during the selection of David Pattison as full-time youth pastor in 1985.

**Brad and Kathy Johnson
(2006-present)**

Both committees interviewed their respective candidates and independently reached the conclusion that they should be presented to the church for a consideration and a vote. Schedules were coordinated, and the evening of 29 April was set aside for the candidates to present their case and the congregation to ask questions. The next day, 30 April 2006, a special congregational meeting was invoked during which the church voted unanimously to call Brad Johnson as Senior Pastor, effective 1 June. Dan Kasey was also called as Pastor of Youth and Family Life by a near-unanimous vote. His call would be effective 1 August.

As he was winding down his ministry at Faith, Pastor Doug began a preaching series on church health. Around this same time the elders and pastors developed short and long-term goals for the church to help the congregation see how the overall vision could be realized. Even during the interim period, Pastor Brad worked with the elders to solidify the vision and priorities into one, two, five, and ten-year goals which would enable the church to fulfill its aspiration to "present everyone mature in Christ." The initial focus would be on prayer, improving worship services, small groups and Sunday school ministries, and taking advantage of evangelistic opportunities. The ultimate goal would be to support two services totaling a maximum of 400 to 450 regular attenders while spinning off multiple daughter churches to accommodate and encourage continued growth. This would also require completion of the building expansion plans.

The next summer Pastor Brad preached through the Free Church's "10 Leading Indicators of a Healthy Church," and challenged the members of the congregation to consider their own ministry health. Small groups were also targeted as a vital ministry, and eight groups were formed to study *The Emotionally Healthy Church* in 2007.

During 2006 the financial condition of the church suffered as giving continued to decline (as it often does during the interim between pastors). Although it was obvious finances weren't healthy, the magnitude of the problem was not understood. Health issues in the family distracted the

Dan and Tara Kasey, Jazmyn and Justin
Pastor of Youth Ministries (2006-2013)
Associate Pastor (2013-Present)

treasurer from timely reporting, and mistakes were made resulting in some unpaid bills and unknown penalties. Once the details were uncovered, it became evident that the general fund was dangerously unhealthy, and the church's financial reputation was at risk. By the time all the bills were paid in March 2007, the general fund was over $27,000 in the red. The rest of 2007 became a time of recovery and rebuilding, and by the end of the year the general fund balance was restored to a balance of about $9,000—still much lower than healthy, but a big improvement.

In spite of these distractions, Dan and Tara Kasey were able to lead the first team of teens to Haiti, ministering to the children and staff of Hope for the Children of Haiti, an orphanage and school with which Dan and Tara had maintained a long relationship. Since that summer, the church has sent teams of teens, adults, and families almost every year, a relationship which has changed the lives of many in the church.

In the fall of 2007, Sunday worship attendance topped 200 for four consecutive weeks, something which had not occurred in many years. While this was exciting news, it was also a wake-up call—200 always seemed to be a kind of ceiling for attendance, the number which could be approached but never exceeded on a long-term basis. The main auditorium had a seating capacity of about 225, with an additional seventy-five seats in the balcony (most of which suffer from poor visibility to the platform). The sanctuary was effectively at over 85% capacity. So, in the spring of 2008, the elders decided to experiment with two morning services for the first time. The format for worship would be identical at both services, separated by a common Sunday School and coffee fellowship.

The approach was well received, and has continued with minor adjustments since that time. The early service is typically attended by fifty to eighty people, mostly without children, and the second service is much larger, including a younger crowd with children. Relationships between people who attend different services are enhanced by the Sunday School and fellowship time. To further enhance the unity of the separated services, special events like baptisms, baby dedications, welcoming of new members, and testimonies are done in such a way that those who attend either service can participate. For example, baptismal candidates give their testimonies at both services, although they are only baptized at one. For baby dedications, a picture of the child is displayed during the service at which the family is not present; members of the congregation at both services are asked to stand and commit themselves to support the parents and family through prayer and ministry.

The best news of all, however, was that the increase in attendance reflected an increase in the number of younger families. One of these new families, Matt and Mariah Straayer, began attending with all of their young children. Mariah found that the infant and toddler nurseries were poorly kept, old and uninviting. But rather than give up and go elsewhere, she dug in and was instrumental in rebuilding the nursery ministries by making them clean, bright, well organized and secure.

During 2008, the elders also increased their emphasis on small group ministries to promote closer relationships and mutual accountability. They were thinking strategically to make the church more visible to the surrounding community and maximize the use of the church building for the Kingdom of Christ. Requests for use of the building were encouraged, provided they were not for activities that would dishonor Christ or the church. Acton Community Chorus had been using the church for their rehearsals since at least 2000. But in 2008 New Life Fine Arts also began to rehearse for their presentations of Christian musicals written by David McAdams, pastor of New Life Community Church of Concord, with whom Faith enjoys a close relationship. Also, the Chinese Bible Church of Greater Boston (now called the Boston Metro West Bible Church), a new church plant in the Acton area at the time, used the facilities on Friday evenings until they were able to move into their own building in 2011. Concurrent with these new relationships were the ongoing ones with Acton Korean Church, Joy Bible Study, a "Moms and Tots" playgroup, and a homeschooler group. There were indeed few days when the church lights were not on.

In 2009, Pastor Dan's role was expanded to include more adult ministry, and his title was updated to reflect this. He was now Associate Pastor of Youth and Family Life. The primary new emphasis was on building and supporting the small group ministry that would involve as much of the congregation as possible.

That year the church also adopted the modified doctrinal statement of the Evangelical Free Church of America which had been adopted at the national conference in 2008.

The Journey to Bethlehem ministry continued to build steam with the addition of a new Inn scene.

After six years of enjoying the first phase expansion of the building, the congregation voted in 2010 to start a new stewardship campaign, called "Finish With Faith," to complete the new addition. The fleece put forward: if the campaign raised more than $600,000, construction would begin. Pledges came in at $630,000, so site work began in December. Attendance continued to climb in both services.

Around this time the congregation finally accepted what they had known for years: a small church cannot do everything, but they can do a few things well. So, they embraced a plan to focus the church outreach on three well-done activities each year, rather than spread limited resources too thin. These ministries targeted needs which had always been the focus of the church's vision: youth, home and foreign missions.

Vacation Bible Camp (VBC) that summer drew about 110 children, only thirty-two of whom were from Faith EFC. In fact, for the first time ever, there was a waiting list! The week drew help from many women, retired men and teens.

Journey to Bethlehem (JtB) drew over 2,000 visitors that year, mostly from nearby towns, but also included more distant towns from Massachusetts, New York, New Hampshire, and Connecticut—sixty-six in all. Attendees represented 286 churches that year. Almost half of the visitors attended for the first time. "JtB" was becoming a community tradition, and people were commenting on the love and friendship they observed among the workers. As always, nearly every family in the church was involved.

The summer mission to Haiti, which by now had become an almost annual event, included fifteen teens and adults in 2009. Some years the team consisted of teens, other years adults, and some years entire families would make the trip to minister to the children and staff of Hope for the Children of Haiti (HfC). HfC also became the mission focus for VBC each year.

Inwardly, the small group ministry was thriving—over 50% of the adults in the congregation participated in ten groups.

In 2011, average annual attendance reached over 200 for the first time ever. This included many babies, indicating that younger families were attending in larger numbers. Site work continued in preparation for the new building addition, but costs had risen dramatically during the years of delay, and the church was unable to secure the necessary financing to begin construction. Lending institutions were still quite skittish about lending after the 2008-2009 financial crisis; they would not lend based on Faith's intentions of yet another stewardship campaign that had not yet started. So the congregation contented itself with paying down the mortgage, completing the design for the new building, site preparation projects, and delivering on commitments to the Finish With Faith campaign.

urney to Bethlehem that year drew over 2,200 people. Under the leadership of Kathy Johnson and others, a new "Mom-to-Mom" ministry was initiated, ministering to eighteen mothers (seven from FEFC) and twenty-seven children. Another eleven people traveled to Haiti that summer.

Faith's first "Scattered Sunday" was held in June. People were encouraged to worship with their small groups rather than at the church (although a service was held at the church for visitors and those who could not attend a small group). This tradition has continued each spring, to encourage people to catch a vision for church planting.

About fifty people left the church in 2012, either to attend elsewhere or because they moved out of the area—a sign that transience continued to affect the church. Enough new families arrived, however, to take their place. Consequently, average attendance dropped by less than a half dozen, to 202.

As Pastor Dan's ministry became more and more focused on small group ministries, counseling, and visitation, the congregation agreed to form a search committee for a new full-time youth pastor, which started meeting in the fall of 2012.

Meanwhile, Pastor Brad completed his Doctor of Ministry degree, and Pastor Dan, his Masters of Theological Studies, both at Bethel Seminary of the East in Auburn, MA. Pastor Brad's thesis examined the challenges churches face as they grow beyond two full-time pastors, a process which Faith was undergoing.

Journey to Bethlehem attracted over 2,600 visitors (the largest ever) and VBC, Joy Bible Study and Mom-to-Mom ministries continued to attract many children and mothers from outside the church. There were now eleven small groups, including over 100 adults, slightly less than half of the adults in the congregation at that time.

Christian and Sara Waltmire, Evyn, Anna, April and Joy
Pastor of Youth Ministries (2013-present)

Christian Waltmire was called as Youth Pastor on 22 May 2013, starting his ministry in August. This marked the first time that the church employed three full-time pastors.

As the Finish with Faith campaign came to an end, the congregation voted to follow it immediately with a fourth (and final) "Continue With Faith" campaign to complete the building. This campaign, directed by Shawn Seitz and led by André Gorgenyi, drew pledges of $806,000. Construction began soon thereafter.

In 2014, the new building addition was completed, with a multi-purpose room, a new kitchen, a new youth room, an upstairs administrative suite with studies for the pastors, a new large classroom and library, and reclamation of the old offices, kitchen, and overflow room. At a cost of $1.8 million, this meant that for the first time since the move to the Acton facilities in 1976, the church would finally have enough education and fellowship space to support a full sanctuary! At the same time, church finances were healthy, as giving to Missions had risen to $86,000, and General Fund giving was about $400,000.

Completed Building Addition, 2014.

More importantly, there were seventeen baptisms that year. The major outreach ministries—Journey to Bethlehem, Mom-to-Mom, and Vacation Bible Camp—were continuing to show the blessing of God.

Pastor Brad marked his twenty-eighth year of ministry at FEFC in 2015; he took his fourth sabbatical that year, including a trip to Alaska to support and encourage missionaries he and Kathy knew there.

Use of the new building space increased quickly and dramatically, with many requests from the community, forcing the elders to draft a policy for outside usage of the building. Journey to Bethlehem drew over 2,500 visitors, supported by the involvement of 166 people from the congregation.

This was also the first year a specific ministry for those with disabilities came to fruition, led by Karen Hanson. This ministry included two facets: serving alongside a disabled child as a buddy during Sunday School and/or Junior Church, and including a special "sensory-friendly" group during Journey to Bethlehem for those who might be overwhelmed by the normal experience. The sensory-friendly group has become a tradition of JtB every year since then. In 2017, two such groups attended.

Also that year, a small group led by Pastor Dan felt the call to become a church plant in the Littleton/Ayer area. With the blessing of the elders, Pastor Dan has been leading the group with an eye to training a leadership core, and building relationships within the communities of Littleton and Ayer. There remains much to be done; the elders are working with Dan and the team, with support from the New England District superintendent, to make progress.

In 2016, giving to Missions topped $100,000 for the first time ever! Also that year, Pastor Dan began a monthly "Witness Stand" segment in the morning worship services, during which someone gives their salvation testimony. This has been a great encouragement to everyone, especially as people share openly about their spiritual journeys.

In 2017, the church sent its ninth team to minister in Haiti, with twenty-two people from Faith EFC and six from Boston Metro West Bible Church. At the same time, the Littleton/Ayer church plant small group was continuing to build relationships and make connections with other believers in the Ayer community.

During the spring, the church was challenged to participate in prayer walks, with a goal toward covering the entire town of Acton and as much as possible of the surrounding towns with prayer. Maps were placed on the wall where people could mark the areas that had been covered with pink highlighter, resulting in a rather colorful map of Acton!

During 2018, the old nursery, toddlers, and kitchen areas were completely remodeled to create a much larger play area for toddlers, and a more intimate area for the nursery. Overall, the children's ministries included up to eight babies, ten preschoolers, and over sixty

Sunday School students from age two through sixth grade. Over forty children participated in a special musical presentation, "Estherordinary Faith," on the story of Esther and the origins of the feast of Purim. Challenge foR Elementary Worship (CREW) helps children from fourth through sixth grade learn about the elements of worship and how to get the most out of the pastor's sermons. Clubs programs (Pioneer Clubs, Christian Service Brigade, etc.) drew about two dozen children of various ages. Vacation Bible Camp (VBC) ministered to 127 children, over 70% of whom were not from the church, and over 40% of whom had no church affiliation. Almost ninety adults and teens volunteered for the program.

Ministries to those with disabilities continued to gain steam, with buddies being available for two children. The church hosted an event from Joni and Friends called "Pathways to Belonging: Welcoming People of ALL Abilities," giving people in the congregation new ideas on how best to minister to those with needs. And Journey to Bethlehem hosted two sensory-friendly tours in 2018.

Unfortunately, civil unrest in Port au Prince forced cancellation of the summer mission trip to Haiti that year.

Also that year, FEFC began hosting a new church plant, Hope Chapel in Acton, which ministers to those of Brazilian descent, with services in Portuguese led by Pastor Marcos DeSouza. The church, sponsored by Hope Chapel in Sterling, MA, began meeting in the large upstairs classroom, and has quickly filled the space.

In addition to the Joni and Friends seminar, four additional seminars were held for the congregation and community at large. In May, the three pastors led a seminar on "Honoring God with Technology." In June, David Spector gave a challenging and informative presentation on safety in an active shooter situation, including how the church can be made a safer place for the children and attenders. In September, Joe and Cherri Freeman came to share a biblical perspective on how to help those with addictions and their family members. And in October, Hope International put on a poverty simulation to help people understand what it is like to be caught in a cycle of poverty.

Despite ongoing protests and unrest, in the summer of 2019 Pastor Christian and Tara Kasey were able to lead a team of twenty-eight people of all ages from nine families to Haiti for the church's tenth trip to serve Hope for the Children of Haiti.

Also in 2019 Dan Kasey became the fifth pastor to be ordained to the ministry while serving at Faith. His ordination council, held in May, included representatives from many area churches and the New England District:

Church	Location	Delegate	Office
Valley Bible EFC	Haddam, CT	Rev. John Westerholm	Pastor, moderator
NEDA District Superintendent		Rev. Sam Huggard	Pastor
Westgate EFC	Weston, MA	Rev. Bruce Daggett	Pastor
Christ Community EFC	Easthampton, MA	Rev. Chad Patterson	Pastor
Hope International Church	Waltham, MA	Rev. Alex McDonough	Pastor
Faith EFC	Acton, MA	Rev. Brad Johnson	Pastor
		Shawn Seitz	Delegate
		Michael Young	Delegate
Chinese Gospel Church	Southborough, MA	Eric Sandberg	Delegate
Cornerstone	Westford, MA	Andrew Bradshaw	Delegate
First Baptist Church	Leominster, MA	Michael Seeley	Delegate

Pastor Dan's ordination service, with the laying on of hands by the elders and members of the ordination council. Photo by Tara Kasey.

Pastor Dan was unanimously recommended for ordination, which was accepted by the EFCA ministerial board. His ordination ceremony was held on 25 August 2019 in which Pastor Brad gave the charge.

In September the small group led by Pastor Dan grew into two groups, with the second group led by Andre and Julia Wu. Together they make up the launch team of the Ayer church plant initiative. Taking the name "Life Church", they held their first public worship service on 17 November at Woody's Barber Shop in Ayer with sixteen in attendance. As an exciting reminder of God's providence, it was reported that the father of the barber who offered his space for the meeting had originally attended Faith Chapel in the late 1970s and was discipled by Rev. Ken Spence!

Ordinary People, Extraordinary Impact: Bob and Barbara Thoresen

Bob, like his older sister Helen Vettrus, grew up in the church. After serving in Korea, he married Barbara and quickly became involved. He held many positions of leadership over the years, not so much because he aspired to them, but out of a conviction that he should serve where he was needed. He was equally likely to be seen working with the trustees, elders or up front as song leader. He was the church's main liaison with Camp Spofford from the time the camp was founded. After March Purinton Jr. stepped down, Bob served many years as the church moderator, where his quiet demeanor helped keep meetings from becoming overly contentious in times of stress. After Pastor Bill Lupole resigned as youth pastor Bob took over responsibility for the ongoing youth ministry.

He was a gifted craftsman with wood, which he put to good use on behalf of the congregation. The cross that currently hangs at the front of the church sanctuary was his creation, as well as the mailboxes and display case in the foyer.

After retirement he took up carving, quickly becoming accomplished at his new craft and winning awards at local carving shows. Always generous with his time and resources, he would gladly help anyone who asked, whether it was an errant golf swing, or passing on his love of carving (he gave the author's son a set of knives and taught him to carve). Each year he would make small carvings as gifts to all of the children in the congregation, which he passed out at the spring family camping trips. His carving gifts to family and friends are still treasured by many.

Likewise, his wife Barbara became the church pianist after the move to Acton, serving in that capacity until a few years before they moved to Alabama in 2014. Her accompaniment for the choirs, special groups, and soloists always greatly enriched the worship experience. Bob passed away in 2018. Barbara still resides in Huntsville near her daughter Elizabeth and son Eric.

Life Church plans to hold public services twice a month during the first half of 2020, working up to weekly services in the summer and a "hard launch" in September. Current intentions are to remain under the umbrella of Faith EFC as a satellite/daughter church until they are ready to become fully independent—an arrangement that is remarkably similar to the original arrangement of the Scandinavian Branch with Trinitarian Congregational church from 1893 until 1920!

As of this writing in 2019, Pastor Brad is in his thirty-second year of ministry at Faith EFC, his fourteenth as Senior Pastor, and Pastor Dan is in his fourteenth year of full-time ministry as associate pastor. The Lord has indeed blessed the church with stability of leadership over the past thirty years under Pastors Doug, Brad, Dan, and Christian!

Faith Evangelical Free Church, May 2019. Photo by Tara Kasey.

Chapter 8:
Ebenezer

Then Samuel took a stone and set it up between Mizpah and Shen. He named it Ebenezer, saying, "Thus far has the LORD helped us."

1 SAMUEL 7:12 (NIV)

It is important to look back occasionally and reflect on the journey one has traveled. But one must not lose sight of the point at which one has arrived with the Lord's help. Where is Faith EFC's "thus far?"

Since the first twenty-nine charter members committed themselves to the work on 29 October 1920, 615 additional people have joined them in membership, for a total of 644. This is a surprisingly small number over a span of one hundred years, averaging only about six new members per year. These are the people who committed themselves to the work of the Gospel through this local church and joined the covenant community. Their faithful, sacrificial ministry, often without any human recognition, has been an essential part of the ongoing work.

As of 2019, there are 122 active members and 342 regular attenders (including children). If we assume a similar ratio of regular attenders to members throughout the history of the church, 643 members would represent over 1,800 people who have engaged in the ministry of the church over the past one hundred years. By any measure, Faith EFC is a small church.

What impact has this small flock of believers had on the surrounding communities, our nation, and the world since its inception? How many souls have been saved? Only God knows the heart, but the records show celebrations of decisions for Christ numbering in the hundreds, from evangelistic meetings, Vacation Bible Schools, youth group activities, Journey to Bethlehem, Joy Bible Study, and individuals sharing their faith. Over fifty decisions were celebrated in the three years alone leading up to the seventy-fifth anniversary celebration! Even the church's furnace room has been the scene of people surrendering their lives to Christ.

The founding documents described the aim and endeavor of the church: to "spread the gospel both home and abroad, and as far as possible support the home and foreign missions." Since 1920, the people of Faith EFC have supported at least 120 individual missionaries, representing over fifty mission organizations. Ten people from the church have been commissioned to the mission field, and no fewer than thirty-five individuals have gone on short-term mission trips, in addition to well over 200 who have gone on special expeditions to foreign mission fields. As of 2019, eighty-five different individuals have gone on ten trips to Haiti. Of these, thirty-six have participated in multiple trips, and built relationships in Haiti that will last a lifetime. Total expenditures for missions since 1920 have exceeded $2.55 million, the equivalent of over $4.3 million in today's dollars.

Since 2002, over 34,500 people have gone through Journey to Bethlehem presentations and heard the gospel of the manger and the cross proclaimed. Of those who submitted comment cards, an average of 50% indicated it was their first time. Many have indicated a desire to learn more about a relationship with Christ or asked for prayer.

Faith EFC has celebrated five ordinations so far, the latest this year's council and ordination service for Pastor Dan. Counting those who were ordained by the Scandinavian Branch (Rev. Ole O. Thorpe and Theodor Jensen), seven people have been set part for the ministry of the Gospel by the church.

The church has always actively supported the national and regional Evangelical Free Church Association, including releasing two pastors to become district superintendents. Many pastors and lay people from the congregation have served in various capacities on the district and Camp Spofford boards. Two from our congregation have served on the Board of Regents at Trinity International University, and one has served on the national EFCA board.

Since 1982, Joy Bible Study, meeting at Faith EFC, has become a predominant Bible study for women in the area, having touched over 900 women from Acton and nearby towns. Its impact on the women of Faith and its outreach to women of all walks of life in the area cannot be overestimated. It has also been a gathering place for women who are new to the community. Many have come to Christ through this ministry, and Joy's ministries of discipleship and leadership development have been a great benefit to Faith and other churches in the area as well.

How many believers have dedicated their lives to sacrificial service of Christ's Kingdom because of the faithful teaching of God's Word over the past one hundred years? Again, these heart changes are God's work, not that of human beings, and some have entered the church's doors already convinced that they were bound for full-time ministry. But it is encouraging to see multiple individuals and families who have gone to the mission field after ministering here. Examples from the recent past include: Tom and Julie (Spurr) Varno, Martin and Cindy (Bennett) Brown, Frank and Veronica Decanio, Daniel and Rachel Lewis, and Thomas and Cassie (Mullane) Van Der Laan.

It is unlikely that the people who dedicated themselves to the establishment of a little Norwegian church in Concord could ever have envisioned where the Lord would lead His church!

Part Two:
Church Planting Insights

Principles from FEFC's History

"Dear Mom, I get it now."

ANNA LUTHER

Chapter 9:
The Birth of a Church

When Is FEFC's Birthday?

Good question! So many were involved in birthing the church that a single date is difficult to pin down. That said, Faith Evangelical Free Church has traditionally considered its birthday as 14 November 1920, the date when the new church building on Lang Street in Concord was dedicated to the service of the Lord. But why celebrate that date above so many others equally as important to the birth of the church? For example:

21 April 1921	The Norwegian Zion Evangelical Free Church was incorporated with the Commonwealth of Massachusetts. From the state's point of view, this was the birthday of the church.
14 November 1920	The church building on Lang Street, Concord was dedicated.
29 October 1920	The first formal meeting in the Lang Street building. At this meeting, twenty-nine people voted to accept a new constitution and bylaws, and become charter members, withdrawing their names from membership of Trinitarian Congregational Church and other churches.
12 September 1919	At a meeting in a tent on Lang Street, members of the Scandinavian Branch of Trinitarian Congregational Church voted to purchase the Lang

	Street property and construct their own church building.
16 November 1893	The Scandinavian Branch of Trinitarian Congregational was formed, and called Ole O. Thorpe as its first pastor. They met in the vestry of the church.
15 June 1879	The first Sunday School class for the Scandinavian community was held at Trinitarian Congregational Church. This class became the nucleus of the Scandinavian Mission Society, which met in the old Wright Tavern in Concord until 1893. This mission could be said to have given birth to two churches— the Scandinavian Methodist Episcopal Church and the Norwegian Zion Evangelical Free Church!

Using the above timeline, it is apparent that birthing this church was a long process that required the faithful ministry and support of many people and multiple organizations.

Ordinary People, Extraordinary Impact

Obviously, it is the Lord Jesus Christ who created, died for, bought, and continues to nourish His Church. But as is usually the case, He used many ordinary people who, desiring to be faithful to the Great Commission, expended themselves for the Kingdom and opened their hearts to the Norwegian people in their midst. Most of them probably had no idea of the impact their service would have on countless people yet to be born. For example:

Elizabeth Hunt

Mrs. William Hunt, in the midst of her own personal struggles, discovered a real love for the Lord and a burden for the souls of the Norwegian people who worked so diligently on her farm. She learned Norwegian so that she could teach them Sunday school in their native tongue. Her efforts may well represent the inception of the Norwegian Free Church movement in Concord, as she awakened a spiritual hunger in the hearts of many and endeared herself those who would eventually plant the church.

Rev. Ole O. Thorpe

Rev. Thorpe, himself a recent immigrant from Norway, loved the Lord and, as a capable preacher, took over the Sunday School class and turned it into a preaching service, helping to organize the small group into the Scandinavian Mission Society at Wright Tavern. He was active in the early free church association, serving as its chairman for at least six years while it was still getting off the ground. He was ordained a minister of the Gospel at Trinitarian and became the first pastor of the Scandinavian Branch. Although the Branch paid him a salary, he continued to serve as a tentmaker, making his living as a cobbler in Concord.

Rev. Gustav A. Dahl

Rev. Dahl, of the Massachusetts Home Mission Society, encouraged and strengthened the group at Wright Tavern after about half of their number left to form the Scandinavian M.E. church. Without his timely visit and fruitful evangelism, the whole movement might have died in 1890.

Rev. Severin K. Didriksen

Rev. S.K. Didriksen, who preached frequently for the Norwegians in Concord, took Ole Thorpe under his wing as a mentor, and helped organize the group into the Scandinavian Trinitarian Congregational Church (Scandinavian Branch).

Rev. George Tewksbury

Rev. George Tewksbury, the longest serving pastor at Trinitarian Congregational, was very supportive of the immigrant group, and welcomed them in as the Scandinavian Branch. In the Lord's perfect timing, he served at Trinitarian for the entire timespan of the Branch.

Lars and Rudolph Petersen

The Petersen brothers, both successful immigrants in their own right, invested their time, money, and talents to purchase the Lang Street property and construct the new building, even though they did not join the new congregation, opting to keep their membership at Trinitarian. They and others in the town were favorably disposed to the new church and helped get them off the ground.

Rev. Edward M. Andersen

Rev. E.M. Andersen, an evangelist from Jersey City, NJ, after a successful tent-meeting campaign on a vacant lot on Lang Street, became so invested in the work that he moved his family to Concord for a year and a half to make sure the church was planted on a firm foundation.

John Swen

John Swen was a leader in the Scandinavian Branch who helped construct the church, then served for years as deacon, elder, member of the String Band, leader of music and the choir, and as a volunteer janitor. If the church was open, he was there. In each generation, the Lord has supplied men like Mr. Swen for the church, including many from the Andersen, Thoresen and Purinton families.

Inga Cahill

Inga Cahill was the daughter of charter members Samuel and Karen Lee, and joined the church as soon as she came of age. She served as the church's first financial secretary, pianist, organist, leader of the String Band, and countless other functions. She poured her heart and soul into the church.

Helping Organizations

There is no question that the Norwegians were greatly supported by those around them, financially, spiritually, and physically.

The Women's Missionary Society was formed by the women of the Scandinavian Missionary Society while they were still meeting at Wright Tavern, and thus predate even the Scandinavian Branch. Their importance in keeping the young congregation together during hard times cannot be overstated. They supported the spiritual life of the Norwegians in Concord for years, and contributed time and money to keeping the church healthy.

Trinitarian Congregational Church

Trinitarian, under the leadership of George Tewksbury, and also with the encouragement of Ole O. Thorpe, did much more than simply provide a place for the Branch to meet. They supplied financial support, not least in the form of rent-free use of the vestry. They provided training and instruction for children in the Sunday School, not to mention a place to call home. In today's climate of division and denominationalism, Trinitarian's willingness to adopt the Scandinavian congregation seems a breath of fresh air. Without their support and care, the church likely would never have gotten off the ground.

The Norwegian-Danish Evangelical Free Church of Boston

Roxbury Free Church, painted by Walter Frank of the Westwood Free Church in 1982, presented as a gift to EFCA national office. Courtesy EFCA Archives.

The Norwegian-Danish Evangelical Free Church in Roxbury (a neighborhood in Boston) was vital to the successful founding and thriving of the Concord/Acton church, as well as many others. In fact, the Boston church was sometimes called the "mother church" of what would become the Norwegian-Danish Evangelical Free Church Association.[1] It was organized on 26 Jan 1885 by David and Severin Didriksen and others, and incorporated with the Commonwealth of Massachusetts on 14 May 1891.[2] They had both been greatly influenced by the theology of Fredrik Franson, an evangelist who worked with Dwight L. Moody. David came to Boston in 1882, and eventually convinced his recently ordained brother Severin to come as the first permanent pastor of the new congregation. The church originally met at 164 Hanover Street in Boston. Their first permanent pastor was Rev. S.K. Didriksen; prior to that, they had been served by various pastors and lay preachers, including Rev. Gustav Dahl of the Massachusetts Home Missionary Society, who was also instrumental in keeping the old Scandinavian Mission Society alive in Concord in the 1880s.

The Boston Church was perfectly situated right in the middle of a thriving Scandinavian community in the Roxbury neighborhood, and home missions was always a priority. They established a presence near the seaports of Boston so that they could contact Norwegian and Swedish sailors as they arrived in town. They launched "preaching stations" in and around Boston, such as in East Boston, Quincy, and Norwood. Young people participated in these missions with their music and singing, as well as testimonies. They also established the Waltham Evangelical Free Church and nurtured the work in Concord.

Gustav A. Dahl and Severin K. Didriksen both took an active interest in the small group in Concord while they were serving in Boston. They saw the potential of a shoe salesman (Ole Thorpe) to become a great preacher.

Another of their pastors, the Rev. L.J. Pedersen shows up frequently among the early minutes and records of the Concord church, as he provided frequent pulpit ministry for the Scandinavian Branch. In 1916, Rev. Pedersen left Boston to found the Trinity Seminary and Bible School in Rushford, Minnesota (later moved to Minneapolis), where he served as president for over twenty years before returning to Boston. This school later merged with the Swedish Evangelical Free Church's school in Chicago, Illinois to become what is today known as Trinity International University.

Pastor Ingvald J. Loe (1919-1927) spoke at the dedication of the building on Lang Street in November 1920.

It wasn't just the Roxbury pastors who supported Concord. Mr. and Mrs. Oscar Levine were leaders in the Roxbury church and members of the Free Church Home Missionary Society. They argued forcefully for the need to support the rural outreach centers and churches throughout Massachusetts. They took a particular interest in Concord. Mr. Levine read Scripture and gave the invocation at the laying of the cornerstone of the new Concord church building.[3]

Every fall, the Boston church—their choir, pastors, string band, and others—was involved in the anniversary celebration of the Concord church. The youth groups from both churches also often worked together. The Concord church, in turn, participated in the Boston church's special occasion celebrations. The Concord String Band played for the fiftieth anniversary celebration of the Boston church in 1932. Ole Thorpe and other pastors from Concord often preached in Boston when their pastor was absent and at their annual missions conference.[4]

Over the years, as the Norwegians in Roxbury became more affluent and transportation improved, many of the congregants moved out of Roxbury to the suburbs. In 1955 the building on Cedar Street was sold to the St. James African Orthodox Church, who used it to serve the now mainly African American community until 2015 when it closed.[5]

Just like most immigrant churches, the Boston/Roxbury Evangelical Free Church found it difficult to escape the ethnic characterization in the community's eyes, and deemed it necessary to reinvent itself by moving to a new community. In 1956 they moved south to Westwood, even as Faith would eventually leave Concord and move west to Acton almost twenty years later.

After initial success and growth, the Westwood EFC fell on hard times, and by 2003 their attendance had dropped to about thirty. In 2003 they closed their doors, much to the lament of all the churches throughout the district, especially those it had helped establish in the greater Boston area. In honor of their faithful labor in planting churches, the New England District Association used the proceeds from the sale of the Westwood property to fund a church planting missionary and provide seed money for church planting efforts around New England.

The Massachusetts Home Missionary Society

The goal of the Massachusetts Home Missionary Society had been to support churches that were not yet capable of standing alone financially. It also supported missionaries who could travel from church to church, providing comfort, advice, and pulpit ministry. Rev. Gustav Dahl was one of two men assigned to help the fledgling Scandinavian churches in Massachusetts. He met frequently with the Scandinavian Branch in Concord, while also preaching at the Boston church until S.K. Didriksen graduated from Chicago Theological Seminary. The Massachusetts Home Missionary Society also gave regular support to the Branch—between $180 and $240 per year. It continued to donate money to the Lang Street church until at least 1923.[6]

Birthing a new church is a huge undertaking, far beyond the abilities of any one person. It is God's work, and He orchestrates it all through individuals and organizations, each doing their part as He prompts and enables them. It is only looking back that we can see His hand in everything!

Other Churches of the Eastern Free Church Association

Although they were spread across the northeast coast of the US, the Norwegian Evangelical Free Churches were a close-knit association. The early Free Church pastors were well known and loved by all the churches. There were many reasons for this, including: 1) the churches faithfully sent their pastors to the annual meetings of the Association; 2) the congregations participated from the earliest days in "pulpit exchange," where pastors would preach at sister churches at least once a year; 3) pastors often helped other churches by preaching for special services, conferences, etc.

New York City was an area where many Scandinavians settled, especially those of the seafaring trade. The large Norwegian neighborhoods were ripe for spiritual harvest, and many free churches sprouted from the end of the nineteenth into the early twentieth centuries. Gustav A. Dahl, who had ministered in Boston and held evangelistic meetings in Concord, was instrumental in founding numerous churches in the area, including Jersey City and the 15th Street church in Brooklyn. Other churches were founded in Hoboken, NJ and Tottenville, on Staten Island. Eventually, the Second Norwegian Evangelical Free Church spun off from its parent church in Brooklyn, ministering primarily to the English-speaking, second-generation Norwegian immigrant community.

In May 1919, these churches joined with others in Boston for the annual meeting of the Eastern Evangelical Free Church Association. Churches from Portland, ME, Boston, MA, Concord, MA, Hartford, CT, Bridgeport, CT, Hoboken, NJ, Jersey City, NJ, Orange, NJ, W New Brighton, NY, Tottenville, NY, and both churches from Brooklyn, NY sent delegates to the meeting. This meeting came at a time when the Concord congregation was experiencing an existential crisis: they had no pastor, and no prospects for a new pastor; Norwegian immigration had essentially halted since the start of the War; attendance was dropping; there was no money in the bank; everyone was discouraged and considered closing down the ministry.

But God had other ideas. We have already recounted how Rev E.M. Andersen came to Concord for tent meetings which resulted in the revitalization of the congregation and ultimately, in constructing the building at Lang Street. To illustrate the level of support of the New York/New Jersey churches for this effort, it is best to give several quotations from the *De Norske Evangeliske Frimenigheders Blad*, a monthly newsletter published by the two Brooklyn churches and distributed throughout the area churches. What follows is a series of quotations from the *Blad* related to the work in Concord. Commentary is provided in brackets [ ]:

> **June 1919:** At the Boston Annual Meeting, from May 21 to May 25, Brother E.P. Backie was the [52nd St] congregation's delegate or representative. [Rev. O.M.] Jonswold also joined and stopped in with friends in Concord, MA Wednesday night as well as the Boston friends again Thursday night. It was a blessed time during the meetings, and especially for those who have wandered in and out among these friends for approximately 8 years. After all, it was like coming home and greeting old and dear ones. God bless the church and pastor in the coming days.[7]

[Jonswold had been pastor in Boston until 1918, when he went to the 52nd St. church in Brooklyn]

> Of the provisions adopted, the Internal [home] Mission was of particular importance. A brother was chosen to travel around our field, and especially to visit the more neglected places, to help the cause of God where possible. The idea was to get a tent, set it up in a city, here or there, where the good news was lacking, and proclaim the Gospel. Let us join in the advancement of this cause and the spread of the kingdom of God, and support it with our resources.[8]

[Support it they did – they gave money for the tent, and one of their pastors, E.M. Andersen from Jersey City, agreed to accept the call as field missionary on a temporary basis.]

July 1919: Brother Andersen from Jersey City will have a four-week tent meeting in Concord, Mass. Let us remember him to the Lord that it might be a great blessing.[9]

August 1919: E.M. Andersen announces in a letter from Concord that they are having a wonderful time in Concord with the meetings in the tent. Not a few have sought the Lord, and it has been a great revival for the faithful. May the good work continue.[10]

[As described in Chapter 3, after the tent meetings were over, the congregation met on 12 September 1919 and, encouraged by the spiritual fruit of the tent meetings, voted to strike out on their own and build.]

December 1919: Pastor E.M. Andersen has a firm call back to Jersey City. It is unknown to us yet whether he will assume it.[11]

January 1920: Sunday the 4th of January the congregation in Jersey City held a farewell party for Pastor Andersen and his family. After a short trip to see his sister in Canada, Andersen is going to Concord for a few months. Brother Eikland is serving the congregation in Jersey for a time until he and his family leave for South America.[12]

March 1920: Prof. Pedersen has answered the call negatively about calling him from Jersey City some time ago.

E.M. Andersen is in Concord for the time being and will probably stay there for a few months until they are done with the church building.[13]

December 1920: [N.W.] Nelsen [from 15th St] participated in the dedication ceremony in Concord, Mass. Sunday November 14. The friends in Concord have built a really cozy little church that can accommodate a few hundred people. Brother E.M. Andersen has done a good job there by the grace of the Lord. They now have their own house to gather in after being with others for over twenty years. We also had a Bible conference which most of the brothers here in the East attended and participated. The following Wednesday, Nelsen traveled to Providence RI for a mission meeting in a Swedish church. Not a few gathered around the Word of God, and several sought the Lord for salvation. In Concord there were also those who asked for peace with God.[14]

This group of churches had invested themselves and their resources in the work in Concord. They prayed for God's blessing on the work, and followed the results closely. Without their support from afar, it is doubtful that the Concord church would have been built.

Chapter 10:
Church Planting Lessons

Every Church Was Originally a Church Plant

It is a truism that every church had a beginning at some point in time, thanks to the efforts of one or more people. If churches were never planted, we would all be worshiping in Jerusalem—or, more likely, Christianity would not have reached us at all.

Very few churches are the result of efforts of a single person or group unaided by others. Most can point to a "parent" church that nurtured, supported, and advised them. The church at Antioch parented many churches in the Roman provinces of modern-day Turkey and Greece. And just as most churches have one or more individuals who go out and plant churches, Antioch sent Paul, Barnabas and Silas.

The roots of Faith Evangelical Free Church go deep. As we have already seen, its congregation took many forms before it was finally organized as the Norwegian Evangelical Free Church of Concord. But at every step, there were people and organizations that recognized the value of starting and nurturing a Gospel work among the local Norwegians. And they were willing to invest time, money, and resources toward that end.

Church Plants Can Take Many Forms

Church planting has become an industry in today's western world. Many models for church planting have become fads, but churches were reproducing long before today's church planting conferences existed.

There is no one "right" model for planting churches. It is a natural result of faithful Christians who "go into all the world, making disciples."

It is helpful to concentrate not so much on the "how" but the "who." Whom are we trying to reach? When we are locked into a method, we risk missing outreach opportunities right under our noses, or try to force a method on the work that is not particularly effective.

Outreach to Immigrant Communities Remains Viable Today

Many churches are planted among immigrant communities simply out of a desire to reach people for Christ before the secular American society draws them into its vortex. An immigrant church can connect with people who are feeling homesick for the old country, provide them with a sense of comfort and community, and meet their spiritual needs.

That is certainly what occurred in Concord. A small group gathered to learn about the Gospel. As the group grew, preaching and fellowship times began. Eventually the group started meeting in the local tavern. Then they came under the wing of a sympathetic local church.

Today, Faith EFC supports similar groups. Currently, a Brazilian group meets in the church during worship service on Sunday mornings. The Brazilians hold their own worship service in one of the larger Sunday School rooms. Sometimes they join Faith for communion, and some of their children attend Faith's Sunday School. The Acton Korean EFC also meets in the building on Sunday afternoons, sends their children to Faith's Sunday School, and participate with Faith in work days and some joint services.

The Chinese Bible Church plant (now known as the Boston Metro West Bible Church, or BMWBC) also used the church building certain weekdays in the past for their Bible studies and fellowship. They have since constructed their own building in Littleton, MA, and no longer need Faith's help, but the two still maintain warm relations; some from Faith's congregation provide assistance for BMWBC's children and youth ministries.

Immigrant Churches Typically Have a Limited Lifespan

Unless there is a constant influx of new immigrants, within two or at most three generations, an immigrant-focused church will typically begin to struggle, as their children become Americanized and absorbed into the American melting pot. The non-ethnic community at large will see them as a closed group (although they probably never were!). To survive, the church usually needs either to reinvent itself or reproduce itself. Faith EFC did the former; the Boston EFC excelled at the latter.

No Single Congregation Can Reach Everybody

Christians are called upon to reproduce themselves. Churches should be doing that as well. No single church, no matter how large, can reach the entire surrounding population.

If Faith EFC were to max out its facilities with multiple services, it could potentially reach about 600 people. According to the 2010 census, about 22,000 people reside in Acton alone. So at best, Faith could reach fewer than 3% of the local population. Even if everyone could be accommodated, the fact is that not everyone would be willing to join in—not even every believer. Many would not be comfortable with Faith's style of worship. Some might prefer more liturgy, others a different mix of music styles or a different ministry emphasis. Still others might disagree with Faith's doctrinal stance on some issues, although hopefully these would be secondary issues and not the central tenets of Christianity. But people tend to fellowship with those with whom they feel most comfortable.

The Kingdom of Christ is bigger than a single congregation. It is bigger than a denomination. People of like faith can worship differently and minister differently. To be sure, there are articles of faith that are non-negotiable for anyone claiming to be Christian. But in this secular age, believers should be working together with brothers and sisters of like faith, regardless of minor differences, to spread the Gospel among their town and surrounding communities.

This has always been the philosophy of the Evangelical Free Church of America, and Faith Evangelical Free Church in particular, as embodied in its original 1920 statement of faith:

> In that we confess these words to be the teaching of the Bible we declare ourselves willing to cooperate with all that have participated in the same faith, and with same will we work together in grace for the advancement of His kingdom.

The Purpose of Church Planting Is Not Sheep Stealing

The purpose of planting new churches is to reach the lost for Jesus Christ more effectively, not to take believers away from other good churches. Today too many new churches are populated by believers from old churches.

When Trinitarian took in the Scandinavian Branch, they were not concerned with the possibility that they might steal people from the mother church. Instead, they were concerned about reaching an unreached group in the community.

When the congregation decided to build their own house of worship on Lang Street, there were people from other congregations in the community who contributed money and skills to help build it. The goal was to further the pursuit of religion in the town. To be sure, there were some who disagreed. But overall in those days, there were many who sought to be benefactors to any group that promoted religion.

You Don't Have to Be Large to Engage in Church Planting

Trinitarian was not a large church back in the early 1900s, and the Boston EFC was no bigger than the Acton church is today. Yet both continually engaged in active plants and satellite churches. Planting a church does not necessarily require huge financial resources or large numbers of people. In fact, churches that think they have to be larger or wealthier before planting a daughter church will probably never plant one.

That is the lesson taught by Faith EFC's own history. From as early as the late 1970s, the plan of the church leadership was to wait until the congregation grew large enough before planting a daughter church. But the congregation never seemed to be big enough.

Any size church can be a mother church. Size doesn't matter. What matters is a heart's desire to see the lost won for Jesus Christ. Without that, no church will ever grow or reproduce, no matter its numerical size.

Ed Stetzer recently wrote, "An informal survey several years ago asked pastors what was the optimal size to plant a church. Across the board, whether the church was large or small, most pastors answered about 25% larger than their existing church."[1] This reminds one of when John D. Rockefeller's response when asked how much money is enough. His answer: "one more dollar." What we have is never enough.

Since Faith's leadership most recently began specific goals for planting a church (around 2005), the yearly average attendance has grown from 132 to over 212, an increase of 61%! And every single family in the current church plant core group (except Pastor Dan) has joined the church since that time. Clearly, the Lord provides the resources to accomplish His plans.

Jeffrey C. Farmer, in his doctoral dissertation, found that sponsoring a church plant, rather than draining resources and vitality, is actually an effective means of revitalizing the mother church. In his study of over 600 church planting churches, he found that the mother churches typically grew in attendance and financially after planting a daughter church.[2] Even planting a church nearby did not adversely affect the mother church.

Being a Mother Church Is a Big Responsibility

In the same way that parents undertake a great responsibility in raising their children properly, a mother church should expend herself for her daughter churches.

Not all church plants require financial investment, but many do. Just as parents gladly spend money to feed, clothe, and educate their children, churches should be willing to expend themselves for the benefit of their church plants. If the goal of any church is to reach the lost and make disciples, and a church plant is part of that strategy, investing money in the daughter church is not a diversion of funds from ministry—it is directly related to the purpose of the church!

On the other hand, many plants do not require significant financial investment. These organic church plants tend to start as small groups that grow in size and number, expanding as families are added and remaining essentially self-funding.

Even if financial help isn't needed, a church plant often benefits from resources, both material and human, provided by the mother church. Oversight, financial accounting, participation in Sunday school and other ministries of the mother church can ensure that members of the daughter church are adequately nurtured as they pursue other ministries. This type of encouragement, which was provided by Trinitarian to the Scandinavian Branch, is critical to the vitality of the daughter church.

Once a church plant begins to hold their own public worship services, the mother church might provide preaching, worship team, and other support on an ad hoc basis, or for a committed period. For example, the senior pastor, Rev. George Tewksbury, often preached and offered other encouragement to the Scandinavian Branch.

All of these approaches were exemplified in the relationship between the Branch and Trinitarian, without which the Branch probably would have floundered. Trinitarian provided them with space, Sunday school for their children, preaching when needed, as well as financial support. They also advocated on behalf of the Branch with the Massachusetts Home Missionary Society. But the Branch paid for what it could whenever possible. When it came time to build, Trinitarian released some of its leaders and members to minister within the new church until they got on their feet. Rudolph Petersen was a deacon at Trinitarian, and although he never joined the Lang Street church, he served as secretary there for over two and a half years, and continued to attend as he was able until 1929, while still maintaining his membership and service at Trinitarian. Lars Petersen also served at Lang Street for a few years, and even helped purchase the property for the building. Once the new church was incorporated, he signed the property over to the new corporation and returned to Trinitarian.

The Roxbury Evangelical Free Church did not make significant financial contributions to the Concord church, but they provided meaningful assistance to the congregation in the form of joint worship and ministry opportunities, encouragement, and prayer.

Other important ways that a church plant can be supported include simple words and acts of nurture and encouragement, and most of all, persistent and fervent public prayer on their behalf. The enemy is certainly unhappy when a new Bible-believing church is born, and the church should be praying for the daughter church's protection and growth.

The Need to Guard Against Discouragement

The 1932 *Church Manual* of Faith EFC states that the members of the Scandinavian Branch hoped and prayed for the opportunity to have their own house of worship, but "were met with discouragement." Some of that opposition came from within the larger congregation of Trinitarian. For example, at the same time that the Norwegian brethren were praying for a place of their own, the mother church was quite naturally becoming more desirous that they would become more assimilated into the life of the larger, English-speaking community.

Yet one wonders if some of the discouragement came from within the immigrant congregation itself. When they first organized in 1893, they did not feel confident that they could make it on their own, so they united with Trinitarian. Should it really have taken twenty-seven years to get ready? The Boston church started with only seven charter members. The Massachusetts Home Missionary Society supported the Boston church for many years until they got on their feet, just like the Branch. The Old South Church in Boston donated multiple thousands of dollars toward the construction of their first building. Surely the Branch could have availed themselves of similar help. Perhaps the relationship with Trinitarian was too comfortable?

One also wonders what would have happened if their aspirations had instead been met with encouragement, help and perhaps a nudge? Could they have built much sooner, rather than waiting more than twenty-seven years? Could the new church have had an easier start if they had built before the War rather than after? In 1913, the Branch appeared to have peaked in its attendance and giving potential. But once the War was in full motion, immigration from Scandinavia and Europe dropped to a trickle.

As Faith EFC takes on a more active church planting role, the lessons from the past should remind us that sometimes we discourage great steps of faith simply by allowing ourselves to become too comfortable with the status quo.

Praying for and Supporting Good Local Churches

Currently there are many good local churches in Acton and surrounding communities, including:

- The Acton Korean Church, meeting within Faith's church building every Sunday afternoon, led by Pastor Chang Soo Kim.
- Hope Chapel in Acton (the Brazilian church plant), meeting in Faith's Sunday School room every Sunday, headed by Pastor Marcos DeSouza.
- The Ayer/Littleton church plant small group headed by Pastor Dan Kasey.
- Apple Valley Baptist Church in Ayer headed by Pastor Steve Wells.
- Boston Metro West Bible Church, now meeting in their own building on Newtown Road in Littleton. Until they were able to build their own worship center, they met in Faith's church building. Some members of Faith continue to help with the English ministries at BMWBC, and the youth group still periodically fellowships with theirs.
- New Life Community Church in Concord, pastored by David McAdam, with whom Faith often fellowships and participates in their musical presentations.
- Mount Calvary Lutheran Church in Acton, part of the Lutheran Church Missouri Synod (LCMS).
- Highrock Church, currently meeting in Acton.

Are these churches competition? Or are they fellow servants in the faith? We do not need to feel threatened by church plants or other faithful churches. We may not agree on everything, but as long as we agree on the major theological doctrines about salvation by faith alone in Christ alone by grace alone, we can fellowship and support one another as brothers and sisters in Christ's kingdom. We should be praying for them specifically and publicly.

Part Three: Church Health

What Can Be Learned from the Successes and Missteps of FEFC?

It's fine to celebrate success but it is more important to heed the lessons of failure.

Bill Gates

Chapter 11:
Stages of Church Life and Church Health

As the centennial celebration of Faith EFC approaches, many realize the importance of giving thanks to God for His leading and blessings thus far. Much more significant than human faithfulness is the faithfulness of Jesus Christ to Whom alone belongs the glory. Nevertheless, one hundred years of service does not guarantee that there will be a 101st year. Faith EFC has experienced both fruitful and dry seasons over the past 100 years, but how will it fare in the coming lean years? By the grace of God, Faith EFC is currently thriving while many area churches have shut their doors.

It could be said that the closing of a church is not a death, but a burial. The closing is an indication that the church had already ceased being a vital ministry. But it can take years, even decades, for people to realize and accept it, and then act on that realization.

Upon close inspection, it is apparent that some churches are still thriving after hundreds of years of existence. Others are merely surviving, often able to function only because they are propped up by endowments. Many church plants do not survive more than a couple of years. Those that do survive beyond infancy often last about the same timespan as an average person, about seventy years.[1] This makes sense, especially when one considers the difficulty of passing a vision from one generation to the next.

No church leader desires to stand before the Judgment Seat of Christ without a good answer for the way they led His Church on earth.

In the past, many people attended church out of a sense of duty— going to church was expected of them. As the culture has become more secular, this type of "civil" religion is all but disappearing. The New York Times recently reported that in Quebec, where 95% of the population regularly attended Mass in 1950, only 5% do so today.[2] Mainline churches are in serious decline. As Albert Mohler described in a recent Briefing commentary on the Times article, "if what you are looking for is feeling good and philanthropy, there are other avenues for that that don't require giving up your Sunday mornings!"[3] Today, many churches are closing their doors—and they are not all mainline liberal churches.

The Scandinavian Methodist Episcopal church in Concord shuttered its doors in the late 1930s after about fifty years. Their building is now a residence. The nearby Wayside Evangelical Free Church of Hudson (and later, Sudbury) closed its doors in 1988. Even the Boston/Roxbury/Westwood Free Church, often called the mother of the Norwegian-Danish Evangelical Free Church, closed its doors in 2003, after almost 120 years. What is to prevent the same from happening to Faith? Indeed, the Concord church seriously considered throwing in the towel in 1972. By God's grace the congregation experienced a revitalization. But such a crisis could (and probably will) happen again.

Why do churches go through times of decline? Clearly, God can use such times to refine and purify his people. But are there lessons we can learn from the past which would help us recognize times when the church has strayed from the path, repent, and get back on the straight path?

In this section, we will take an unflinching look at the health of Faith Evangelical Free Church from two perspectives: the life cycle of a congregation, and vital signs of church health. Through this review we hope to glean insights into what was done well, and what we can learn from past mistakes.

The rest of this chapter will provide a definition of the life cycle of a church, and set forth some principles by which we can evaluate the health of a church. Chapter 12 will revisit the history of the church from the perspective of these principles, looking for signs of strength and weakness. Chapter 13 will examine various surveys and evaluations conducted by the pastors and elders. Chapter 14 will look specifically at pastoral transitions throughout the years, recognizing that these intervals put additional stress on a church, and the way a congregation responds can reveal a great deal about the health of the church. In Chapter 15 we examine attendance and membership trends to see how they line up with our analysis. Chapter 16 wraps up the entire section with a summary of lessons learned.

The Life Cycle of a Congregation

The local church is a living organism, and as with all organisms, it progresses through birth, cycles of health and sickness, and possibly death. There are many books and articles which detail these stages in different ways.[4] For our purposes here, we will consider five stages:

1. **Birth.** This is the exciting stage of a church plant, where a group of people committed to a new work put everything they have into starting that work in a community. The group rallies around a common vision, and everyone is willing to do whatever it takes to help it succeed. Survival of the work is by no means assured, but there is a real sense of fellowship—people share the burden and benefits of working together.

2. **Growth/Adolescence.** The work is succeeding and growing. People from outside the core group have joined, and are catching the vision. Some organizational structure is added to ensure everything is done decently and in order. New ministries are started; some fail but excitement prevails.

3. **Maturity.** This is the "well-oiled-machine" stage. The organizational structure is set, and everyone is comfortable in their role. But complacency can begin to insert itself at this point, evidenced by an inward focus of the people. Facilities need to be maintained or expanded; the constitution is often rewritten to reflect "the way we do things."

4. **Decline**. At this point, the original core group is dying off or moving on. Some of their children or the early adopters are continuing the work as before, but not necessarily with the same vision and commitment. The old way of doing things doesn't carry the same attraction to the next generation, so few new people are joining, resulting in declining attendance and resources. Eventually some ministries need to be shut down, contributing to the departure of even more people. The inward focus becomes more pronounced, as those who remain are focused on keeping things going rather than on the original mission.

5. **Death.** If the decline is not arrested and reversed, the closing of the church is inevitable. It is no longer able to maintain a

viable ministry or pay the pastor. This stage can take years to complete.

Is death a foregone conclusion for every congregation in decline? Perhaps, but it is not optimal, and certainly not inevitable. Christ warned the church at Ephesus that they had abandoned their first love and called on them to remember the place from which they had fallen, repent, and begin again doing the works they had done at first (Rev 2:1-7). He did not counsel them to accept the death of the congregation; He warned them and gave counsel on how to avoid it.

Vital Signs: Indicators of Church Health

Often attendance and/or financial data are used to gauge church health because these are easily measurable. It is more challenging to measure spiritual health. So many books and articles have been written about church health (as a Google search of "signs of a healthy church" will show), that it's easy to be overwhelmed. Further, most of these sources reflect the trendy fads of today and are not unhelpful in evaluating a church over a long period of time.

But one Scripture passage that we all read with some sense of envy is the description of the early church in Acts 2:42-47:

> And they devoted themselves to the apostles' teaching and the fellowship, to the breaking of bread and the prayers. And awe came upon every soul, and many wonders and signs were being done through the apostles. And all who believed were together and had all things in common. And they were selling their possessions and belongings and distributing the proceeds to all, as any had need. And day by day, attending the temple together and breaking bread in their homes, they received their food with glad and generous hearts, praising God and having favor with all the people. And the Lord added to their number day by day those who were being saved.

Luke describes the church in glowing terms. What did the disciples focus on? We can see four activities that they intentionally practiced:

1. **Devotion to God's Word**—Not just preaching, but expounding the whole counsel of God, and the applicability of

Scripture to all of life. Leadership can model this by basing church decisions on scriptural principles. A congregation that strongly believes Scripture is the Word of God will also seek to help others interpret and apply it to their own lives, i.e., a healthy church is an intentional disciple-making church. And by disciples, we mean helping Christ's followers to obey the Great Commandment and the Great Commission.

2. **Genuine Fellowship**—A friend once pointed out to me that true *koinonia* is not just sharing a meal (breaking bread) or having a good time, but being fellow-shareholders in a work. We sometimes can better experience true fellowship while working shoulder to shoulder rather than sitting face to face. Genuine fellowship is also expressed in hospitality and a recognition that the church is a covenant community, not just a group of individuals. Genuine fellowship cannot thrive when the members of the congregation are seeking to protect their own individualism and autonomy.

3. **Steadfast Prayer**—The early church was faithful in prayer because they truly believed God answers prayer. They believed this because they witnessed prayers being answered before their very eyes.

4. **Worship**—Worship is not just about sound preaching and singing but includes a constant reminder of the holiness of God and the immeasurable riches of His grace toward us. This would include not only singing psalms, hymns, and spiritual songs (whatever style), but frequently celebrating the Lord's Supper— a constant reminder of the grace of the Gospel, resulting in joyful, sincere praise. Presentation of the Gospel of grace is not just for unbelievers. We all need to be reminded that we were once dead in our trespasses, "having no hope and without God in the world. But now in Christ Jesus, you who were once far off have been brought near by the blood of Christ." (Eph 2:12-13)

By focusing on these things, the early church saw results:

1. **A Sense of Awe**—They sensed the presence of God and saw evidence of His work as God answered prayer and performed miracles among them. Not all of God's works among them were

dramatic, but they were sufficiently in tune with God to see Him at work. They gave testimony to those works, generating praise, joy, encouragement, and fear. A healthy church sees God at work and seeks to join Him in that work.

2. **Generosity**—A healthy congregation is committed to supporting the local church using all its resources, including financial. Leadership handles finances in a God-honoring, transparent manner, with proper checks and balances in place. The congregation should be willing to give their pastors "double honor" by paying them well enough so that they can concentrate on the study and preaching of God's Word without worrying about caring for their family. "The laborer is worthy of his wages (1 Tim 5:18, NASB)." Looking outward, the congregation is willing to help the poor, widows and orphans.

3. **A desire to be among God's people**—The disciples in Jerusalem were together "day by day"; they never tired of being with each other. Paul describes an important indicator of saving faith as "love toward all the saints" (Eph 1:15). The members of a congregation should order their lives so that they have time to minister and participate in church functions. In a healthy church, a large percentage of the congregation is involved in small groups or other opportunities to build accountable relationships. Corporately, the church recognizes that Christ's Church includes more than their local assembly and seeks to fellowship and partner with other like-minded congregations.

4. **Fruitful Evangelism**—The Lord blessed the early church with "favor with all the people." A healthy congregation seeks to adorn the Gospel of Christ by interacting with the community in a winsome way. As Pastor Spence put it, this is the result of believers living out their lives in such a way that it shows people what it means to be a Christian. We look for ways to share Christ, training members to do the work of evangelism, and providing opportunities for the congregation to invite neighbors and friends. God gives the increase; we are only required to be faithful. Numerical growth in the congregation is the expected result; this should be conversion growth, not merely organic (babies) or transfer growth.

The first four traits of a healthy church cited above are those on which the early church was actively focused. The second four are effects, of the working of God among them. As such, they can be measured. But they are not necessarily what leadership should focus on as they develop and communicate vision. If one or more of these effects is missing or weak, it is a sign that all is not well. But weakness in any of these areas probably reflects weakness in one of the first four foci of the church.

It is also important to remember that healthy churches are not immune to cycles of growth and stabilization. Even in Jesus' ministry, there were times of great popularity, followed by times when many were offended and fell away. Not everyone is ready to accept the cost of discipleship. Rapid growth may be a sign of the Lord's blessing, or it could signal a tendency to tickle itching ears. In the same way, declining attendance may be healthy if the church is going through a period of purification, where "hangers-on" drift away because they are not willing to take the next step into accountable discipleship. But long-term attendance decline is rarely a sign that things are going well.

Church Health and the Life Cycle

What, if any, is the relationship between vital signs of church health and its life cycle? Is it possible for a thriving church to be unhealthy? Or conversely, is it possible that a declining church is actually healthy? The answer to both questions is yes but...not for long! A church that is beginning to lose its vision may appear to be thriving because the "well-oiled machine" is still being blessed by God with visible results. But in time, the "machine" will run down. More specifically, the "machine," geared toward what is effective for the older generation, may eventually be found irrelevant by the younger generation. On the other hand, a congregation that is in the process of recapturing its vision and reason for existence, may lose people who had become attached to the church, but who do not share the new vision. This "cleansing" of the church may be a painful necessity. Jesus Himself was not shy about helping people recognize that their commitment to Him was shallow. Many walked away at His hard sayings!

How should a church respond to decline? Is it ever okay to allow a church to die? What is the alternative?

Russell Burrill, in his article cited above, summarizes George Barna's conclusions about revitalizing congregations in decline:

> George Barna surveyed churches across America, looking for an adequate number of "turnaround churches" to include in his study. To his amazement, he failed to find a sufficient number of successfully transformed churches to make his research statistically valid. His conclusions point out that it is rare for a church in decline to turn around.
>
> In the turnaround churches examined, Barna found that change occurred with the arrival of a new pastor who brought new vision to the church. Such turnabouts required great sacrifice on the part of the pastor, who worked an average of 80 hours per week during the transition. Barna concluded that it takes so much energy for the pastor to accomplish the turnaround that only younger pastors should attempt it, and that only once in a pastor's lifetime![5]

This does not mean that revitalization is not worth the effort. Rather, it is an admonition to deal with problems early, before a decline should become so steep that nothing can be done. As long as it is not too late, a church can reinvent itself by recapturing its vision and mission. Burrill instructs that:

> There are three vital questions that church leadership needs to answer as it negotiates revitalization with existing churches. (1) Why are we here? (2) Where will our present course take us? (3) If this is not where we want to go, what must be changed?
>
> Note that the first step is not change, but the reestablishment of mission. Answering clearly the "Why are we here?" question is the most important step in the process of revitalization. The dream cannot be birthed until this question is fully explored. Leadership must then move on to the remaining questions...[6]

This involves more than just remembering the Great Commission. The congregation must own the mission of reaching the lost today, not the lost from the previous generation. What worked in the past will not necessarily work now. The church must re-establish their reason for existing, not in conformity to the world, but recognizing that cultural changes may require different methodologies. The specific mission may remain the same or it may change, but the commitment to Scripture, the Gospel, and reaching the lost must prevail. At the same time, the new generation may worship, fellowship, and minister differently than their parents.

Once the vision and mission have been re-established, more drastic action may be required—what could be called "repotting" or reinventing itself. This is essentially what the Concord church accomplished: it moved to Acton, changed its name to Faith Evangelical Chapel, and refocused outreach on its new neighbors, thus reinventing itself. The Boston/Roxbury church did this as well when it moved to Westwood, as did the Wayside EFC when it moved to Sudbury.

Chapter 12:
Report Card

In this chapter we will take another look at the major seasons in the history of Faith EFC, this time with an eye toward indicators of church health. Where possible, we will focus on actual evaluations by pastors and leadership. Through this review, we are struck time and again by how God worked in the life of His church through (and sometimes in spite of) its leadership and the body to accomplish His plan.

The Early Years: Healthy Vital Signs

The only information we have to evaluate the health of the church during its early years on Lang Street is from the official records, since no one from those years is alive today. These records are in the form of minutes of congregational or board meetings and annual reports. As is often the case, congregational business meetings tend to focus on the "business" activities of the church. But we also get glimpses of other facets of church life in those early years. Many of these were outlined in Chapter 11.

Devotion to God's Word

By the grace of God, His Word has always been a central focus of activity.

In the 1914 annual report of the Trinitarian Congregational Church, Rev. Tewksbury makes the following observation of the Scandinavian Branch:

> These meetings include, except occasionally Wednesday evening, a sermon, which is earnestly evangelical, imbued

with the spirit of loyalty to Christ and his Cross, which our friends brought with them from Norway.[1]

After Rev. Huseby resigned in 1919, Anton Hoff, who had been acting as treasurer, wrote the following in his report about the Scandinavian Branch and Rev. Huseby:

> Rev. Adolph O. Huseby, who, coming from Wisconsin, began his work with the Branch at the beginning of 1915, continued in its charge until the spring of 1919. His preaching was thoroughly evangelical, marked by sincere belief, and a strong desire to advance the work. While here, he made 1,248 calls, baptized 20 children, and received 11 members into the church...[2]

By this we can infer that his preaching was centered on the Word of God and the Gospel of Jesus Christ. We may also be confident that he desired to do his best for the congregation. He was not simply "mailing it in." However, Arlo Odegaard, in his work on the early history of the Norwegian Free Church, *With Singleness of Heart*, gave a negative review of Rev. Huseby's service to the church, mainly because he was not supportive of the Free Church movement.[3] A disagreement or vacillation about the direction can cause the sheep to wander off. The report is also evidence that official church reports seldom address issues and concerns directly, so we must be cautious in interpreting them.

Sunday school was always a major component of the life of the church, even for the Branch. When the new church opened at Lang Street, Sunday school was held on Sunday mornings, and the adult preaching service was held in the evenings, just as they had been at Trinitarian. As the church grew and stabilized, the Sunday school program expanded to include adult classes, usually taught by the pastors.

The laying of the cornerstone in May 1920 became the occasion for a week-long Bible conference. The annual anniversary celebration was often accompanied by multiple-day Bible conferences. Although the subject of these conferences is not described, it is likely they centered around evangelism, the need for personal conversion and prophecy, as was common among Free Churches.

Business meetings were always opened with Scripture reading, a devotional related to the passage, and a time of prayer, much as is done today.

Infant baptism was practiced for many years. As the number of children in the church increased, especially after the Second World War, the pastors began to hold regular Bible Instruction/Confirmation classes for young teens.

Genuine Fellowship

As explained previously, fellowship is more than the sharing of meals. But it is not less than that either. Even a cursory scan of meeting minutes shows that fellowship was always an important part of their meetings together. If we define *koinonia* as a shared sense of ownership of the work of God, the congregation at Lang Street had it in spades.

The ladies of the church, before and after the construction of the new building at Lang Street, met as the Women's Missionary Society for the purpose of furthering the outreach mission of the church. They played an important role in supporting the work of the church financially, as well as with their talents.

The initial construction of the building was supported by many in the congregation, and even in hard times, many men were always willing to donate their time and resources to ensure that the work continued. People like John Swen, who served in different leadership roles, such as moderator, deacon and elder, also volunteered his time to maintain the facilities and keep the church clean. In many ways, Swen's involvement was like Peter Hanson's or Jack MacLellan's today. If the doors were open, he was there. If there was a need, he filled it.

During World War II, the ladies of the church ensured that the young men who were serving overseas remained in the hearts and prayers of the whole congregation through letters, Bibles and reminders.

After the war, a Couples Group was formed to provide fellowship for the adults of the church. This group performed a fruitful outreach also, as they attracted people from the community who did not otherwise attend regularly.

There is ample testimony to a vibrant body life, concern for reaching souls for Christ, and sacrificial devotion to God and His church:

> The church has had four business [sic] meetings this last year ending 1930. The meetings have been in a very Good Brotherly way with one mind and Love to try and help to uphold the work of wich [sic] our Christ has given us to do.

And may we so more do this the coming New Year [sic] Be more fully in the Will of our Lord and Savior. John Andersen, Sec.[4]

No doubt the fact that many were related to each other helped this sense of unity!

Steadfast Prayer

Every meeting opened and closed with heartfelt prayer. The members understood the importance of the work, and set their hearts on it—but they also recognized that it was far beyond their abilities. So they depended on God for strength and wisdom. Mid-week prayer meetings were well attended and prayer groups were typically held in private homes during the week.

Worship

It is difficult to evaluate the worship services of the past. Based on the few extant programs, they were traditional non-liturgical, and included plenty of music. For the first twenty-five years at Lang Street, the church had no organ. Instead, Inga Cahill, the pianist, formed a String Band which led the congregation in song. In a sense, this was the early church's worship team! The worship and song leader, as well as choir director, were elected offices from the earliest years of the church, an indication of their importance to the congregation.

A Sense of Awe

It is evident that during the early Lang Street years, people marveled at the way God was working among them. They had seen souls won for Christ, and favor earned with the community, as people from all over town contributed to the work.

Generosity

Finances always figure heavily in the meeting minutes, as would be expected for a small, fledgling congregation trying to make ends meet. But even with budget concerns, there are many entries such as, "John Andersen volunteered to pay the interest on the church mortgage," or "John Swen gave $15 towards its support of Brother Swenson, a missionary." Most years ended with an entry such as, "A letter of thanks has been sent to all those not members of the church who have given help this past year."⁵ A preoccupation with finances does not necessarily point to misplaced priorities. There is ample testimony to a vibrant body life, concern for reaching souls for Christ, and sacrificial devotion to God and His church.

A Desire to be Among God's People

For many years, the worship service (called the "Gospel Service") was held on Sunday evenings. Sunday morning was reserved for Sunday School. In the twenty-fifth anniversary program, listed services included:

- Sunday—Sunday School 10:45 a.m.—Gospel Service 7:30 p.m.
- Mid-week Prayer Service Wednesday 8 p.m.
- Young People's Society Friday 8 p.m.
- Rebecca Sewing Circle 1st Thursday each month 8 p.m.
- Missionary Society Meeting 2nd Thursday each month 8 p.m.
- Church Business Meeting 2nd Monday each Quarter 8 p.m.

Many special services were also held, such as the annual anniversary celebration, watch-night services and other holiday services, special Bible conferences, and evangelistic crusades. The annual anniversary celebration always included invitations to other churches, and they frequently met together with other local churches in the community for ecumenical services. The Roxbury EFC was especially close, but they also met with the Waltham and Hudson/Sudbury churches, as well as Carlisle Congregational.

Before Lang Street, the Scandinavian Branch maintained close ties with the Norwegian-Danish Evangelical Free Church Association, and all nearby churches. Once the church opened on Lang Street, they continued to fellowship with Trinitarian and the Scandinavian Methodist Episcopal church and joined in ecumenical services with these churches and others in the surrounding towns.

Fruitful Evangelism

From the earliest days, the primary focus of local outreach was on new arrivals from Norway. Evangelistic activities concentrated on the immigrant community. Therefore, when immigration declined during

World War I, membership growth became almost non-existent, as shown in the 1917-1918 Annual Report of the Scandinavian Branch of the Trinitarian Congregational Church:

> We have received into the Branch, on confession, two members, namely, Mr. and Mrs. John Andersen.
>
> The average attendance has been: Sunday evenings, 39; Wednesday evenings, 15.
>
> Had the times been as before the war, the attendance would surely have been much larger. Since the war broke out in Europe, we haven't had a single new-comer among our church people. And besides that, some of our old "church-goers" have moved away, and still others have died. Thus, after all, we are satisfied with the numbers we have had.[6]

This focus on the Scandinavian community continued throughout the early years at Lang Street, but as the younger generation grew up, the church actively sought avenues for evangelistic outreach to the larger community. For example, at the 20 September 1926 meeting, the minutes stated:

> Voted that Annie Olsen, John Swen, Mr. Hoff, Pastor Johnsen, and myself [Mabel Holm] serve as a committee to meet with the different churches, to see what can be done to create an interest in religion.[7]

As can be expected from a church that was birthed as a direct result of evangelistic tent meetings, hardly a year went by without planning for outreach or evangelistic meetings or Bible conferences, some of which were very fruitful. The church worked hard to be creative in terms of the speakers they invited. During interim periods between pastors, they made good use of well-known professors from Gordon Divinity School. In the end, however, special services were attended mainly by those of Norwegian descent or who had married into Norwegian families.

The warm relations that the Free Church maintained with other churches helped maintain the church's reputation within the community. But as long as they remained in Concord, they never proceeded beyond the point of an ethnic church or a "servants' church."

Global missions was always forefront in the minds of the congregation. From its beginnings as the Scandinavian Branch, even when money was tight, there was always something to send to missionaries. The WMS, founded during the Scandinavian Mission Society years, met for the purpose of supporting missions. Although the Scandinavian Branch had to rely upon support from the Massachusetts Home Missionary Society, they still gave sacrificially to missions. And at Lang Street congregational meetings, the first order of business after devotions, prayer and reports, was almost always the reading of missionary letters and discussion of missionary needs.

In summary, the early years of the Concord Free Church were fruitful. And as far as we can tell, the congregation, although not large nor rich, was faithful, healthy and well-balanced. Although it never experienced a period of rapid growth until after World War II, it quickly became stable and self-sustaining after its founding at Lang Street.

The War Years: Continued Faithfulness

1941 was the first year annual reports were printed and distributed prior to the annual meeting. The earliest printed reports focused on finances and activities of the various departments of the church. The pastor's report included a short devotional section and an attempt to summarize the spiritual health of the congregation.

During the War, the attention of the congregation was clearly upon events on the world stage, and their thoughts and prayers often strayed to those from their midst who were serving overseas. But the work continued faithfully. Major priorities continued to be preaching the Word, teaching children in Sunday School ("the church of the future"), and supporting missionary efforts around the world.

The Baby Boom Years: Ministry Growth

With the arrival of Gunnar Gundersen, the people began to think of themselves as a mature congregation, ready to take their place among other Free Churches. In the 1949 pastor's report:

> The year 1948 has been a good year, in a material sense—as evidence from the reports of the various organizations and officers of the Church. We have experienced the blessings of unity, progress, and Christian love; we have been instrumental in the bringing of some souls to a knowledge of Jesus Christ, and have been spared from the pitfalls and

inroad of things detrimental to a healthy spiritual life and condition. For all these evidences of God's favor and approval we bow humbly in adoration and thanks to our "great shepherd of the sheep," who has through "the blood of the eternal covenant" made these things possible.[8]

In this same year, we see the creation of an adult Bible class on Sunday mornings (remember that preaching services still took place on Sunday evenings at this time). This class was taught by the pastor and attracted about a dozen adults.

A 1948 report describes how the Young People's Society was beginning to attract newcomers and was developing into a true outreach opportunity.

Older members from the early days were beginning to die or become less active because of frailty, but the next generation was becoming more involved.

In 1949, Pastor Gundersen began to direct attention toward the need to expand the facilities, because various ministries were growing so quickly. This Sunday School report is almost breathless:

> The year 1949 has been the greatest year in the history of our Sunday School. As we compare certain statistics of 1948 and 1949 it causes rejoicing in our hearts to see this important, yea most important, branch of our work progressing. We have seen the enrollment swell from less than sixty to eighty-five; the missionary offerings have increased by over 65%; and much favorable comment has come regarding the efficiency and sacrificial labors of our Sunday School staff. Comment heard rather frequently would be: "you do so much for the children," "'Johnny' just loves to go to Sunday School," or "it's amazing how much they can learn in a short time.."..[9]

The main emphases of the church continued to be Sunday School and Missions. As Pastor Gundersen stated in his 1950 annual report:

> We must never forget—a growing and effective Church is a missionary-minded church. Let us continue this trend, and also pray God that He may see fit to call of our Young People and Children some who may be willing to say, "I'll go where you want me to go."[10]

The introduction of a morning worship service in the fall of 1950 indicates that leadership had evaluated the church's impact on the community, and found it wanting. The primary purpose for initiating this change was to attract parents of the Sunday School students, and others in the wider community. One of the arguments in favor of the change was that other churches that lacked a morning service were dying.

In 1951, after Pastor Gundersen had resigned to become the superintendent of the Eastern District of the newly formed EFCA, he penned the following report:

> I have endeavored during these four years to guide you in your worship and service for Christ here. Many are the times of blessing which I look back upon in the study of the Word, in seasons of prayer, and in activity for Him! Some members were added to the membership, about twelve in number. During this time a number of the older ones have gone to their reward, so the overall gain is not large. Your pastor has had the privilege of interesting a few outside families, some of whom are attending more or less regularly, and others have become members of the Church. Even though your pastor's ministry has not been of the sort which has always inspired the type of family unity which not a few of our members may be interested in, he has endeavored and he trusts in some measure succeeded to instill in your minds the necessity of not just "keeping warm" oneself, but to have the interest and that very actively in winning members of the immediate community to Christ, and doing our part in putting the Church "on the map" in Concord. It has been of great inspiration to see some souls come to know Jesus Christ as Saviour, and also to see some of those younger in years and experience come to a deeper walk with Christ and greater activity for Him![11]

During these years when many youth were coming to Christ through the programs of the church, many adult conversions also took place. These were not necessarily the result of specific church ministries, but rather the activity of the Holy Spirit in the lives of individuals. For example, the story is related of Marjorie Andersen who trusted in Christ at a home Bible study she attended. Afterward, she was encouraged by Elizabeth Watson, a member of the study group and also of Lang Street, to attend the Free Church, where she could grow in Christ. Marjorie took Elizabeth up on her invitation, even bringing her family with her. In the excitement of her newfound faith, she led all of her immediate family and many members of her extended family to Christ! Janet Stuart, daughter of Marjorie and Krist Andersen, is still a beloved member of the church.

Losing Focus?

Pastor Richmond's Final Report

During Pastor Richmond's time at Concord, the church was extremely busy, and on the surface it seemed as if the church was thriving and doing all the right things:

- Sunday School attendance increased from a low of about fifty-five in 1953 to 125 in 1958.

- Pioneer Girls and Christian Service Brigade programs were started. In 1954, Pioneer Girls enrolled forty girls. More than half were from non-church homes.

- The new youth programs were bearing much spiritual fruit, with a significant number of decisions for Christ.

- There were twelve new names in the Cradle Roll in 1954.

- In the mid-1950s, construction began on a thirty-by-fifty-foot addition to allow for more Sunday School space. Most of the work was performed by members and friends of the church.

However, the growth that was occurring was the result neither of conversion nor transfer growth, but due mostly to the ongoing baby boom. Attendance did not change significantly during this time, except almost entirely among children's ministries. A morning service, added in 1950 to attract parents of children who attended Sunday School, resulted in some membership growth until about 1955. From that point on, though, there was a small but steady decline in membership. Even the spiritual fruit of the youth programs was either among the children of people who already attended, or whose parents did not have significant involvement in the church.

Every time the church embarked upon a major project such as a building addition or the move to Acton, some people decided to leave. This is not unexpected. There will always be those who are not prepared or willing to devote their time and resources to such an endeavor. The new construction undertaken during the late 1950s was no exception. Because members generally are more committed to the work than non-members, a decrease in membership represents an even greater loss to the church.

As history would prove, the congregation overextended themselves in acquiring the extra land and taking on construction costs. To save money, most of the work was carried out by members of the congregation and much of their energy went into the new construction, as documented by business meeting minutes from the time. Given the decrease in membership, those who remained were saddled with additional responsibility.

Pastor Richmond did much work on the addition himself. It was said (probably a bit of hyperbole) that he would work with a hammer every day and would come to preach straight from the work site. This was his choice, but it shows that more attention was given to the construction than winning new converts and reaching the community.

In 1955, finances had gone into the red to the point where the church was having difficulty paying its bills and was forced to cut back on special speakers and conferences. The pastor offered to give back his raise (ten dollars/week), but that was rejected. There was discussion about the need to take action on "non-active and non-resident members" (i.e., people who had moved away). This is further evidence that the membership roll was inflated by inactive families who were no longer participating.

At one meeting it was suggested that the church publish their expansion plans in the local papers. The thinking was that some people in the town, especially former attendees and members, might take an interest and help with the work or donate finances. The suggestion was rejected, an interesting decision given that when the original building was constructed, many people from the town donated time, materials, and money toward the work—even people from First Parish (Unitarian). Back in the 1920s there were many people in town who sought to support "religion" as a public good, regardless of the denomination. Not so in the 1950s. By not publicizing the work, the church was showing that it recognized its relationship with the town was no longer as fruitful as it should be. But at the same time, it was missing an opportunity to build curiosity in the community and help them catch the excitement about what was happening on Lang Street.

With some cajoling, giving increased and construction was completed. Significantly, the new sanctuary actually reduced seating capacity from 140 to about 120! The new facility was beautiful and more comfortable, but less able to handle growth. The church appeared to be losing its focus on the mission. Additionally, people were clearly tired and body life was suffering, although the ministry was still bearing spiritual fruit. It all came to a crisis point in the latter half of 1959.

Pastor Richmond's final annual report before his resignation in 1959 spoke of a moving of the Spirit, but it was clear that the church had been experiencing some difficult times. An extended quote follows:

> The year 1958 is now history. The records of our stewardship are best known to God alone, but we rejoice in the manifestations of His rich blessings which we behold in many realms.
>
> We have enjoyed greatly increased attendance in nearly all of our groups and services. Finances are in excellent condition in all departments. Our giving has continued at record heights. For the second year in a row over $10,000 has been accounted for and the General Fund balance has improved.
>
> We have enjoyed many Spiritual blessings as well. Testimonies abound of the growth in grace of many of God's people. A goodly number of our young people have professed faith in Jesus Christ as Lord and Saviour. Many others are evidencing an increased interest in spiritual things. The Bible study class has been well attended and the many discussions and testimonies have caused our hearts to rejoice and believe that this venture was truly of the Lord's leading.
>
> We have sensed a desire on the part of some to be better witnesses and true soul winners. We have expanded our missionary horizon with an enlarged budget and particularly through the Jubilee Fund of the Program of Progress. Last but not least, our building has come to a state of near completion.
>
> For all of these things we should be grateful and offer our praise to God. However blessings are seldom unmixed

with sorrows and Satan has also been busy but God is greater than the enemy. The spirit of love, brotherliness, humility, forgiveness and Christian good will is desperately needed, if God is to fully bless us.

Brothers and sisters in Jesus, let us all humbly confess our faults to Him, Who alone can cleanse and Who longs to restore to His fellowship. Let us earnestly seek the filling of The Blessed Holy Spirit that we may show forth His fruits of love, peace, longsuffering, gentleness, meekness, etc. and let us truly LOVE one another-overlooking, understanding and forgiving each our faults, remembering that only in Christ will we find perfection!

NOTE: Since the above was penned we have held the week of Prayer services which were well attended and last night was our Official Board meeting. It is a real joy to be able to report that we experienced the Holy Spirit's presence and blessings in a remarkable way! We had what was pronounced "the best meeting we ever held." We all felt convicted of our own faults; tears flowed; we all humbly confessed our sins to the Lord and prayed for forgiveness and love for one another. Prayer was answered for we all felt the Holy Spirit moving and a REAL spirit of love prevailed. We all went forth rejoicing in the Lord! Let us all continue to pray that this spirit of Revival shall continue!...[12]

Shortly after this Pastor Richmond resigned and was replaced by Rev. Donald Barns. The next year, Pastor Barnes opened his ministry report with the following comments:

Since we have been serving the church less than three months, it is extremely difficult to give an accurate evaluation of the past year's occurrences. However, we are positive that 1959 has been a momentous year to all. It has been a year of such self-evaluation, self-analysis and heart-searching for many. God is sovereign and what He ordains and decrees is for the purpose of His own glorification. Man may, as many of us do from time to time, step back and wonder why God permits such events to transpire. Why should he send hardship, heartache, and tribulation to his children? Possibly the Scriptures throw some light on this question: "You are guarded by the power of God operating through your faith, till you enter fully into the salvation which is all ready for the denouement (final revelation) of the last day. This means tremendous joy to you, I know, even though at present you are temporarily harassed by all kinds of trials and temptations. This is no accident—it happens to prove your faith, which is infinitely more valuable than gold, and gold as you know, even though it is ultimately perishable, must be purified by fire. This proving of your faith is planned to bring you praise and honor and glory in the day when Jesus Christ reveals Himself." (Phillips). Thus we are told that increased faith and endurance ultimately brings with it praise, honor, and glory towards our Saviour and Lord, Jesus Christ.[13]

These two reports, taken together, along with the meeting minutes reported elsewhere, indicate that, although spiritual fruit was visible, there had been some significant conflict within the church, either resulting in or caused by Pastor Richmond's resignation, which was poorly handled (as will be described in Chapter 13). In the interim period, some healing and repentance occurred. But significant damage had been done, from which, as Pastor Westa's comments testify below, the church had still not recovered five years later.

At this point, many people of Concord considered the little church on Lang Street to be irrelevant. It was still "the servants' church," a small ethnic enclave formed by the domestic servants and farm hands who worked for the elite of the town. Although the church was active, with many effective ministries, conversions, a strong commitment to missions and preaching the Word of God, there was no effective outreach to the local non-Norwegian community. Meanwhile, church leadership was so busy maintaining programs and building the addition that they weren't addressing the question of how to reinvent themselves to become relevant to a wider audience.

During Pastor Barnes' tenure the church spent much of its energy rewriting the church's constitution and bylaws—drawing attention inward and away from the issue of how to reach the local community.

It is clear the church was entering into a period of decline, even though its activities were still bearing significant spiritual fruit.

Time to Move?

As early as 1961, many in the congregation understood that the church had reached a plateau and was beginning to decline. They recognized that the Lang Street property in Concord was an impediment to expansion. There was no room for parking, little room for growth, and the facilities required significant maintenance investment. At the January 1961 meeting, where twenty-seven members out of about eighty were present, a motion was made to form a "site committee" to investigate potential new locations for the church. After "some favorable discussion," the motion carried. Of course, this motion did not commit the church to actually do anything specific.

Thus began a long period of time during which three camps formed within the congregation. On the one hand, there were many, especially among the older members, who favored making things work at the current Lang Street location. Many of them had invested their own sweat and labor in the new addition and remodeled sanctuary during the 1950s. Their parents had built the original edifice at Lang Street. They saw the building as the fruit of their hard labors, holding forth an historic Gospel to an historic town. An indication of the intensity of their feelings can be seen in the fact that every year since 1920 the church had celebrated the anniversary, not of the organization of the church, or of its incorporation, but of the dedication of the building.

On the other extreme were those who saw the old location as an albatross that prevented "real progress." At the April 1961 business meeting, a number of men "voiced an overall need for progress through spiritual love, faith, and vision" and a need to "progress by starting a 'new location and new building fund.'"

In the middle were a great many people who did not want to move but knew that God was leading them in that direction, and they wanted to be faithful to His leading. But they were in no hurry to make it happen.

In 1963, Rev. Westa convinced a majority of the members to purchase the Macone property next door. This represented a last gasp attempt to remain at Lang Street, which so many desired. However, it created new debt for the church, delayed the move for another decade, and almost proved fatal to the church. It frustrated many who were anxious to move. At the same time, Grace Chapel in nearby Lexington was beginning to see fruit from its dynamic youth programs, attracting people away from Concord. Grace Chapel was built upon a strong youth ministry emphasis, like the Lang Street church, but without any ethnic baggage. The loss of the Tavilla families (related by marriage to the

Hoffs), who were very active in many outreach programs in Concord, was a particularly bitter pill to swallow.

Meanwhile, the activity of rewriting the constitution and buying and renovating the Macone property took attention away from strategic planning on how to reach the community. And the one thing the church was doing that families in the community were interested in—youth ministry—was in trouble.

Pastor Westa's Evaluation

At a special congregational meeting on 30 June 1964, a few months before he resigned, Pastor Westa took the floor and bared his heart about the state of the church. His remarks and the comments that follow in the minutes of the meeting are quoted here in their entirety, because they help illuminate the difficulties the church faced at that time:

> Pastor Westa next asked to have the floor... [He] stated where there is no vision people perish. he said we have to analyze ourselves, take a good look at ourselves. The membership has remained the same for quite a few years— between 60 and 70. There are 79 members now. He said our membership list should be reviewed. He regrets losing the families we have lost—George *[son of John]* & Ruth Andersen, Christine & Ronald Jackson, Ernie & Ginny Tavilla, Joe and Pauline *[daughter of Olga Hoff Olsen]* Tavilla, Gardner & Emma Benson. There are others who have been inactive—Dot Swen *[wife of John Swen]* to name one. Pastor said we ought to consider this membership list and contact these people. There are others also who in view of the way things appear to them will seek Sunday School elsewhere. Pastor and people should be concerned. Look at the situation with open hearts and minds. He said he and Mrs. Westa have been much in prayer, earnest prayer. He named Jean and Geo. Hodgson and Jonja & Lou Marinelli as not being satisfied with the church. Pastor said the time has come when this church needs a constructive analysis and evaluation. He said he had sent out a questionnaire and had very little response, and this speaks to him personally. He said look at our finances—we are in dire circumstances. People have not responded. A church operates only when it has money in the bank. He said that Sun. night he did not

give a letter of resignation, it was a request for prayer and he still requests prayer. This is the time for heart searching, asking this church and those who have mixed feelings to seek God's will.

Moderator Purinton next asked if anyone else had any comments. Trustee Stuart Scott said it would be a crime if the remarks made here at this meeting we let go out the window—it would be a tragedy. We should all take hold now, this is the time to do it. Eleanor Thoresen said she is with the Pastor, he has done a wonderful job and she for one will try to do more. Marjorie Andersen said we should all take account of our own lives, take account and stand on a mirror, surrender our hearts, not our minds. Several others gave excellent testimonies and if we all stand behind our Pastor the Lord will bless us and we'll overcome this crisis we are now facing.[14]

Reinventing the Church

The Decision to Move to Acton

The decision to buy the Macone property put financial stress on the church and discouraged those who favored a move. Many of these people left during the early 1960s.

By the time Pastor Condit arrived, the decision to buy property in Acton had become inevitable. By 1965 most of the people attending the church lived in West Concord or Acton, and almost no one attended from the actual town of Concord itself. If nothing were to be done to reverse that trend, the future looked bleak. However, it was also inevitable that a move would be opposed by many who favored remaining at the Lang Street location.

The meeting to consider purchasing the Hosmer Street property was well attended, with thirty-eight members and four adherents present. The vote was twenty-three in favor, thirteen opposed, with two blank ballots—well over the majority needed to pass, but far from a united vision for the future. The weightiness of the decision being made, its financial ramifications, and the intensity of emotions all signaled that the vote would likely result in another exodus of people who disagreed with the vote.

The situation was exacerbated by significant trials which beset the congregation, including moral failure within the leadership, and the death of George and Eleanor Thoresen's daughter Catherine (George was a key person advocating the move to Acton). Some in the congregation began to experience buyer's remorse—or rather, those who had been opposed began to vote with their feet. There were greener pastures nearby—Grace Chapel in nearby Lexington was entering another season of strong growth, with vibrant youth ministries and resources to meet diverse needs, and many were being drawn from nearby communities like Concord. Mission Evangelical in Maynard also offered sound Bible teaching.

In the 1971 annual pastor's report, Pastor Condit attempted to address the issue directly:

> "Have I not commanded thee be strong and of a good courage: be not afraid, neither be thou dismayed; for the Lord thy God is with thee wherever thou goest." Joshua 1:9 [KJV]
>
> Difficult decisions are hard to make. The decision that we made on September 15, 1971 was a difficult decision. It was not one that was made in haste, it was not one that was foisted upon us. It was a decision that was a long time in the making. It began two years ago when the Church board formed a site committee which was voted for and accepted at our quarterly business meeting. Now you don't form a site committee unless you are seriously considering the possibility of looking for land and are seriously thinking of relocating. Jim Goodemote, a trustee and a member of the site committee, located land in Acton on the corner of Hosmer Street and Rt. 2. This site consists of a house, a two-car garage, a barn, and 4 1/2 acres of land. After a great deal of discussion, after much prayer, after much evaluation, a vote was taken and the majority voted yes, purchase the land in Acton. The land is now owned by the Evangelical Free Church of Concord.
>
> If we have any concept of the body of Christ, if we have any understanding of the Lord's leading in His church, then we must accept this as the Lord's will for our church. Now that this decision has been made, there should be complete harmony among all members. There should be a sense of unity and of striving together. Moving at best is difficult. It will be a big change for the Pastor and his family as well as

for the whole congregation. Making alterations, adjusting to new situations, is not easy. Therefore, it would be a help if we all worked together to make this move as smoothly as possible.

It would be easy at this time to belittle this decision. It would be easy to say, "it was a big mistake." We could visibly point to many weaknesses such as our lack of youth program and our lack of musical activity. We are saddened by these turn of events, but yet we are continually looking to the Lord for His understanding in His own way and in His own time. When the Israelites went from Egypt to Canaan, the biggest problem was not "the enemy without" but the "grumbling and the murmuring of the people within." Too many wanted "instant success." Too many were reluctant to wait upon the Lord. Too many looked back wishing they had never decided to go. This was the biggest problem that Moses faced. The attitude of the people. Let us learn from this and begin the New Year with a clean slate. Right now thank God for His leading, thank God for the decision that he enabled us to make and thank God for the continual leading and victories He is going to give in the days ahead.

The year ahead looks to be transitional. The pastor and his family will be moving to the Hosmer Street property. The house on Lang Street will be rented. Our meetings will be held at both the house and at the church. It is our hope that even while we wait for further leading from the Lord as far as the building program is concerned, it is our hope that we might use the land during the summer months for some group activities such as DVBS and perhaps something geared for young people.

More than anything, we covet your prayers and your cooperation. The Lord's work will only be accomplished as we work and think together as one...[15]

In retrospect, forging ahead on the strength of a majority vote was perhaps not the best approach. It would have been more prudent to stand down, and work toward building more of a consensus on such an important decision.

By contrast, when the Roxbury Free Church voted to sell their property and purchase the new site in Westwood, the vote was twenty-six in favor, one opposed. Votes to purchase a new parsonage and sell the old one were unanimous. Everyone was behind the change, and willing to expend their resources to make it happen.[16]

It would have been much harder to build that kind of consensus, but it would have been worth the effort.

The departure of those who disagreed with the decision, along with the loss of those affected by personal trauma, brought the church to its knees financially. After Pastor Condit left, leadership seriously considered giving up and closing the church's doors. Attendance had declined during the search for a new pastor to between twenty and thirty. Finances were in trouble, and multiple pastoral candidates declined the offer after visiting the church. In fact, attendance, finances, and confidence had declined to a point below which the Westwood church had sunk when they closed their doors in 2003. On the other hand, almost all of those who felt strongly about remaining at Lang Street had already left the church. This meant that those who remained were relatively unified in their vision. The executive board was determined that the main criterion for the next pastor was that he have the "ability and burden to move the church to Acton." Pastor Spence was that man. By the time the congregation voted to move to the Conant School in Acton, all but two members present voted in favor of the move.[17]

In hindsight, the congregation had been struggling for many years to spread its message to Concord, and they were unable to reach consensus on how to change their circumstances. The result was a series of meetings with low quorums and divided votes, and people began to vote with their feet. It might not have been possible to create a true consensus on such emotional issues at the time, but vacillating between two alternatives clearly made the situation worse. Split leadership meant there was no real direction apart from the pastor, and he received insufficient support and backup from the board, leaving him unprotected from second guessing by the congregation.

The church was at death's door. But God had other plans.

Pastor Spence's Evaluation

Ken Spence's primary task was to re-establish the church's mission and keep the congregation focused on its goals. His first pastor's report for the January 1974 annual meeting outlined his goals for the church to be centered on Paul's description of the Thessalonians: "Remembering without ceasing your work of faith, and labor of love, and patience of hope in our Lord Jesus Christ." (1 Thess. 1:3, KJV). He challenged the church to avoid the temptation to criticize how things were being done, and instead to commit themselves in allegiance to the Lord, showing the local community what it means to be Christians. The following year he challenged the congregation to

> become a faithful dynamic witness to all around and to see our outreach begin to reap fruit this year. To this end I have committed myself this year and I would prayerfully ask you to join with me in the outreach of our church so that we may truly experience growth in the community and in the lives of every individual within our congregation.[18]

Even with the encouragement of numerical growth, Pastor Spence's emphasis each year centered around reliance on the faithfulness of God, and faithfully serving Him. The congregation began to recapture this vision, and a renewed vitality was ignited in many hearts. The church had been brought back from the precipice.

What was different about Pastor Spence's ministry that attracted so many new attenders, after so many years of stagnation? Some were attracted by the idea of a new church—at least the adventure of one that was seeking to reinvent itself. Others were simply curious, and liked what they saw once they came. Interestingly, although the congregation included a number of new believers, the church did not conduct many explicitly evangelistic events at that time. By his own account, Pastor Spence did not issue many invitations or altar calls either. However, he endeavored to present and clearly explain the gospel each week, allowing many of the new believers to grow in their faith. He made it a priority to "touch everyone that touched us"—in other words, if anyone visited the church, they would be visited soon afterward.

But as the church grew, the unified vision of leadership began to dissolve. New leaders understood the goals but disagreed about strategies to employ. In the spring of 1977, the pastor challenged the board to hold a retreat, during which they would consider the state of the church and set new goals and vision for the future. The retreat was held, but there is no record that it resulted in any consensus.

In Pastor Spence's 1978 report, he noted that despite the number of new people who were added to the congregation and who had followed in believer's baptism, a large number of people had also drifted away. He was beginning to see cracks in the foundation. It is true that many of the new attenders had become members, and entered the leadership of the church. Each of them, however, had definite (and different) ideas of how to proceed, and the unity that characterized the original core team was fracturing with no consensus about future direction. Knowing that he would be reading his resignation letter at the 1979 annual meeting, the closing prayer of his report was:

> For the church, I pray that this year of varied emotions would produce a new year that will be characterized by greater unity, a deeper quest for a spiritual intimacy with Jesus Christ and a resulting growth that will glorify our Father in Heaven.[19]

Pastor Fife's Evaluation

The early years in Acton had brought the church back from decline and possible demise. But although there was superficial unity, there was no agreement on how the church should proceed after the successes of the late 1970s. And because most people were new to the church, the familial relationships that could help smooth disagreements were lacking.

When Pastor Fife arrived in 1980, he quickly recognized that leadership was favoring an organizational path that was significantly askew from what he felt was healthy. From his perspective, leadership was over-organizing and running the church as a business, ignoring the important spiritual and relational aspects of church life.

In his first annual report to the congregation, Pastor Fife listed 7 emphases of ministry that he felt were needed by a healthy church:

1. Building a church family rather than running a business. Emphasis upon developing a nucleus of committed, interdependent people who are loyal and truly caring of each other.

2. Creating an atmosphere of growth rather than necessarily a product of excellence. Our efforts in the Lord's service should always be our best, but surrounded by the love of God's people, the church should be a place where talents can flourish and potential fruit develop. A place where one can fail, grow and try again in the absence of destructive criticism.

3. <u>Valuing people above programs</u>. We are fortunate as a church to have excellent administrative personnel on most of our committees and we certainly need and value their management skills, but the individual and his specific needs, created in the image of God will always take precedence over any program.

4. <u>Magnifying the Word of God</u> through preaching and teaching—this above all else should be our foundational distinctive.

5. <u>Expecting Great Things—Attempting Great Things</u>. We are blessed with people of vision and burden in our church. During the past nine months God has brought in 20 or more people, and if we just extrapolate this growth we would have a full church each Sunday morning (300) by 1983! If we pledged ourselves to vigorous outreach, under God's guidance this could be achieved much sooner.

6. <u>Encouraging vital worship</u> rather than dead formality—we are constantly re-examining our Sunday morning, evening and Wednesday services in the light of this goal.

7. <u>Showing the joy of Christ</u> while teaching the disciplines of our faith. Our call is to preach and live the Gospel so it is attractive to those around.[20]

Clearly, Pastor Fife was concerned that the church was drifting into a business *vis-à-vis* a family or Body-of-Christ orientation. Indeed, in future years during some pastoral searches, several interview candidates and interim pastors would comment (not as a compliment) that the church seemed to be a "well-oiled machine."

On the other hand, the changeover in the church body and leadership from the old days in Concord, as well as the transience of people and the increase in church size, drove the need for a way to capture the collective "memory" of how and why ministries were conducted. Both perspectives had validity, but no one knew how to reconcile them. This is reflected in the church moderator's report in 1982, after Pastor Fife's resignation:

Early in the year, the church board spent several Saturday mornings working on focus and direction of the ministry for the future. We discussed areas of strength and weakness in our ministries and tried to develop a view of where the Lord would have us move in the future. Even though we learned some things about our church body, we were never able to make a clear statement about future direction.[21]

Leadership was looking to stabilize and solidify the organization after a period of rapid growth, and create a new constitution and bylaws that reflected the way the church wished to operate. The pastor was trying to capture the vision and principles of a healthy body life that were missing for many. Neither the pastor nor leadership were able to attain a balance between these perspectives. At the very least, the conflict created a distraction from ministry, and, in some cases, a toxic atmosphere among leadership.

Pastor Marty Crain's reports to the congregation in subsequent years makes it clear that many of Pastor Fife's original concerns were valid, but leadership was also beginning to understand and work with Marty to address them.

During the interim between Pastor Fife's and Pastor Crain's tenures, Elder Frank DeCanio reported at the 18 May 1982 business meeting:

> ...the church is coming through a hard time with problems with Pastor Fife's ministry and also with the resignation. These problems seem to be dissipating. People seem to be pleased with Rev. McCowan's ministry. We are trying to work out the problems of contacting and visiting new people. Three couples have requested a membership class.
>
> The elders are concerned that many people are overworked especially the Pulpit Committee. They are going to review the church's programs and the effect on the spiritual growth. The most important thing we need to work on within the church is communication to build up mutual trust.[22]

In September, the elders expressed concern that there were still "not enough people for all the ministries" required by the bylaws. But they were committed to discipleship. To this end, the elders prioritized the Navigators' Colossians 2:7 program over all committees and other ministries, so that anyone who wished to join a 2:7 group would be encouraged to withdraw from all other activities for the duration. The investment in discipleship was worth the strain on other ministries.

Pastor Crain's Evaluation

One common complaint of the pastor and elders during Marty's entire pastorate was the lack of willing and able workers to run many of the church's ongoing ministries. Indeed, the elder board itself was shorthanded for most of Marty's time at Faith.

The elders, deacons, and pastor spent a great deal of time praying and considering the state of the church, and developing a vision and focus for church ministry. At the January 1983 annual meeting, the elders and Pastor Crain further refined their focus:

> The elders and pastor had a retreat in which they discussed the mission of the church. They decided that the purpose of the church is to glorify God, and there are three aspects of worship. They are personal, corporate, and offering the entirety of life. The purpose of the body is to be a catalyst in developing individual spiritual growth within this threefold concept of worship. The direction that we should take is in personal discipleship concepts. The church is not to do everything for everybody, but we are here to help believers do what God has called them to do.[23]

With respect to worship, Pastor Crain and the elders had detected that the morning worship time had somehow lost its focus—it felt like people were just going through the motions. Changes made to the service were well received, and Pastor Crain led a sermon series on worship, followed by a Sunday School class devoted to worship taught by Mike Young. Ongoing concerns included the content and style of music, and how best to encourage people to prepare for worship (a common thread of concern from the earliest days of the church).

In his 1985 report, Pastor Crain noted a large turnover and malaise among the congregation:

> ...A number of active families transferred out of the church leaving some questions as to personnel resources. Yet the Lord was faithful in bringing into His Body at Faith Chapel an even greater number than had left. As the dust is settling, it appears that approximately twenty percent of our constituency has changed! In this respect, the year was transitional for many, and we continue seeking to assimilate the newcomers into our ministry.

What, then, is the current state of the church? I believe we have great potential for continuing both spiritual and numerical growth. Momentum seems to be building in the spiritual life and health of the church which frequently results in expansion. A simple indicator in this is the number of individuals seeking baptism this fall—with more already scheduled for the near future! Nevertheless, weaknesses and needs exist with which we must deal if we are to realize our full potential for Christ. Some of the congregation seem to be characterized by an unbiblical fear of numerical growth combined with a lack of reasonable vision. Others appear unwilling to give up personal predispositions in favor of the furtherance of Christ's kingdom. Some need to re-evaluate their attitudinal responses to the duly authorized leadership of the church. Recalcitrance is not attractive in the Christian. May our relationship with Christ never merely be one of convenience. Rather, may we all be open to God's work in us and among us, whatever it may be. May we respond to Him with enthusiasm, optimism, and all the energies with which He has blessed us. Finally, may we continue striving together for the faith of the gospel![24]

At the same time (as described in Chapter 6), the congregation seemed to be catching a renewed vision for missions and outreach.

In January 1987, Pastor Crain continued to elaborate on his evaluation of the church, as shown in the meeting minutes:

Pastor reminded us about the purpose statement that was made 2 1/2 years ago, of which the key issue was the church direction statement of Faith Chapel. The theme of which was motivation of the church family to please God... The question arose on how can we motivate people. Stability: There has been a great turnover of people in our church. We must come to grips with that issue. Friendship is the most common reason someone will stay in the church. Another concept is inclusion in the ministry, mostly again through friendship.[25]

In May, he expressed pleasure with the slate of candidates to be voted on that evening, reflecting a change from previous years, when there were often vacancies that could not be filled. He also elaborated further on what he felt was the primary need within the congregation:

Concerning church direction: the root issue common to many perceived needs at F.E.C. is lack of individual motivation to please God. Therefore, our current emphasis will be to stimulate each believer's individual spiritual health, the depth of his understanding and experience of God and his surrender to God. The results will be felt in personal discipleship, and his relationship with others, his ministry in the body and his witness in the community.[26]

There remained an ongoing concern that all was not as it should be. On 28 September 1988, after Pastor Crain's departure to become superintendent of the New England District Association, the deacons' report stated:

The deacons are concerned as to what could be wrong with the way we as a local body approach ministering to people. As a result, they are banding together in prayer that God would reveal any fundamental problem and provide solutions.[27]

The importance of leadership (elders, deacons, and especially pastors) communicating a vision and guiding the flock cannot be overstated. If for no other reason than their connections with the daily life of the church, the pastor has the clearest insight into the spiritual health of the congregation, and is in a unique position, along with his leadership team, to set a direction and guide the flock. God provides pastors with different skill sets and gifts at various times, each suited to the needs of the body. But if the pastor and leaders allow themselves to be distracted by the "tyranny of the urgent," the seeds of malaise can be sown which take root later. We have seen examples where the spiritual challenges of the congregation were not adequately addressed because leadership was focused on organizational or building concerns, which, although important, should not have been their primary focus. If left unaddressed, these challenges may threaten the life of the congregation. We are reminded of the apostles' insight when they announced, "It is not right that we should give up preaching the word of God to serve tables." (Acts 6:2). The issue then and now was not whether these things should be done, but by whom. Delegation is necessary if the shepherds are to focus on leading the sheep.

Fellowship and Body Life Challenges

During the Concord years the congregation was mostly homogeneous, made up of Norwegian families who had known each other for decades, at times even intermarrying. While many children of the founders married outside their ethnicity, they usually remained within the church. The people conformed not just in their faith, but in many other ways. They were comfortable together. Sure, there were disagreements and conflict, but they were still family.

With the move to Acton, many of the old families had left, and many new people arrived, who were neither Scandinavian nor from a traditional, evangelical background. Many had only recently come to Christ, and still carried scars from their past lives. Suddenly everyone was different. The only bonds they shared were their common faith and relationship to Jesus Christ. This was a good thing! But this new "family" needed to learn what love looks like when everyone in the family is adopted, and when worldviews collide.

It is tempting to evaluate fellowship and body life of a church by measuring conflict or lack thereof. But true fellowship does not imply uninterrupted concord. We don't expect families to be totally free of conflict. Rather, healthy conflict happens within a context of mutual commitment and love. When God moves and people are saved, new believers bring their experiences and background with them. Everyone—the new believer and the old—must get used to each other.

One example gives an especially intimate view of how the congregation learned what love looks like. The following account is included by permission of Ann Brannon and her children.

Ordinary People, Extraordinary Impact: Ann Brannon[28]

Ann Brannon was providentially led to Faith Chapel during a time of personal crisis. Shortly after her husband had walked out on her, an old friend called to see how she was doing. Upon hearing the sad news, she sent Ann a round-trip ticket to her home in Texas. While there, Ann trusted Christ as her Savior. Her friend

instructed her, "find a good Bible-preaching church and go there." When Ann asked if she knew of any near her home, the friend answered, "I don't know, but God will help you find one." Upon Ann's return to Acton, she received another phone call from a previous neighbor who had also recently trusted in Christ in the midst of personal trial. She invited Ann to join her at Faith Chapel, which at that time was meeting at the Conant School in Acton.

Ann's arrival would initiate a positive disruption at Faith. Although Ann was not the only divorced person in the church, she was the only one going through a divorce at the time, and in such a transparent fashion. Evangelical churches at the time often treated divorce as a scandalous, taboo subject. As in any church populated by sinful people, Faith had had its share of broken relationships and moral failures over the years, but unfortunately these subjects were seldom discussed or addressed outright except as examples of sinful behavior. Ann was a brand new believer, with a voracious appetite for spiritual things, always wanting to do the right thing in her circumstances. She had much to learn as a newly single mother of three, she needed a job, and did not know the rudiments of budgeting or personal finance. So she shared openly and asked a lot of questions. This took many people in the congregation well outside their comfort zones.

> "Ken Spence was the pastor of that time. He counseled me on a weekly basis—teaching me God's Word, finances, and how to live a Christian life. He baptized me in Lake Spofford. I had told him my head does not go under water— his response was if you can trust Jesus with your life, you can trust him being under water."

Although the pastor and congregation were generally welcoming and loving, some were not so gracious. In fact, some were overtly hostile. There were women who viewed her with suspicion because she was single—"I was told, 'keep your hands off my husband.'" Once, in a Bible study on the subject of the roles of men and women, she asked about a pending promotion she was expecting which would put her in a position of authority over a man. One man responded, "with the sin of divorce in your life, that's the least of your concerns." The remark was intended to instruct, not hurt. But it cut deeply. On another occasion, "a guest preacher in his presentation said that children of a single parent would be dropouts, druggies, or end up in jail. My three children sitting with me were extremely upset! (The preacher was asked not to return to speak that evening).”

Other affronts were unintentional, but equally injurious. The congregation was very family oriented. For example, the Couple's Club was still active, and would schedule “sweetheart dinners” and activities that were not inclusive of single parents. “It was difficult just going to such a family-oriented church.”

Most people would have left in anger. Many young believers might have decided that if this was what it meant to be a Christian, forget it. But Ann was strong and committed to her new faith. She discussed the issues with leadership and individuals who were unintentionally offending her. She never stopped asking questions and never gave up on the church. Generally, the congregation wanted to do the right thing. They loved her and wanted to show it. They just needed help.

The Couple's Club was renamed Adult Fellowship, and the organizers began planning events that could be enjoyed by singles and single parents, as well as couples. In fact, Ann was involved in planning many of these events.

> “We used to have adult fellowship nights—so much fun— out to dinner, progressive dinners, talent shows, Yankee swaps, 40th birthday “surprise” parties, borrowing the green dinosaur from the Discovery Museum, winter retreats and rodeos. We were a fun social bunch!”

Ann helped the congregation learn not to take themselves too seriously (there are those in the church who still have the vision seared in their brains of deacons doing pirouettes in tutus!), while taking God and His Word very seriously. The author, who was at one time a deacon assigned to Ann's care, remembers a call from her where she said, “Ok deacon, it's time to ‘deac!’ I have enough money to buy groceries or give my tithe. What should I do?” She didn't want to hear the easy answer; she wanted to hear that God was faithful and would supply her needs; His eye is on the sparrow, and He clothes the lily of the valley. Ann was more faithful in giving than many in the congregation who had plenty of money. She wanted to honor her Savior.

Ann did not give up even on those who had hurt her. Rather, she won them over. The man who had invoked “the sin of divorce in your life” to her became so close to the family that, years later, he walked Ann's oldest daughter down the aisle at her wedding and officiated at her oldest granddaughter's wedding. When reminded of the story after Ann's death, he did not remember having said it, but remarked, "I wish I had known, I would have wanted to apologize to her and ask her forgiveness." He rightly called her an "aggressive friend" who never gave up on their friendship, even across distance and years of separation.

Ann opened the eyes of people in the congregation to what it means to support one another in love, and to extend grace to those around us:

> Over the years the pastors and congregation supported us in so many ways. An unknown paid for my children to go to Camp Spofford for two summers. My son was in Boys Brigade and several men volunteered to help him with projects like woodworking and electrical areas. There was a list of people to call if I had problems with my car, my refrigerator, plumbing and whatever. Financial help was provided by the church and unknown individuals.
>
> My children were all saved at Faith Chapel—through youth leaders, pastors and Sunday School teachers. They are all married, gave me eight grandchildren and are following Christ.
>
> Faith Chapel has been a huge, blessed part of my life. The pastors and the congregation have helped me grow, have loved me and have prayed for me for many years. Over the past year I have been supported by prayer, visits, meals and love. I am so thankful for so many friends at church. God has blessed me through this church.

The congregation at Faith is thankful for Ann's presence over the past forty-five years. She truly had an extraordinary positive impact on the body life of the church and she will be sorely missed.

Why Ann's Story is so Important

Ann taught the church much because she was a special person. She didn't give up on the church or Jesus Christ when people offended her. She strove to make the church more like its Savior, who accepted the woman at the well with compassion.

Why is her story so important to tell? Because today, as God moves and draws more people to Christ, the church will find people at its doors who do not conform to the sterile, upright image that we try to project. It is said that "ideas have consequences, and bad ideas have victims."

The church has a calling to show the love of Christ to those victims, and if we are faithful, victims will begin walking through our doors. Many may carry much deeper scars than a broken home. When they do come, the church must learn—and never forget—what love looks like. People are not the scandals, but victims of the scandalous ideas that the world has sold them.

Ann's story is also important because it serves as a constant reminder that there is always room for improvement in how the congregation ministers to individuals, couples, and families that are often forgotten in the day-to-day activities of a church. Women with unbelieving husbands, older couples whose adult children are no longer nearby, people who are caring for ill and aging parents—all of these need extra care and support as they navigate the struggles of life. Every church must cultivate an environment where people look outside their own bubble of friends and seek opportunities to minister to the larger community.

Chapter 13:
Insights from Surveys and Evaluations

At various intervals throughout the years, the elders have evaluated the health of the congregation by conducting surveys. Most of these surveys focused on the ministry of the pastors and were used as input into pastoral evaluations. Occasionally, a survey would focus on the various ministries of the church. The danger of carrying out surveys has always been to "lead from behind," allowing perceived needs of the congregation to dictate the direction of the church. But these surveys have proven to be valuable aids that confirmed what the elders already knew or suspected, even if they did not typically provide new actionable data. In hindsight, we can appreciate the insights they provide into the health of the church at that time.

During the years immediately before and after the turn of the century, leadership scrutinized the health of the church using various evaluation methods. As a result, it became clear that the church was beginning to enter another period of decline. This decline had not yet progressed nearly as far as the one in the 1960s and early 1970s had, but still merited attention. It is to the credit of the leadership that the signs of decline were not ignored. These evaluations are described below.

1997 Church Body Life Survey[1]

In 1997 the elders conducted a church ministry survey designed to give people in the congregation an opportunity for maximum feedback in five major areas of church life: Worship and Prayer, Fellowship, Discipleship and Training, Evangelism and Outreach, and Service and Ministry. In each of the five categories, there were six questions:

1. In general, how do you think we are doing in this area (Excellent, Good, Fair, Poor, Don't Know)
2. What are we doing well?
3. In what areas would you like to see improvement, and how?
4. What new ministries or activities would you like to see added?
5. What ministries or activities would you like to see de-emphasized?
6. General comments

This was not a simple survey that would yield easily analyzable results. Considering the complexity of the survey, the elders were encouraged to receive sixteen responses from the congregation. The results provide interesting insights into the state of the church around the end of the twentieth century.

Worship and Prayer

Survey responses in this category fell into three main groups rather than two: Music, Overall Worship Experience, and Prayer.

Music had captured the attention of the congregation because worship services were trending away from hymns and toward choruses led by a worship team. Opinions about the new format were almost evenly split, as shown by an equal number of requests for more worship team vs less worship team.

Apart from music, there were requests for more attention to elements of liturgy, such as reciting the Apostles' Creed and the Lord's Prayer. This reflected an ongoing desire among many that the flow of worship should reflect a drawing of people together to honor and adore God, as well as reaffirm their allegiance to Him and His Word. At various times in the past (for example, during Pastor Crain's ministry), the need was felt to refocus the congregation and the flow of worship periodically in an effort to prevent services from being reduced to "a few songs, a prayer, and a sermon."

Prayer was seen as a mixed bag at this time. The church-wide prayer chain was being put to good use. It was being handled entirely by telephone—each person was assigned a list of other people to call. Of course, with the ubiquity of email today, the prayer chain has become more efficient and immediate. Anyone can ask to be part of the email prayer chain. Prayer requests are sent to one person who is then responsible for sending emails out to the list of "prayer warriors."

The church had also begun periodic concerts of prayer by this time, which were usually well attended. These prayer meetings often coincided with special occasions and are still held occasionally today.

However, the normal midweek prayer meeting continued to suffer from poor attendance, as it does to this day. This has been an issue since at least the mid-1960s (as indicated by Pastor Condit's first report to the congregation) and continues to be a struggle to this day.

Fellowship

Responses regarding fellowship centered mainly on group functions rather than small groups or work opportunities. The variety of offerings was affirmed, with a note of caution about not forgetting single adults in fellowship planning.

The elders were concerned by the priorities implied in the response of some that we shouldn't let worship time interfere with coffee time! In 1997, there was a single service of morning worship, followed by a fellowship time and Sunday school for all ages.

Discipleship

Comments about discipleship clustered into two main categories: small groups and Sunday school. Leadership had encouraged the development of numerous small groups, many of which met on Sunday evenings, and others throughout the week. Immediately prior to this survey, all existing groups were encouraged to study *Experiencing God* by Henry Blackaby. Once a month the entire church would gather on a Sunday evening to discuss what they were learning. This church-wide study had a significant influence on the way the congregation would seek God's will regarding the expansion of the facilities. The survey reflected satisfaction with the small groups, and a desire for more groups and better participation.

Sunday school was seen as the best opportunity for discipleship and training, and there was a push for greater diversity of subject matter, especially for adults. People voiced a desire for meatier topics, more

Bible book studies, and foundational theology courses—including the creation of a complete adult curriculum.

Evangelism and Outreach

Feedback on evangelism and outreach was interesting, as this was an area that leadership was most concerned about. The congregation felt that Youth Group, Vacation Bible Schools, and clubs programs (Christian Service Brigade and Pioneer Clubs) were effective outreach tools for the youth. There were ongoing ministries at the Concord prison farm, women's ministries and Community Supper, which were seen as important avenues for adult outreach. Many felt the need to improve Faith's "interface," or presence, in the community. Apparently, some people in the community even thought that Faith was a Korean church (because of ambiguous wording of the signs at the entrance)! There seemed to be some agreement that older, traditional models of outreach which sought to entice the community to "come to us"—as opposed to "us going to the community"—were no longer effective in the wider culture. New ideas were needed.

Service and Ministry

Service and ministry dealt mainly with the willingness of the congregation to be involved in ministry opportunities within the church, including facilities maintenance. The main concern: most of the work was being performed by a small minority of the people. Even the all-important coffee time on Sunday mornings was beset with lack of people to help with setup and cleanup, although there seemed to be no shortage of those who were willing to consume the coffee and snacks!

Church Health Evaluation in 2004[2]

In 2004, the church leadership (Elders and Deacons) completed the "10 Indicators of a Healthy Church" evaluation based on a survey produced by Barna. Some were not comfortable with the apparent focus on modern church leadership fads that could skew the results. Nevertheless, it was a useful diagnostic tool during a time of general malaise and dwindling attendance.

This survey was given only to leadership, not the congregation at large. The survey included one hundred questions grouped into ten different categories: Centrality of God's Word, Passionate Spirituality, Fruitful Evangelism, High-Impact Worship, Great Commission Driven (Vision), Leadership Multiplication, Church Planting, Stewardship of Resources, Intentional Disciple-making, and Loving Relationships. Each question required a 1 (weakest) to 5 (strongest) answer. The answers for each question were averaged and added together to provide a total score for the category. A perfect score for a category would be 50. The results were tabulated and evaluated according to the Barna criteria. Tabulated results are shown in the graph below:

2004 Church Health Survey

The survey guide suggested the following interpretation:

Score	Health	Explanation
41-50	Above average	Your church is doing well compared to other churches. This is an area of strength for your church
33-40	Average	Your church is average compared to other churches. On average, however, churches in the US are plateaued or declining.

10-32	Below Average	Your church is below average compared to other churches.

Based on these results, the elders concluded that the church's strengths were the Centrality of God's Word, Leadership, and Stewardship, and the largest weaknesses were Evangelism, Worship, Vision, Church Planting, and Discipleship. Since at that time the church's ministry emphases were Worship, Discipleship, and Outreach, it was troubling that the church's weaknesses were the very areas that were most important. This indicated that a significant change was required.

The Church Planting result was neither a surprise nor a concern, since Faith had intentionally laid that goal aside for a time. But the overall results indicated that the church was challenged in many other areas. In Worship, the congregation was still trying to figure out how best to evolve musically. People were also struggling to be faithful in corporate prayer outside of the worship service. It was also clear that the elders needed to do a better job of articulating the church's vision and mission.

For the next few years, the elders focused on principles of a healthy church, and re-establishing the three-fold vision of Evangelizing, Equipping, and Exalting. Commitment to the still-new Journey to Bethlehem outreach was redoubled, and the pastors drew the congregation's attention to what it means to be a Great Commission/Great Commandment church. At the same time, a renewed personal focus on missions began with preparations for the first trip to Haiti, and everyone was encouraged to join a small group ministry.

Church Health Evaluation in 2007[3]

Three years after the 2004 evaluation, leadership completed a follow-up evaluation using a similar survey from Barna. Almost all of the questions were identical between the two surveys, making it possible to make comparisons and look at trends. The new results showed improvement, but continued areas of concern.

The differences between 2004 and 2007 show some improvement in every category except Stewardship, but especially in the categories of

Evangelism, Worship, Vision, Leadership, and Church Planting (although the latter was still very low). The decrease in Stewardship was understandable given that in 2004, the church had just exited the first Act on Faith stewardship campaign. There was still much to be done in the areas of Evangelism and Discipleship, even though perceived improvement was evident. Question 2 in the category Centrality of God's Word was worded so differently in the 2004 and 2007 surveys that the difference is irrelevant.

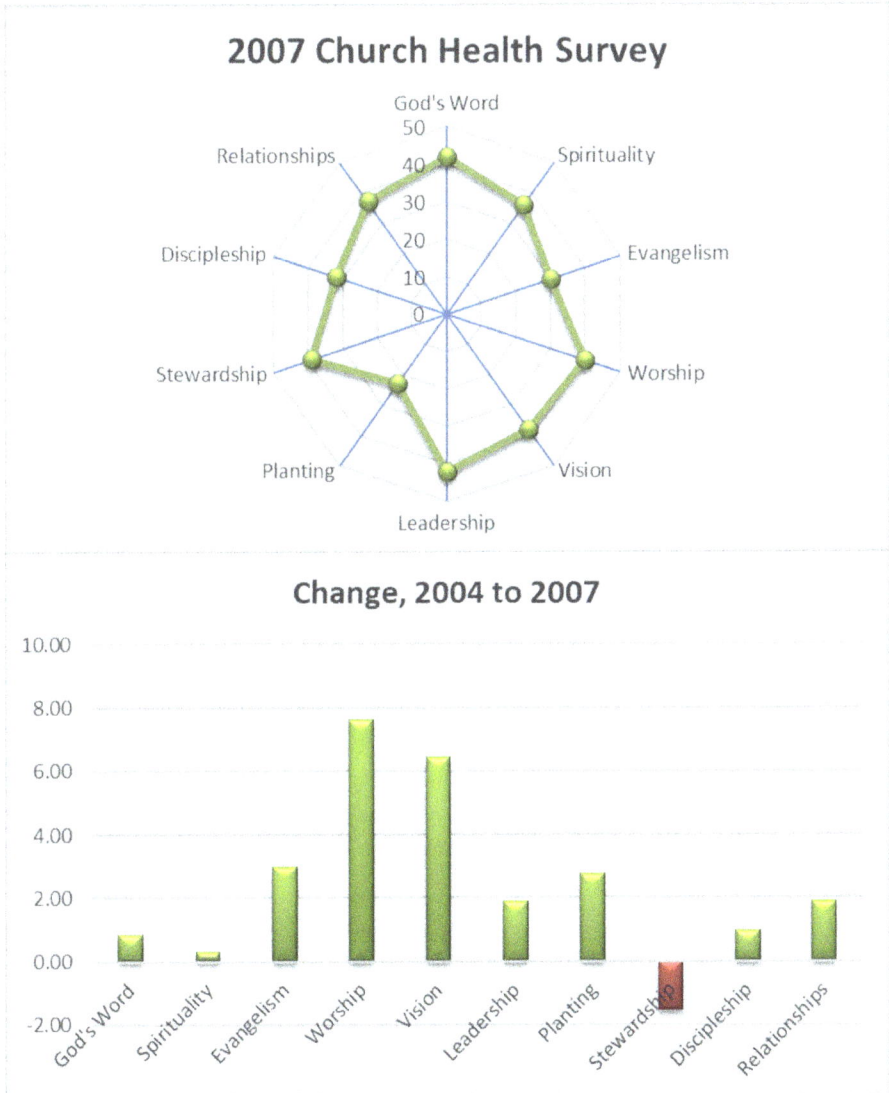

2007 Church Health Survey

Change, 2004 to 2007

Today

Over the past ten years, the church has entered a season of general excitement, as the congregation has seen God work in many areas. With the final completion of the building addition in 2014, the facilities were no longer a hindrance to ministry. And looking back at how God provided the funds and paved the way for construction, it is surprising to recall the fear and trepidation most had felt going into the project!

There continues to be a general feeling of unity among the brethren. That is not to say that there are no disagreements, but rather, all is done in a general atmosphere of mutual commitment and love. Ministries like Journey to Bethlehem and Vacation Bible Camps, which depend on scores of volunteers, have taught many that true fellowship occurs when Christians work together, not just eat together.

Thanks to major outreach ministries such as Journey to Bethlehem, and other avenues like Acton Community Chorus which rehearses in Faith's sanctuary each week, the community is finally becoming aware of who Faith is and what it stands for. At present, the church enjoys a good reputation with the town—it is becoming known as a welcoming church that truly believes.

Church planting has finally taken over the imagination of some in the congregation. Pastor Dan is leading a small group that has felt the call to plant a church in the Littleton/Ayer/Shirley area within the next few years. This is the closest the church has ever come to reproducing itself. It is long overdue. In addition, the church is still supporting other church plants by opening its facilities for their use free of charge.

Almost 50% of the congregation is currently involved in one or more small groups, with more being formed all the time. These groups sometimes study the same materials; at other times they do their own thing. Participation in such groups fosters closer relationships, accountability, fellowship, service, leadership training, and mutual support in prayer. In fact, many of these small groups have become a major focus of prayer ministry.

While there are still ongoing concerns and disagreements about the flow of worship, the services are well attended and generally appreciated. The worship team has become a welcome and appreciated presence in the services (compared to 1997!). A general balance has been achieved in which each service contains both hymnody and spiritual songs and choruses. Although there are now two Sunday morning services, Pastor Brad leads both in a way that forges a sense of community between the groups—as opposed to feeling like separate congregations.

While there has been a great deal of numerical growth over the past decade, much of it has been transfer or organic growth, not conversion growth. Corporate outreach ministries like Journey to Bethlehem, Vacation Bible Camps, Youth Group, Community Supper, Joy Bible Study, etc., provide opportunities for individuals to connect with their neighbors, but real conversion occurs mainly through deeper, personal relationships. The elders have encouraged personal evangelism through small group studies (Sharing Life series), a Great Commandment/Great Commission sermon series, and a special training course from New Life Community Church called "Conversations for Christ."

In 2017 and 2019 the church was invited to participate in prayer walks throughout Acton and surrounding communities. About 75% of the town of Acton and large sections of Maynard, Boxborough, Stow, Concord, and Littleton have been bathed in prayer.

A final area of concern among the elders is that numerical growth increases the need for development of new leaders. God has brought some into the church who are ready to assume leadership positions, but many younger believers still need to be mentored for this purpose. This will be an area of continued prayer and ministry focus going forward.

It is usually the case that the pastor, elders and deacons can see qualitatively whether the congregation is spiritually healthy or not. However, sometimes it is difficult to recognize the root causes of concern. When a person feels poorly for no good reason, they are encouraged to talk with a doctor or nurse, who examines them and performs some tests to determine the root problem. In like fashion, church leadership can employ diagnostic tools such as surveys and evaluations to determine what is out of balance. These tools are useful, but they are a means to an end, not an end in themselves. The goal is not to help people feel better about themselves, but to help ensure that the flock is united, healthy, and moving toward the next pasture that God has selected for them. The Indicators of a Healthy Church surveys were an important step that helped Faith's pastors and elders determine the cause of malaise that had infected the congregation for so long, and helped point to changes that could be put in place to put things back in balance.

Chapter 14:
Insights from Pastoral Transitions

Pastoral transitions are unsettling times for any church. They are stressful in the best of circumstances—and stress either reveals inner strength or exposes problems that otherwise lie hidden. Sometimes the interim period is relatively short; other times it can last for well over a year.

During transitional times, congregations may be tempted to shift into neutral, coasting along as the focus shifts toward internal matters. When the vision and leadership have been vested entirely in the previous pastor, the interim period can be paralyzing. In any case, introspection and self-analysis are important during a pastoral search. Depending on the circumstances surrounding the resignation, a time of repentance, recommitment and restoration may be required.

In this chapter we will look at a selection of pastoral transitions at Faith EFC and how the church responded to them. In the case of "successful" transitions, we will attempt to see what strengths the congregation was able to fall back on. For the difficult transitions, we will look for clues and indicators of why things did not go well.

Except for the ministry of Pastor Olaf Johnsen, most early pastors at Lang Street served two to seven years, probably a typical tenure for pastors nationally at that time. The church was stable and healthy, growing slowly but steadily. Changing pastors was not that uncommon, and many in the congregation had a long history with the church, so they were not unsettled by transitions that occurred every few years.

Indeed, for most of its first three decades, the church did not consider the pastor or his family to be members of the church, and they did not vote at membership or committee meetings. Church leadership was selected from the laity; the pastor, while having the influence of the pulpit and a strong voice at all meetings, was still just an employee of the church. So a change in pastorate was perhaps less disruptive than in more recent years. To be sure, his opinion necessarily carried weight simply because of his ordination and call to ministry, and he was uniquely gifted and sought after for spiritual counsel and advice in all matters. It was not so much that his leadership was considered less important, as that the laity recognized their own responsibilities more acutely than may be true today.

For the most part, searches for new pastors were short, with the district superintendent or a local professor from Gordon Divinity School supplying one or more names for consideration. The church board usually conducted the search and presented the candidate to the congregation for a vote. Interim periods rarely lasted a year.

Successful Transitions

Even "successful" transitions are difficult, and emotions can run high. Calling the following transitions successful is not meant to imply that there were no issues or stress. Rather, these are transitions where the congregation, while recognizing the gravity of the situation—and experiencing some level of uneasiness, fear, and sorrow—navigated the interim and emerged on the other side without undue interruption in ministry and body life.

Olaf Johnsen to Otto Rafos

When Rev. Olaf Johnsen resigned after serving for twelve years, the church first asked him to reconsider, then wasted no time in calling a new pastor, as shown in the following excerpts from business meeting minutes:

> On Sunday, July 12, 1934, Pastor O.M. Johnsen sent in and read his resignation. Shortly after this the elder of the church called the members together and it was unanimously voted at this session to ask Pastor Johnsen & family to continue to remain with us if they possibly could. John Swen and John Andersen were elected to carry this message to Pastor Johnsen.
>
> August 1934. The business session opened with song and prayer. This meeting was called in order to call another

pastor as Pastor Johnsen felt it was God's will that he should leave. It was unanimously voted that the church call Mr. Otto Rafos from Brooklyn, New York for God's service here, beginning the first Sunday in September. John Andersen to send letter to him. Meeting adjourned with prayer.

Shortly after the last business session a Farewell *Fest* was held for Pastor O.M. Johnsen and family at the church. The friends from Boston were with us and Pastor Pedersen conducted the service. Many kind words and thoughts were expressed by many friends for the kindness, patience, and inspiring help of Pastor Johnsen & family. It was a hard blow for the friends of Concord to have Mr. Johnsen & family leave us as we had grown very fond of them in the twelve years that they were with us and had become united as one family in each other. The service adjourned with prayer after which refreshments were served.

Mr. Otto Rafos from Brooklyn arrived in Concord the first Sunday in September to begin God's work here as new pastor of the church.

On Saturday, November 2, a Welcome *Fest* was held for Mr. & Mrs. Otto Rafos. The friends from Boston were with us and Pastor Petersen conducted the service. Several selections were enjoyed by the Boston choir. Rev. Theodore Jensen also brought a welcome message. Many kind words of welcome were expressed by various friends. Service adjourned with prayer after which Mr. and Mrs. Rafos were introduced to the many friends by Mr. & Mrs. John Swen.[1]

Otto Rafos to Harry Odland

When Mr. Rafos resigned in June 1940 (effective 1 September), it was not to accept a new pastorate, but rather to become a chaplain in the Navy. He moved to Somerville, but continued to have a close relationship with the church, including preaching when the pastor was absent. By July, the church had already settled on Mr. Harry P. Odland as a candidate for pastor, and chose to call him on a trial basis as an interim/candidate for three months starting as soon after 1 September as possible. By November, they voted to call him as permanent pastor.

Apparently, during this transition Mr. Rafos was actually involved in the selection of his successor.

David Fife to Marty Crain

After Pastor Fife resigned, a new search committee was formed. As described later in this chapter, the search committee for Pastor Fife had been ill-prepared and ill-equipped for their task, and multiple mistakes had been committed which ultimately damaged Pastor Fife's ability to minister effectively.

The new search committee, formed under the newly-approved constitution and bylaws, consisted of two elders, two deacons, and three members-at-large. Elder Mike Miller served as chairman. Under his capable leadership, the committee first went through a thorough process of evaluating the needs of the church, polling the congregants, and determining what was required in the next pastor. A profile of the type of person to look for was then created.

The committee was given extra time for this exercise because the church wanted to "do it right this time," and interim pastor Rev. Kenneth McCowan was providing excellent pulpit ministry, which minimized the pressure for quick results.

Before beginning the actual search for a new pastor, the committee also agreed that they would not present any candidate that they did not unanimously agree was God's man for the job. This also implied that they would only present one candidate, and if the congregation rejected that candidate, the committee would resign and request that a new committee be formed.

This search committee broke new ground in how to search for a pastor, at a time when the denominational resources for pastoral searches were not plentiful. It became the model for all future searches that the church has conducted.

When the committee presented Martin Crain as a candidate, the congregation voted by a wide margin to call him. And leadership, having learned a lesson from their mistakes with Pastor Fife, was more willing to listen to many of Marty's suggestions!

Marty Crain to Doug Welch

Marty's resignation to become New England district superintendent created many opportunities for things to go wrong. But Marty prepared the church for his departure, and helped the congregation support Brad Johnson during this transition. Using the model developed by Marty's search committee, the new search committee spent time determining the needs of the congregation and building a profile of what was desired in a pastor. As per the congregation's prior commitment to Pastor Brad, he was invited to participate in this process, ensuring that he would be able to work well with the incoming pastor, who turned out to be Doug Welch.

Doug Welch to Brad Johnson

Doug had served as pastor at FEFC for sixteen years, the longest tenure in the church's history, when he tendered his resignation. Many in the congregation had never personally experienced a pastoral transition at Faith or indeed at any church. Some were apprehensive, having witnessed other churches stumble through the process. For everyone it was a painful time—many families had grown very close to Doug, Jeri and their children during the years they served at Faith. This held equally true for some in leadership, as well as the congregation at large.

During this time, the elders called the congregation to pray for the church and for leadership. The elders themselves were in heartfelt prayer that God would direct their footsteps to avoid the landmines that certainly surrounded them in times such as this. They also called a special "summit" that included the current elders and all those who had served as elders in the past, so that they might provide wise counsel and join in prayer.

The fact that Brad and Kathy Johnson were still serving at FEFC, and had actually been serving there longer than Doug and Jeri, provided a much-needed anchor for many who were anxious about the transition. Pastor Brad agreed to act as interim since he had already been delivering some of the preaching over the previous couple of years.

By this time Brad's ministry goals had evolved, and he was interested in becoming senior pastor himself. He made it known that, depending on what kind of pastor the search committee was looking for, he might be interested in throwing his hat into the ring. He made sure the congregation was aware of this before accepting the interim position.

Some, fearful of a long process, wished to short-circuit the search process, call Brad and be done with it. Others, remembering Brad as a young youth pastor with no aspirations to preaching, were more hesitant. Sometimes it is hard to recognize how much a person in one's midst has grown over the years.

Wisely, the congregation instructed the search committee to undergo a time of introspection, determine what the church needed in a new senior pastor, create a desired profile, and present it to the congregation for comments. This was done without input from Brad. Once the profile was completed, and after prayerful review, Brad submitted his name for consideration.

The search committee interviewed Brad, discussed his philosophy of ministry and what he believed he could bring to the position, and addressed various concerns with him. They then unanimously decided to present him as a candidate for senior pastor.

This process—which for some seemed exasperatingly long, and for others seemed unnecessary ("we already know him, he's been candidating for 17 years!")—was nonetheless critical because it resulted in the church calling Brad on his own merits and based on their due diligence. The final vote was unanimous to call Brad as senior pastor.

Difficult Transitions

There were, however, a few difficult transitions that seemed to shake the congregation to its core.

Rev. Olaf Thompsen to Rev. Olaf Johnsen

When Olaf Thompsen left in 1922 after only a year of service, the congregation was still very young and insecure. His resignation was a surprise to all. This reminded members of the many times at the Scandinavian Branch when pastors would come and go quickly. It was difficult to keep the ministry going with such rapid turnover.

The search for a new pastor took over a year. Since their new home had been dedicated, the church had spent as much time without a pastor as with one! Youth ministry suffered the most during this time, as the adults had little time to devote to it.

Rev. Hyland Richmond to Rev. Barnes

Pastor Richmond's resignation seems like a classic case study of how not to go through a pastoral transition. Looking on the surface, it appeared that things had been going well at the church. Much was happening: the facilities were expanding; Sunday school classes were bursting at the seams; and many new programs were being put in place. But as described elsewhere, the church had begun to lose focus on its vision and mission.

In July 1959, while Pastor Richmond was on vacation after attending the EFCA national conference in Colorado, the church board was made aware of his intention to resign shortly:

> Concerning a report that Pastor Richmond was preparing to terminate his services at Lang Street Church, the Secretary was asked to write our field superintendent Rev. Urang explaining our position and seek his advice or recommendations as to securing another minister under the present compensation and preferably thirty five years or over.[2]

At the next quarterly business meeting on 20 July[3], the secretary, Mr. Robert Carson, resigned his position after reading his report. A letter requesting membership transfer was read and acted upon. An offer to have an outside speaker come in for a special meeting was declined "because of our unsettled condition." A discussion ensued about potential salary for an incoming pastor, and then the consideration of an interim. "This was defeated on the basis that our present pastor had not yet resigned."

Apparently, they were in a hurry!

The pastor did eventually resign, and the church board met again on 30 July[4] to act upon his resignation, effective 1 September. But they decided it should be effective immediately, and he would no longer serve in the pulpit. They set a date of 8 August for a special business meeting. The pastor would be paid for the entire month of August, but the board proceeded to work on securing pulpit supply for 16, 23 and 30 August, and 6 September.

At the special business meeting (which actually took place on 11 August)[5], Rev. Richmond's resignation was "accepted with regret." The congregation decided to pursue an interim pastor, preferably from Trinity or a Free Church man. Since the Eastern District superintendent had already sent recommendations for four men, it was decided to have three of them come in as candidates in September. In the meantime, one of them, Donald Barnes, would be asked to serve immediately as interim pastor.

At the 9 September[6] board meeting, it was reported that Inga Cahill had resigned as financial secretary and organist, effective 1 September.

It is not clear whether her resignation was related to the way Pastor Richmond was treated, but the timing is suspicious.

What happened? Clearly Pastor Richmond's resignation was bungled, as word leaked out prematurely. But why then did the board act on that knowledge? They seemed far too anxious. The result was the resignation of several leaders, and fallout continued as people decreased their giving and involvement, causing ministry to suffer going forward.

Why did Rev. Richmond resign? The 1959 annual report is missing from the archives, and the board minutes do not elaborate. There may have been an undercurrent of discontent on both sides that was masked by all the busyness of the church. Perhaps Rev. Richmond was burned out from being so involved in the construction, as well as many new ministries. In any case, the transition was handled poorly, and a number of long-time members of the church withdrew from leadership—some left the church entirely.

Over the next six years, from 1959-1965, the church experienced several transitions, and pastoral searches were becoming more difficult. Finances were tight, due in part to considerable repair expenses. The congregation and board meetings focused on finances.

While the meeting minutes do not state explicitly why Rev. Barnes or Rev. Westa each resigned after only a few years, they appear to have been struggling against a general malaise in which people were unresponsive to leadership. Attendance dipped, and expenses were outpacing income, forcing cutbacks in ministry. It also appears that the membership roll was in some disarray, resulting in confusion as to who was still actively supporting the church in 1960:

> In order to keep accurate membership record, a request was made from the Chair to have the Secretary send letters and cards to members, indicating his desire of re-evaluation of membership on our Church Roll. The purpose is to find out how many inactive members care to remain on our membership roll. We have 77 members and approximately 20 inactive members...[7]

As discussed in chapter 5, Rev. Barnes' call was actually a four-way vote of preference, unique in the history of the church. Only twenty members attended the meeting, and one-fifth of them voted "none of the above." Although Rev. Barnes received more than the (then) necessary two-thirds majority for the call, it is significant that the new constitution, which was approved in 1960 changed the threshold for a pastoral call to 75%.

Rev. Barnes to Rev. Westa

When Rev. Barnes resigned, the church did not announce it to the public. His last day was 27 August 1961; Professor Pfeiffer began as interim pastor in March 1962, after it became evident that the search process would take a while. Yet there were no announcements in the Concord Enterprise regarding Rev. Barnes' resignation until 14 March 1962. Even that consisted of only a short, terse statement with grammatical errors at the bottom of the page. The wording of the announcement reflected a lack of concern for the church's reputation within the community, a poor reflection indeed of the church at that time.

> ### NEW PASTOR HERE
>
> Concord—Rev. Donald Barnes is no longer pastor at the Evangelical Free Church and taking his place is the intern pastor Mr. Charles F. Pfeiffer. The church serves the people of Concord, Carlisle and the Acton.
>
> — *Concord Enterprise,*
> 15 March 1962, p1.

After Rev. Barnes' resignation, it took about six months to settle on Rev. Westa as the desired candidate, and another six months before he began his ministry. The first candidate had withdrawn his name from consideration, and the second candidate was rejected.

Rev. Westa served as pastor from 1962 to 1964. During this period, the church continued to experience a season of malaise. Although membership stabilized, it did not rebound. At the October 1962 business meeting, nominations for boards and committees were difficult to come by, as many people declined their nominations from the floor.[8]

Rev Gordon Condit to Rev. Ken Spence

The resignation of Rev. Condit in 1972 came at a critical time for the church. There was dissention in the ranks about the move to Acton. The church was hemorrhaging people, including a significant number of leaders, to other churches. Finances quickly deteriorated. On the immediate horizon were the daunting tasks of a building program and moving the church. As a result, serious consideration was being given to shutting down the church.

The difficulty of this transition was not so much the way in which it was handled, or the result, as the context in which it occurred. Many candidates were considered, and a number who were brought in received positive votes. But pastors who were already established in their ministries were loath to leave their relatively comfortable surroundings to take on such challenges. The board, however, continued to press forward, and seek God's man. They focused their search on a single goal: finding a man with the ability and burden to move to Acton.

Meanwhile, the church was sinking further into a death spiral. It was almost a year before an inexperienced youth pastor, Ken Spence, realizing that he had nothing to lose, and seeing the potential of a small group of dedicated leaders, decided that he was up to the task.

Rev. Ken Spence to Rev. David Fife

During the rapid growth years in Acton under Ken Spence, the church outgrew its constitution. New committees were formed, and old committees were refocused based on current needs. At some point the old constitution became so irrelevant to the daily activities of the church that it was ignored. There was talk of rewriting or amending it to reflect the way things were now being done, but that work took a back seat to ministry.

So when Pastor Spence left, a search committee was formed to find a replacement. Previously, the church board had served as the search committee. And by looking at the various meeting minutes of the past, the search process typically involved finding some candidates, bringing them in and having the congregation vote on them. Sometimes the congregation was asked to vote on multiple candidates at the same time. Also, candidates were brought in based on majority vote of the board—that is, there was no real sense of endorsement by the search committee for a candidate. The new search committee followed the tradition of previous searches. When they presented Rev. Fife for consideration, they did not unanimously endorse him. Rather, their stated position was that he met the qualifications for the pastorate and did not disqualify himself in any way. When the church voted after the candidating period, he received a two-thirds majority. The search committee believed that this was sufficient to call, but the 1960 constitution and bylaws stated that a 75% majority was required. Although there was some discussion that two-thirds was perhaps too low a bar, it was deemed sufficient to call, and Rev. Fife accepted the call. It wasn't until after the call was made and accepted that someone noticed the error, but it was too late.

As a result, Pastor Fife arrived with two or three strikes against him already. First of all, Ken Spence was a tough act to follow. Secondly, it is challenging to minister when you know that one out of three people in every pew voted against you. And some of those people were feeling frustrated that leadership had overruled the bylaws, albeit unintentionally. Finally, it must be remembered that the reason Pastor Spence left in the first place was because of growing discord over how to chart a course for the future. In fact, the biggest impediment to ministry at that time was the ongoing philosophical differences between the pastor and some members of leadership regarding how best to guide the church.

In the end, for the sake of unity, Pastor Fife withdrew. But the different perspectives of how the church should operate did not disappear, and it was left for Pastor Marty Crain to navigate through the minefield.

David Pattison

Pastor Fife struggled in his relationship with the leadership of the church, while enjoying a generally good relationship with the congregation as a whole. Youth pastor Dave Pattison's problem was not so much with leadership, as with the congregation—specifically, the parents of some of the teens.

Pastor Marty Crain always insisted on regular evaluations for staff as an important means of ministry improvement. In 1981 the elders performed a telephone poll of people in the congregation regarding the strengths, weaknesses, priorities, and character of Pastor Crain and Dave Pattison. The report for youth pastor was as follows:

> He was found to be a good teacher. Also good at defining creative activities with the teens. There is a neglect of fringe kids. Biggest weakness is communication with parents. On priorities, he is a role model for the teenagers. On charac-

ter, he is in harmony with biblical passages. On Goals, there should be more in the way of discipleship, and there should be more development with youth and young adults. A motion was made by Fred Gluck to telephone poll another 18 to 20 people for further comment on Dave by the next business meeting. This was seconded by George Werber. Methodology to be determined by the elders. All voted yes.[9]

At the next quarterly business meeting, held 26 May 1987, the elders reported back to the congregation:

Elders report: The elder ministry was involved with the National Day of Prayer, Home Groups, Board of Youth and Education for the summer ministries. Also discussed were the Korean church relationship with our church. They also planned the farewell service for the Pattisons. As directed at the last business meeting, the elders pursued 18 members of the church pertaining to the evaluation of Dave Pattison. The following are lessons to be learned by the feedback from the congregation:

1. Pastoral responsibility for staff issues and relationship with the church.

2. Greater objectivity in pastoral staff evaluations.

3. Timely communication of potential conflicts with the congregation for evaluation and resolution.

4. Difficulty in determining satisfaction or dissatisfaction with pastoral staff ministry.

5. Challenge ourselves to greater commitment to prayer concerning tensions in ministry.

6. Appreciation for elder responsiveness to the congregation while seeking to provide leadership and direction.[10]

Pastor Dave report: He has been preparing the youth and young adults for the transition when Dave plans to leave in June....[11]

The nature of the issues is not totally clear from the meeting minutes, but clearly there were missed expectations between the parents and Dave. And the elders failed to address or even acknowledge those issues until they had festered beyond healing. The relationship was so damaged that it resulted in Dave's resignation.

The mishandling of this situation was not merely an internal affair—the news of Dave's resignation, coming on the heels of Pastor Fife's treatment, spread to people outside the church. At least one person from Faith, when attending a function at another local church, was confronted with the comment, "Oh, you go to that church that doesn't know how to take care of its pastors!" It can take years for that kind of reputation to heal.

It is normal to desire to avoid conflict, but avoidance can make things worse in the end. Later in 2004, the church held a special one-day conference with Ted Brewer on biblical conflict resolution. At the time of the conference, there were no major conflicts within the church, but leadership understood that it was better to talk about these things when cooler heads prevailed rather than when there was actual conflict to resolve!

In a sense, the resignation of a pastor is to the local church what having a loved one pass away is to a family. In the stress of change, what is healthy will rise to the surface, but so will anger, bitterness and strife if they had been formerly suppressed. Faith EFC has had its share of both positive and difficult transitions. Navigating these rough seas requires much prayer, open communication, and careful setting of expectations so that people can grieve and move on, and so that the new pastor will be given the opportunity to lead.

Chapter 15:
Insights from Attendance

Thus far we have refrained from looking at attendance and membership records as a gauge of church health. A spiritually healthy church can be small, and a very large church can be rotten to the core, if attendance comes at the cost of fidelity to the Gospel. In the history of Faith EFC, it could be argued that at the time when only eleven families voted to call Ken Spence as pastor, the congregation was as healthy as it had ever been. Their number may have been small, but they were all of one mind and vision, and they consecrated themselves to the work.

That said, it is also true that a long or steep drop in attendance probably indicates that something is wrong, and requires investigation and possibly some changes. Lower attendance is usually synonymous with financial hardship which hampers ministry. As Pastor Westa said during his last report, "a church operates only when it has money in the bank."[1] So while it is not the most important gauge of church health, attendance statistics are still useful diagnostic tools.

The church at Lang Street kept no attendance records for worship services, although some figures are available for Sunday School attendance. However, in January 1924, the annual meeting minutes end with the following entry: "The Sunday evening attendance has been very good. May the Lord richly bless its works."[2]

In the absence of attendance figures, the membership roll can be an equivalent measure, especially if we remember that the important measure is trends, not absolute numbers. Membership changes tend to lag attendance by at least one or two years, however. Sometimes the lag between someone leaving the church and being removed from the membership list was even longer, especially when the church was lax in maintaining the roll, as happened in the 60s and 70s.

The following graph[3] shows annual membership figures for a period of almost one hundred years, including the number of people received into membership, the number removed, the net change (red line), and the total number of members on the rolls. For the years when inactive membership was reported, the blue line shows the actual number of active members.

FEFC Membership History

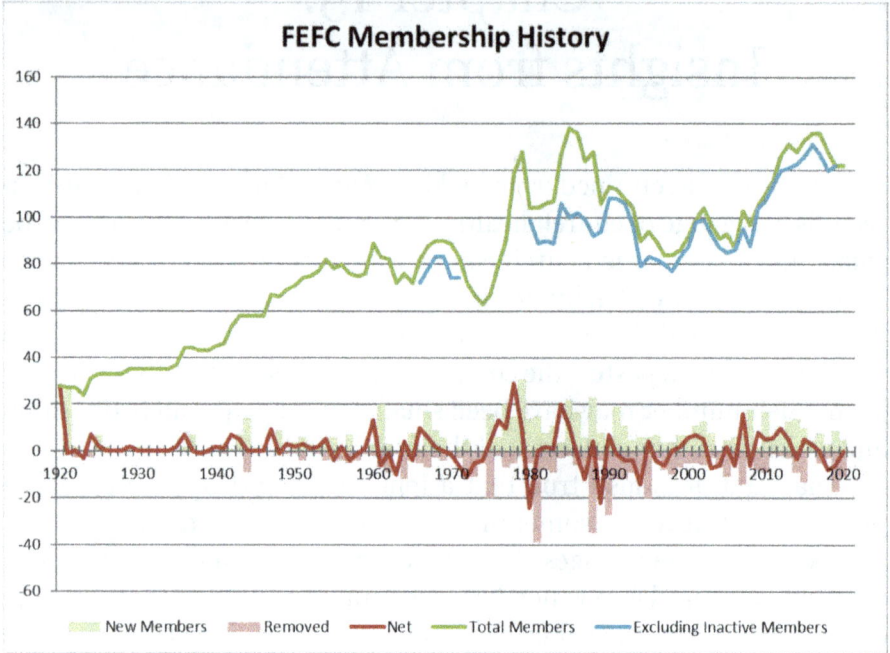

From this chart we can see the following:

- As seen in the New Members and Removed activity of the chart, starting in the 1960s the transience of the congregation (i.e., the movement of people coming in and going out) begins to increase, reaching a crescendo from the mid-70s (when the church moved to Acton) through the mid-90s, but continuing to this day. This cultural phenomenon was addressed previously.

- In the late 1950s, total membership began to level off with a slow net decrease until the late 60s. New people were joining during this time as the old guard was leaving. The beginning of this decline coincides with the latter half of Rev. Richmond's and Rev. Westa's ministries. These years include a major addition to the building and renovation of the parsonage and sanctuary. During Rev. Westa's ministry the church bought and renovated the Macone property, followed by Rev. Condit's ministry during which the Acton property was purchased. Also at this time, the church membership roll began to be cleaned up after a number of years of neglect.

- From the late 60s to the early 70s there is a precipitous drop in membership. These are the later Condit years leading up to the purchase of the Acton property, before the first services were held at the Conant School. As drastic as the membership drop appears, reality was even worse. By the time Pastor Spence arrived, attendance was in the twenty to thirty range,[4] but membership never dropped below sixty. During this time the church was not actively managing the membership roll, so only those who specifically requested action were removed.

- The rapid growth in the late 70s along with the drop in 1979 through 1982 marks Pastor Spence's ministry in Acton, and his departure in 1979. The smaller peak in total membership in the mid-80s reflects newcomers who arrived during Marty's ministry, but also includes a large inactive component, which was cleaned up in the late 80s.

- The large increase starting in the late 2000s and continuing to the present reflects the expansion of the church building, the addition of a second service, and new or revitalized outreach ministries such as Journey to Bethlehem, Vacation Bible Camp, Youth Group, Boys and Girls Clubs, Women's Ministries and Joy Bible Study.

Attendance Record

From the fall of 1976 to the present, attendance records for Sunday morning worship services have been maintained, as seen in the graph below.[5] From these records we can see trends that mirror the membership records. For example, the average yearly attendance figures mirror the active membership graph from 1977 to 2018. With the addition of a second service the church finally broke the "magic" 200 barrier for average attendance (NOTE: averages exclude the months of July and August, when attendance typically drops 10-20%).

These numerical metrics can be a good indicator of whether things are going well or not, but they do not provide insight into why. Declining attendance should prompt leadership to take an honest, deep look into what might be causing people to leave. But rising attendance does not necessarily mean everything is going well either. Large upswings in attendance, while always welcome, could signal a need for new discipleship ministries and ways to bring new people on board with the vision of the church.

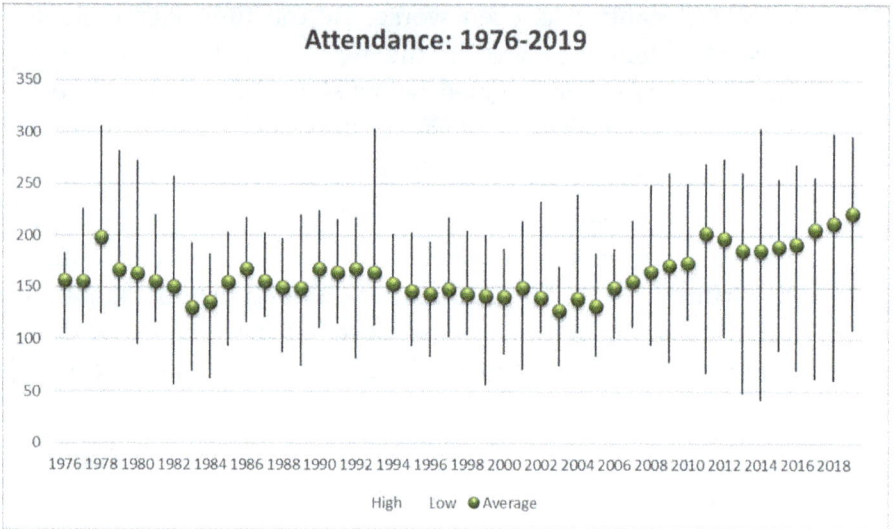

Attendance: 1976-2019

Chapter 16:
Lessons Learned

The previous chapters chronicle many things that Faith has done well over the years, as well as instances when the pastors, leadership, and congregation have fallen short of what Christ desires for His people. Some mistakes of the past have cost the church dearly, and harmed her witness in the community. Others have cost time as the congregation was distracted from her mission. Through it all, the Lord has remained faithful, forgiving and blessing the church greatly. But it is important that the congregation and especially leadership periodically take stock of where we have been and where we are, to repent of any mistakes and sins, and resolve, in the grace and strength which God provides, to remain faithful to Him.

This chapter is not intended to be an in-depth analysis of the church or solutions to problems. Whole books could be (and have been) written on each subject. The intent here is to list some broad topics of discussion suggested by Faith's experiences, which the leadership of any church would probably find familiar. Some of these may serve as warnings of courses of action to avoid, while others may provide insight on how to prevent future issues before they arise.

Building Consensus vs. Leading By Consensus

In a congregational church government, most major decisions are taken by vote of the membership. The pastor and leaders will often advocate a course of action, but the congregation has the final say. Much has been written about the pros and cons of this model, and we won't address them here. Congregational government is a foundational principle of the Evangelical Free Church movement.

A major hazard of congregational government is assuming that the will of the people is the will of God. A brief look at the history of the Israelites after the exodus from Egypt should disabuse anyone of that notion. Therefore, the leaders of a congregational church must never confuse building consensus with leading by consensus. Building consensus is the process of educating the congregation in order to gain widespread understanding, agreement, and approval for a strategy or course of action. Leading by consensus is leading by survey, or being satisfied with a simple majority vote for all major decisions. In effect, leading by consensus is nothing less than an abdication by the leaders of their responsibility to educate and lead.

Jim Van Yperen, in his book *The Shepherd Leader*, points out that the Middle-Eastern shepherd leads his sheep from the front, he does not drive them from the rear.[1] He sets a direction for them to go, then leads them at a pace that is appropriate for them. This is not to say that he ignores those who are wandering—rather, he calls them by name.

It is vital to build consensus, to help everyone understand the reasons and benefits of a course of action. But what happens when the congregation is divided about two potential strategies? Two examples from the history of Faith illustrate the problem.

The decisions in the 1960s and 1970s to purchase land in Acton, move the services to Conant School, and sell the Concord properties were difficult to make. So also were the decisions to expand the facilities in Acton in 1997 and 1999. The decision to buy land in Acton resulted in the departure of many people from the church, and almost caused the church to close. Years later, the decisions to expand the facilities cost a couple of families, but the vast majority were on board. What accounts for the difference in results?

The business meetings to discuss the move to Acton were marked by two things: the number of members participating in the discussion was often significantly less than half the total membership; and there was no clear consensus on the ultimate direction. In fact, it appears as though there were two factions in the church—one that favored staying at Lang Street, and one that favored moving. One group was bound to be disappointed. Making matters worse, leadership was also equally split, leaving no clear direction for others to follow. In this vacuum, Pastor Westa decided that remaining in Concord was the easier choice, and convinced the congregation to invest further in the existing property. This frustrated those who believed a move was necessary. Later, under Pastor Condit, a group of lay leaders convinced the congregation to revisit the decision. This frustrated those who were committed to remaining in Concord. The result was the withdrawal of many from both factions.

Similarly, in 1993 many in the congregation recognized the need to expand the facilities, but they were apprehensive about the cost. A "seed" project proposed to raise money for architectural plans, but it fell short of the required $14,000. Ultimately preliminary architectural plans were drawn up and approved, but progress halted until 1997, when the elders asked the small groups to study Henry Blackaby's *Experiencing God*. This prepared people for the decision-making process regarding expansion. Recognizing the need for consensus, leadership provided a detailed presentation and the congregation held an evening of focused prayer before the special business meeting to consider the motion to expand. Although the bylaws required a simple majority, the leadership and congregation agreed to seek an 85% affirmation to proceed. The resulting 75% affirmative vote (enough to call a pastor!) indicated that although God was at work, true consensus had not yet been reached. So the building committee continued to meet and communicate the vision and goals. Finally, in 1999 the building committee put forth a new proposal. In keeping with the commitment in 1993, an 85% vote was required, but the vote failed with 83.3%. A subsequent vote with seventy-three members present (a 90% quorum!) easily passed with over 85% affirmation.

A few people still left the church after the vote, but by and large the congregation was committed to the new direction.

The lesson learned here: there must be a balance between consensus building and leadership from the front. During deliberations about moving to Acton, the congregation was clearly divided, and neither side was willing to be persuaded. In such a situation, consensus may be impossible to reach, yet simple majority rules can be counterproductive, factious and hurtful. By the time someone begins leading from the front, the flock has scattered.

As for expanding the facilities, the disagreement was not so much whether expansion was necessary, but when it would be appropriate to start. Leadership's desire for near unanimity to expand the facilities extended the process by almost seven years, during which the church struggled to maintain momentum, and attendance declined somewhat. Yet by setting the standard of consensus so high, leadership was forced to educate and campaign for the desired outcome. This resulted in more clarity about the benefits and risks of the endeavor and allowed people to become confident that their leaders knew what they were doing. On the other hand, the 83.3% vote was so close; there were also ambiguities in how abstaining votes should be counted. So it made sense for the board to promptly call another meeting to reconsider, knowing that there were many in favor who had not been able to attend the first meeting. Having a revote so soon after the regular meeting upset a few people who were against proceeding and wished to consider the issue settled. The board recognized that total unanimity would be impossible and there would always be some who would be reticent, and who might vote with their feet if they felt strongly enough. But they also knew that it would be wrong to let one or two families hold the whole congregation hostage to their view.

Overall, the vote to expand was handled far better than the vote to move. Building a consensus is never easy, and it can be frustrating for those who think they already clearly see God's will for a matter. But it is worth the effort, as long as everyone remembers that God's will is not democratic, and that eventually there comes a time when action is necessary. The challenging part for leaders is to recognize when consensus is possible and when it is necessary to lead from the front.

Handling Conflict

Like every church, Faith EFC is populated by fallen people. Even the best of men are men at best. People are finite, fallen, and sinful. Therefore, wherever two or more are gathered, there will eventually be differences of opinion. It is acceptable and even beneficial to disagree—"iron sharpens iron, and one man sharpens another" (Prov 27:17).

But when disagreement in the church blooms into conflict and discord, God is dishonored, ministry suffers, and the onlooking world shakes its collective head. A reputation for discord and failing to care for the pastors is hard to repair, and can cost years of fruitful ministry.

Handling conflict in a God-honoring and loving manner is difficult. The Faith congregation has not had to deal with open strife in many years, but it has had its share at various times in its history. There are three main sources of conflict in a church:

Conflict between pastor(s) and the congregation, especially leadership

The circumstances surrounding the resignations of Pastor Richmond, Pastor Fife, and David Pattison come to mind here. In all of these cases, fruitful ministry was occurring, but there were missed expectations between pastor and laity. There was a philosophical disagreement between Pastor Fife and some members of leadership regarding style of ministry and how to balance organization with relational ministry.

With David Pattison, the disagreement was due to missed expectations of the parents. It is worth noting that a similar kind of missed expectation occurred at the beginning of Pastor Brad's youth ministry, when some parents were disappointed that he did things differently than they preferred. In Pastor Brad's case, he had fully vetted his ideas with the elders, who came to his defense and asked parents to be patient and give his plan a chance. In time, the parents came around. In Dave Pattison's case, the elders were oblivious to the problem, or refused to address it until it got out of hand.

Factions within the congregation

Factions occur when there is disagreement about vision, or when leaders disagree publicly, drawing people to their side. This occurred when the church was considering the to move to Acton. As discussed in the previous section, this might have been handled better if leadership had worked more intentionally and diligently to build consensus. Yet consensus may have been impossible, given the entrenchment of the people. But in either case, leadership exacerbated the problem by vacillating between the two choices, rather than charting a clear course.

Conflict in the home and extended family

Even when a church is functioning well, with no overt conflict, families often have to deal with the same relational issues. Regardless of the source or parties to a conflict, the ability to handle it well is a skill that everyone should master. The special seminar on conflict management that was held in 2004 was important. But a one-time training session is not sufficient; perhaps periodic study of the biblical "one another" passages would help?

The Relationship Between Pastor and Leadership

If the pastor and elders or other leadership do not get along, ministry suffers. When reconciliation is not possible, it is better to part ways. Incompatibility at one church does not necessarily reflect negatively on either the pastor or leadership. Chuck Swindoll did not have a good experience at Waltham, but went on to a long and fruitful ministry in Fullerton, CA. Pastor Fife and Faith's leadership struggled to see eye to eye, but he went on to a fruitful ministry in Rockport, MA.

Focus on Root Issues

This topic is easiest to explain using an example. In 1987 Pastor Crain and the elders stated that the "root cause common to many perceived needs at F.E.C is lack of individual motivation to please God."[2] Does it ever make sense to tell people they need to be motivated? That's probably as ineffective as telling a person addicted to drugs to just stop taking them! If there is a general malaise in the congregation, it is redundant to explain it in terms of a lack of motivation. Motivation is not something a person can just decide to have. It is the result of an inner conviction about the importance of a cause or course of action. The congregation had lost sight of the value of Christ's indescribable gift, and the vital importance of proclaiming the gospel to the lost.

The elders had often succumbed to the temptation to focus on symptoms rather than root causes. This resulted in failure to improve the situation. When Paul addressed the problem of division in the church at Corinth, he did not just tell them to agree (though he did do that), he helped them recognize and address their root problem of arrogance (1 Cor 1:10-4:21) and pointed them toward Christ's command to love another.

All Things to All People

In a small church, there are never enough people to take on all of the ministry opportunities that face the church. Through the years Faith EFC often succumbed to the temptation to do too much, and spread itself too thin.

Currently, Faith EFC focuses its corporate outreach on three major annual events: Vacation Bible Camp, Journey to Bethlehem, and Hope for the Children of Haiti. There are many other outreach ministries, such as the youth groups and the practice of opening the church to community activities, as well as others that individuals and small groups support. But everyone is encouraged to participate in VBC and JtB. The mission emphasis in VBC is always Hope for the Children of Haiti, and in addition people are encouraged to join or support the teams that travel to Haiti. For its current size, Faith EFC has struck a good balance.

The fact that a small church cannot be all things to all people is also a big incentive for planting new churches, which can each have their own ministry emphases.

Grace With Accountability

The church is often accused of being the only army that shoots its wounded. Sometimes it deserves that moniker.

Of course, the church desires to be known as a hospital for the sick and wounded, an island of grace to the broken and brokenhearted. Jesus showed grace to those caught in sin, who recognized their need (Luke 7:36-50; John 4; 8:1-11). Yet this same Jesus also taught the church to hold its people accountable and to exercise discipline on the impenitent.

Discipline is an unwelcome word today. As fallen creatures we all suffer from the inclination toward rebellion, and especially in the West, we hold tightly to our sense of personal liberty. The very idea of discipline implies that someone other than ourselves (the church, our parents, or God) is in charge.

Yet discipline is the heart of discipleship. By definition, as disciples of Jesus Christ we are bringing ourselves under His lordship, His discipline. A major facet of new life in Christ is an implanted desire to please Him (Jer 31:33; Eph 2:10; Phil 2:13; 1 John 3:2-3), and we are taught to live in a manner worthy of our calling (Eph 4:1-3; Phil 1:27; Col 1:10; 1 Thess 2:12). The church is instructed to rebuke and, if necessary, discipline those who bring scandal (public, high-handed sin), dissention, and false teaching (Mt 18:15-20; 1 Cor 5:2; Tit 3:10-11; 1 Tim 1:20).

Discipline may seem unloving and heartless and, especially in this age where personal autonomy is supreme, many people respond with indignation at the audacity that someone should be held to account for their behavior. Yet ignoring sin is expressing disregard for the sinner as well as those against whom the sin is committed. Properly handled, public discipline is the grace of God calling someone to acknowledge their sin and come in repentance to the throne of grace.

So what is the proper balance of grace and accountability? While this is not the place for an in-depth analysis of the topic, there is a clear pattern in Scripture that we can use as a guide: Jesus extended grace to those who recognized their sin and spiritual bankruptcy, and reserved his condemnation for those who trusted in their own righteousness and presumed upon God's favor regardless of their behavior.

All churches are made up of sinners. Faith EFC is no exception. Over the course of a century it is unfortunately to be expected that there would be times of scandal and dissention. There were times when evil was ignored or swept under the rug, and other times when the wounded were not cared for. All too often, certain sins have been treated like they are unforgivable, hanging like a big scarlet letter around the neck of the penitent. Some episodes of dissention almost destroyed the church. Some scandal was never confronted, yet there were still whispers. Getting it right has been a continual struggle, and Faith has a spotty record of success.

But the discipline episode from 1995 to 2000 (described in chapter 7), while heartbreaking, was a real success story, resulting in repentance and restoration. Proper handling of discipline requires leadership that is in tune with the heart of God and the needs of the people. In the 1995 episode, Pastor Doug Welch expertly led the congregation through the process with compassionate, yet firm resolve, showing the grace of Christ while faithfully holding to the teachings of Scripture. He taught the members of the congregation their responsibilities and their limits, building a foundation of prayer for all involved, as well as a respect for privacy. His admonishments to the congregation were forthright, and he prohibited idle gossip. And when restoration was in order, he helped everyone celebrate in a way that gave appropriate honor to God.

Pastor Doug was the man for the job at the time. But what if the pastor himself had been the one in need of discipline or reproof? Would the leadership of the church have been ready and able to do a similar duty?

Thankfully the need for public discipline has been rare. While that is certainly a good thing, leadership must remain vigilant and ready to do the hard work when necessary. If there is hesitance or inability to act, they should be willing to call in objective help from outside the church.

We often think of church discipline as consisting of only the last step in Matthew 18 ("tell it to the church"). But the process includes necessary prior steps which are private. Only when these private steps fail is public discipline appropriate. If public discipline is rare, it should be because private discipline has been successful.

Therefore, although the need for public discipline is (fortunately) rare, the need for accountable grace among the body is constant. As the culture around us deteriorates, and the idolatry of personal autonomy invades the church, it is vital that leadership encourage and train the body to more effectively support one another in mutually accountable relationships, continually pointing each other to the grace and mercy that has been so richly lavished upon us (Eph 1:7-8), which results in our desire to live a life worthy of this great calling (Eph 4:1).

Engaging the Community

Community presence involves more than just reputation, although it certainly includes that. The most basic question is: does the community even know the church exists? At one time a member of the congregation reported that some people in the community thought Faith was a Korean church because of the Acton Korean Church sign under the Faith Evangelical Free Church sign. Rather than realize there were two churches meeting in the same building, many thought it was one Korean church. After all these years trying to shed its Scandinavian ethnicity, its adopted hometown thought they were Korean! (This problem was solved with a simple change to the signs.)

Opening the church building to Acton Community Chorus, basketball, and other activities, such as National Alliance on Mental Illness (NAMI), have helped put the church back on the map. Journey to Bethlehem has been an even more effective method for promoting the church in the eyes of Acton and surrounding towns.

Assuming the church's presence is felt by the populace, the next question must be: is the church a force for good in the community? In other words, to townsfolk appreciate that the church exists in their neighborhood?

Admittedly, it is not always possible to have a warm relationship with the community. The gospel is a stumbling block to those who are perishing, and the world does not always like to hear the truth of God. For example, another member of the church once reported that she heard someone say they would never set foot in an "evangelical" church because of its political views—an interesting comment given the church's policy of not advocating stances on political issues!

Does this mean that the church should hide the fact that it is evangelical? Should the name of the church be changed again to eliminate the word "Evangelical"? Of course not! The church today must never compromise its commitment to the centrality and sufficiency of God's Word and the cross—"folly to those who are perishing, but to us who are being saved it is the power of God. (1 Cor 1:18)."

We must be winsome, but faithful. As Pastor Ken Spence put it, "it is to be expected that people will hate you because of Christ. But never let it be the case that people hate Christ because of you."

The people of Christ can go even further. It is still true that the best way to reach the community is to engage it. The Gospels are filled with stories of Jesus being "moved with compassion," as in the time He reached out and touched a leper and healed him (Mark 1:40-41). If the people of God are truly filled with the Spirit of God, they should also experience Jesus' compassion for the lost and needy. As people at Faith have become aware of needs, they have reached out in compassion to those in the Concord prison system, to Community Suppers, to shut-ins in nursing homes, families dealing with addictions, and the disabled. In so doing, lives are changed—not just those being ministered to, but those who are ministering. As people become involved in everyday activities in the towns in which they live—clubs, charity races, etc.—they are showing the world what it means to live as a Christian. It has been shown that people today tend to become insulated from opposing viewpoints as clubs and social media create "bubbles" and echo chambers. Churches can help their members step outside their own bubble and engage with those around them as ambassadors for Christ.

The elders should always look for ways to expose the congregation to the needs around them, and give opportunities for acts of mercy.

Handling Adversity

The Church of Jesus Christ may be heading for a time of adversity in the West. It may not be so extreme as to cost lives, but we are already seeing examples where those who hold fast to biblical truth are called racists, bigots, and deplorables. The day may be coming when adherence to Christ may cost one's job or livelihood. Even in times when Christianity is popular, it is important to prepare and equip the saints to be willing to suffer for Jesus' sake. How much more so in times of unpopularity? The Apostle Paul warned Timothy that "all who desire to live a godly life in Christ Jesus will be persecuted (2 Tim 3:12)."

In addition to equipping the saints with the whole armor of God (Eph 6:10-20), the elders must ensure that the work of the gospel can continue even when it is hard to attract people into the pews. Outreach that focuses on attracting people to church is not going to work when the church is seen as undesirable or unsafe. Rather, the saints have to go out into the community and engage people where they are, even in times of opposition (Mt 28:18-20).

And what if, God forbid, it became impossible to hold large church gatherings, either because of safety concerns or natural disaster (think of the impact of Hurricane Katrina or Ike)? Does the work of the gospel shut down when the building is closed? Of course not! We must never forget that the most important ministries of the church are never tied to a building. That simple fact can (and should) be pivotal in determining congregational priorities.

Whose Work Is It?

Perhaps the most dangerous time for a church is when it goes on autopilot. Ministries and programs continue, but they become mechanical. The congregation begins to trust in its own abilities. The people begin to think of the work as their work rather than God's work in and through them.

Sometimes this reveals itself as a loss of the sense of God's presence among His people, or when worship becomes rote.

We must always be evaluating the congregation's sense of the holiness of God and His reign over all that the church does. We need to ask ourselves, are we doing God's work or our own?

Communicating Vision Effectively

God always knows what He is doing in the church. But sometimes the congregation isn't so sure. The congregation needs to be reminded periodically why they are there.

The vision for Faith has changed over the years, but missions and outreach to youth have always been highest priorities. Even when the vision is clear, it is not easy to keep the congregation focused on it. Since the 1960s, there has always been significant turnover in the church membership. Frequently during its history, a 50% turnover occurred at Faith in the course of only a few years. During Pastor Crain's ministry, leadership found it necessary to refocus on basics simply because of transience.

Leadership must be ever mindful of the importance of communicating over and over again the vision of the church to its congregation so that it is not easily forgotten or abandoned. Newcomers must also be helped to understand and own that direction. The elders must live out the vision and show how every decision is related to it.

Succession Planning

Pastoral transitions are a fact of life. Lay leadership and membership changes are also a fact of life. Today, there remain only a few active members who were part of the church when it moved to Acton. People move away. People pass away. Planning for transitions is simply a wise thing to do.

The apostles were acutely aware of the need to plan for the time when they would no longer be alive. Paul invested in Timothy and charged him to invest in others (2 Tim 2:2). Peter said, "I think it right, as long as I am in this body, to stir you up by way of reminder, since I know that the putting off of my body will be soon... (2 Pet 1:13)."

Planning for Congregational Turnover

Succession planning for congregational change involves setting in place mechanisms for passing on the legacy of those who came before. This may include things such as teaching the history of the local church, but it must include discipleship programs, and communicating the focus and vision of the church.

Another way to help with congregational turnover is to have written policies for each committee and board. These "manuals" should not be thought of as dictating how things should be done, but rather passing along to the next generation an understanding of why things are done the way they are. If the next generation decides to modify a practice, at least they will know why it existed in the first place.

Planning for Leadership Change

The lay elders and deacons serve only a maximum of six years before they are required to take a sabbatical year. This forces leadership to always plan for transition, investing themselves in those who will come after them.

Through the years, Faith EFC has been blessed with strong, mature leaders. The relationship between pastors and lay leadership has usually been very close, but at times it was excessively confrontational and at other times too passive. Sometimes, the lay leadership was argumentative and uncompromising with the pastor, while at other times the elders were blind to issues with the pastoral staff, resulting in eventual eruptions of ill will and conflict. But overall, the elders have had warm, accountable and supportive relationships with the pastors, working closely together to "present every person mature in Christ (Col 1:28)."

To their credit, the elders and deacons have tried to learn from their past mistakes, but there is always room for improvement. The issue is how to retain and pass on collective wisdom and experience to the next generation of leaders. Deacons have an Associate Deacon program for this purpose, but typically there has been no intentional, formal training or mentoring in place for the elders. To be sure, the elders and deacons have often studied books together, and, for example, the current senior pastor, Brad Johnson, meets regularly with and disciples numerous men in the church. But no curriculum is in place to ensure that leaders are equipped for their responsibilities. And with the "tyranny of the urgent" always commanding attention, there is often little time to consider necessary issues that can fester over time.

Leadership must always be reproducing itself (2 Tim 2:2). If repeating old mistakes is to be avoided, each generation of leaders should be passing on the wisdom and lessons of the past to the next generation (1 Cor 10:6,11). There should be an intentional plan in place for discovering, training, and mentoring the future leaders of the church. This need has become more urgent at Faith as we recognize leadership needs for the new church plant initiative.

Finally, it is important that leadership avoid becoming cocky or overconfident. Constant prayer and seeking the Lord is necessary to ensure that future leaders are prepared to lead the church through the challenges of the future, to be faithful to the Gospel of our Lord in all circumstances, and to share the love of Jesus Christ winsomely to the surrounding community. And we must always be praying for the Holy Spirit to guide the church one step at a time.

Planning for Pastoral Change

One thing that is certain for any church—there will always be changes in leadership. Pastors come and go, and even the lay leadership changes over time. As William Vanderbloemen and Warren Bird point out, "all pastors are interim pastors."[3] At Faith, Pastor Brad Johnson has served in one capacity or another for over thirty years. But he has already made known his desire to retire within the next few years to pursue other ministry avenues. Pastor Dan Kasey has also served for over fourteen years, and as the church's current church planting pastor, plans must be made for the time when he will commit himself to the plant full-time.

No matter how strong or prepared the church's lay leadership is, the role of senior pastor is vital to the health and ministry of the congregation because he is the primary expositor of the Word of God and is the focal point for communicating God's vision for the church and exposing those areas which need to be addressed. The right pastor can strengthen a church and guide it through all kinds of trials. But the wrong pastor or lay leader can seriously weaken a church. It is far better and easier to ensure that the church calls the right pastor than it is to have to let the wrong pastor go or help him improve his ministry where there is little or no gifting.

It is important to remember that individual pastors may have different strengths and gifts. Pastors are a gift to the universal Church (Eph 4:11ff), but they serve in the local church. Different churches have different needs, and a single church will have different pastoral needs at different times in its lifecycle. The church must choose their new leadership wisely.

Traditionally congregations have ignored succession planning until a pastor resigns. Once that happens, there follows an interim period during which the church decides what they are looking for, and then begins the search process. Many times, the interim period can last well over a year. During that time, many churches go into a kind of autopilot mode. Existing ministries continue, but progress slows.

Interim pastors can be profitable and even necessary.[4] If the church is not healthy interim pastors can help such a congregation through a time of introspection and healing. Even in a healthy church, an interim can help the church transition between the past and the future, especially when a highly regarded, long-term pastor leaves. The interim period creates a buffer period which can help the church adjust and move on. But an otherwise healthy church can lose its edge if the search process drags on too long. Some churches do not survive a lengthy pastoral search.

Faith EFC is in the enviable position of being able to prepare for Pastor Brad's retirement in advance and with his help. He has been transparent with the congregation about his desires and future plans, and encouraged the church to be proactive so that the transition will be smooth and with minimal disruption.

Regardless of the approach and timing, a well thought out and documented search process is vital. Faith EFC has had some difficult pastoral transitions, and some very successful ones. The congregation should be thankful for those who have gone before and documented their experiences, mistakes, and successes.

While in Concord, the church's pastoral search process was much less formal. In the early years, the search process was usually short, probably because there were few Norwegian pastors, and they were all well known. Often, the church simply selected whomever the district superintendent suggested. Later, the church formalized a search committee (which usually consisted of the elders and deacons), who presented one or more candidates for consideration. Sometimes multiple candidates were presented at once, and the favorite was chosen.

Since 1982, pastoral staff candidates have been sought by a search committee consisting of two elders, two deacons, and three members at large. Before resumes are even looked at, the committee prayerfully goes through an exercise of determining the characteristics of an ideal candidate according to Paul's letters to Timothy and Titus, and by assessing the congregation's desires (via survey) and leadership input. From this input, the committee puts together a list of qualifications and desirable gifts, which is presented to the congregation for confirmation. At this point the committee begins to review resumes and contact people of interest for interviews. A single candidate is then chosen and brought in for a public candidating period. The search committee will not present a candidate unless after a great deal of prayer and discussion, they unanimously believe he is the right person for the job, so there is an explicit endorsement of the candidate. After the candidating period a special congregational meeting is held for a vote. The call vote requires a 75% quorum, and a 75% affirmative vote.

This process does not guarantee that the best candidate is called, but it provides time and encouragement for the search committee to consider the felt (survey) and real (leadership input) needs of the congregation when evaluating applicants. It is important that the leadership are faithful to cast light on the real needs of the congregation rather than simply following the congregation's will and felt needs.

Avoiding Landmines

At numerous points in the history of Faith, it appeared that things were going well, and the church was busily involved in fruitful ministry. If one were to have asked the leadership at that time about the state of the church's health, they would have responded that it was indeed doing well. Yet within a few months or years, the church ended up walking off a cliff, so to speak, and things fell apart.

It is easy for people to become complacent when things are going well. But Paul's admonition for individuals applies also to churches: "therefore, let anyone who thinks that he stands take heed lest he fall (1 Cor 10:12)." Leadership must cultivate the habit of looking out for potential pitfalls before they become real issues. The elders' constant prayer should be that God would guide each of our footsteps and help the church avoid any hidden landmines.

Body Life is Everybody's Business

Many people think that fellowship is something that just happens—that it's an automatic result of like-minded people being together. It is true that the bonds of love that unite us with Christ also tend to tie us to one another as a family. Christ had compassion on the outcast and the needy. But His disciples could sometimes be oblivious to the needs around them. In the early church love and fellowship abounded. But some people were being "neglected" (Acts 6:1-7):

> Now in these days when the disciples were increasing in number, a complaint by the Hellenists arose against the Hebrews because their widows were being neglected in the daily distribution.

It's not that the Hellenist widows were not welcome or unloved, they were just being overlooked. No one noticed their need.

In the case of the Hellenist widows, somebody started murmuring, or muttering under their breath about the situation. Gossip! And it came to the attention of the Twelve. They solved the problem by commissioning others (the Seven, whom we call the first deacons) who could lead in the care of the faithful.

Likewise today, even when everyone seems to be united, we must always be on the lookout for those who are being overlooked. At Faith the deacons are charged with that oversight. But no one can know or do everything. The purpose of the office of deacon is not to expect them to do all the caregiving, but to help the congregation make sure care is given to those in need.

Deacons must faithfully model caregiving and maintain contact with all of their families. But the congregation itself must take ownership of looking out for one another. If anyone knows of a need, that person should attempt to meet the need, or enlist the help of others. Leadership, especially the deacons, should be made aware.

The key is that everyone should be looking beyond their own immediate circle of friends to recognize and come alongside those in need. Otherwise, eventually the unity and fellowship of the congregation will suffer under the weight of "murmuring" and complaining. One of the leadership goals for equipping the congregation must be in this discipline.

The Importance of Wise Counsel

When Pastor Doug Welch resigned in 2005, it was the first time in sixteen years that the church had experienced a pastoral transition. Even though this was not the first transition the elders had experienced, there was a sense that the board and the congregation were ill-prepared for developing events. So the elders reached out to all those who had served as elders in the past, asking them to join in an extended time of prayer and counsel. This resulted in good discussion, renewed mutual commitment, and a wonderful time upholding the leadership and the congregation before the throne of grace. Leaders of the past have much to offer the leaders of the present.

Epilog:
Looking Ahead

But we have this treasure in jars of clay, to show that the surpassing power belongs to God and not to us.

2 CORINTHIANS 4:7

"I will build my church and the gates of hell will not prevail against it (Mat 16:18)." When we read these words, we naturally think of the universal, invisible Church of Jesus Christ throughout the ages. Yet that Church (capital C) is made visible and effective in local churches (lowercase c) which come and go in various places and at various times. At its best, the local church shines the glory of the Gospel brightly in the proclamation of the Word and in ministry to the community.

Faith Evangelical Free Church is a latecomer in the grand plan of Jesus Christ for his Church. It is not large. It is not alone; it is not unique. It is one of many churches that seek to faithfully proclaim and preserve the glorious faith that was once for all delivered to the saints (Jude 3). We are merely a small flock of His sheep seeking to hold forth the word of life to those in the Boston MetroWest region. We serve alongside many other churches of like profession, most of whom do not share our denominational ties. The Lord has blessed us and graciously allowed us to serve Him for a century in the Concord/Acton area.

Our goal has always been to bring glory to Jesus Christ and proclaim the Gospel faithfully. God has worked mightily in and through us. There is much to be grateful for and much to praise God for. We have not always succeeded as we would wish, and there have been occasions for repentance and renewal. But in God's grace, He has not finished His

275

work in us and through us. George Whitefield famously wrote, "we are immortal until our work on earth is done."[1] The same holds true for local churches as well as individual believers.

Having considered whence we've come and where we are, it is natural to ask, what now? What does God have in store for us? Obviously God keeps His own counsel, and predictions of the future are fruitless and unnecessary. But we can also see glimpses of what is on the horizon. And, as Paul cautioned the Ephesian elders, it is incumbent upon church leadership to "pay attention to yourselves and to all the flock, in which the Holy Spirit has made you overseers, to care for the church of God, which he obtained with his own blood (Acts 20:28)."

Demographic Changes

As described in Appendix C, the towns of Concord and Acton are experiencing gentrification, and communities to the west are experiencing more growth. At Faith this is seen by the changing geographical spread of the congregation from a nucleus around Acton, Concord and Maynard to a much wider area that centers more on the communities to the west of Acton.

Similar demographic changes forced the church to move from Concord to Acton in 1975. Is this an appropriate response today, or should the church look for new ways to remain relevant to Acton and the immediately surrounding communities, while planting new churches in the western communities?

In addition, the ethnic makeup of the local community has been changing rapidly in recent years. Currently the church is similar in makeup to the community at large, but as the Asian population continues to grow, how will the church reach out? With the ongoing trend of planting new churches among immigrant communities (in much the same way that Faith was started!), how can Faith best help shine the light of the Gospel to everyone?

Culture Wars

While the church was meeting in Concord, it struggled to attract people from outside its ethnic and socio-economic boundaries. While supporting the idea of having a church for the "servants," most people from outside the Norwegian community wouldn't attend there because it wasn't the right place in which to be seen. The issue was not so much the message but the ones who bore the message.

Today the issue is not ethnicity but worldview. How should the church respond to the cultural revolution around us? Until recent years, the church enjoyed operating within an environment where the larger community had at least a cultural understanding of Christianity and usually recognized the positive influence of Judeo-Christian values. Within only a few years this has changed to the point that Christians who seek to be faithful to Scriptural revelation are often regarded with ridicule and even hatred by the culture at large.

And yet the church itself is not immune from the idolatry of personal autonomy and self-gratification that is endemic to the culture. In many ways those who identify as evangelical do not behave differently from those outside the church. As the culture becomes more secular and enslaved to harmful behaviors, how can the church reach out to the victims of destructive ideas, be welcoming and winsome to the community while continuing to hold its own members to personal holiness and mutual accountability? These are issues that the worldwide Church has encountered throughout the ages, but the American Church has largely been spared—until recently.

Reproducing the Vision

The history of Faith EFC serves to reinforce the understanding that the problems at Ephesus at the turn of the first century (Rev 2:1-7) are universal. That church had successfully passed on the important doctrines of the faith to the next generation, but failed to pass on their first love. Similarly, the second generation at Faith remained fully committed to the historic Gospel of the Lord Jesus Christ, but had not figured out how to reach their (now Americanized) generation with the message. The methods of the previous generation did not work as well, except for those who were already raised in the church. Over the course of twenty years, the church came close to death while people debated how to re-establish its mission. By God's grace, the church did not die, but reinvented itself with the move to Acton. But thirty years later there were early signs that revitalization was needed again.

It is probably safe to assume that the need for revitalization will come at least every thirty years, or even sooner if sin creeps in. It is incumbent upon the leadership to keep an eye peeled for signs of malaise or sin and address it effectively.

We are not talking here about changing the message in any way, but rather recognizing that some methods may need to change. For example, the author learned about Faith in 1977 by looking in the Yellow Pages. How many people today even remember what it means to "let their fingers do the walking?" This generation is much more likely to use Google to find a website or social media to find a church.

Today's secular culture is far less likely to understand what we are talking about if we always use theological terms that previous generations understood. Yet we must be careful to communicate the same theological truths through words and actions.

Sacred music concerts, evangelistic "revivals" and cold door knocking—that at one time drew many to Christ—are far less effective than they used to be, and often counterproductive in New England today. Instead, individual and small group relationships are much more effective (they probably always were). What will be the most effective way to reach the next generation of seekers and believers? The church has thousands of years of resources for teaching the doctrines of the faith, but each generation must work out how best to teach them without compromise.

Most importantly, each generation must capture anew the realization that without Christ, our friends are lost to an eternity in hell. Love and compassion compel us to reach out to them anyway we can. Whenever we find that our decisions are based more on our comfort than on their need, the church is in danger.

Final Thoughts

It is hoped that this review of the history and ministry of Faith caused the reader to pause and praise the Lord Jesus Christ, whom the Father has "given as head over all things to the church, which is His body, the fullness of Him who fills all in all (Eph 1:22-23)."

A frequent topic of prayer among the leadership at Faith is that the Spirit would move mightily in New England, that there would be a new

Great Awakening in this area that was historically so devoted to Christ, but is now known for its indifference and even hostility toward the Gospel. We pray that God would give our neighbors eyes to see, ears to hear, and hearts of flesh to believe and obey. And we pray that God will find us ready and willing to be used by Him in His great work of reconciliation as we strive to live out the Great Commandment and Great Commission He has given us.

May He find us faithful as long as He tarries, but may He come quickly.

Amen.

Appendix A: Biographical Sketches

All of the charter members listed here stood to identify with the new Norwegian Zion Evangelical Free Church of Concord on 29 October 1920. Their names are in boldface. Other members and friends mentioned here who were not charter members appear in plain text.

Karin Olsen

Karin Olsen was born in Løten, Norway on 14 November 1886. She emigrated to the United States from Liverpool on the vessel Saxonia bound for Boston, arriving on 6 October 1904. In Concord she found employment as a domestic servant for Hugh and Edith Leith, who lived at 64 Main Street. She started attending the Scandinavian Branch sometime around 1913, and gave regularly to the cause. She became a member of Trinitarian through the Branch on 2 May 1915. As a domestic servant, she was not wealthy, but she donated at least $100 toward the construction of the new building at Lang Street, a sizeable sum in 1920. On 29 October 1920 she stood to become a charter member of the new Norwegian Zion Evangelical Free Church. She declared her intention to become a naturalized citizen on 11 December 1924, and took the oath of allegiance sometime before 1930. As of 1940 she was still employed by Hugh Leith, and she died sometime ca. 1950. In 1926, she and Karen Lee were voted to be on a committee of two "as a sick or visiting committee."

John Mikkelsen Family

John Mikkelsen was born on 24 October 1862 in Norway, the son of Mikael Andersen and Kristine Knudtsen, and came to the United States in 1890. On 12 June 1892 he married **Oleanna** Knudtsen, born ca. 1867, daughter of Severin and Bertha Knudtsen. Rev. George Tewksbury from Trinitarian Congregational Church performed the ceremony. John and Oleanna lived on Monument Street in 1896. He started out as a farm laborer, but by 1910 he had his own fruit farm on Strawberry Hill Road in Acton. John became a naturalized US citizen on 25 October 1905. His sponsors were Emil O. Thorpe (younger brother of Ole O. Thorpe), who was a fish dealer in Concord and a member of the Scandinavian Branch, and Martinus O. Helsjer (Helsher), who was a charter member of the church. John and Oleanna had four children: Bertha, Christine, Soren, and John Otis. There is no indication that John and Oleanna ever formally joined Trinitarian or supported the Scandinavian Branch, but John donated $100 toward the construction of the new church on Lang Street. He and his wife stood with the others to declare their desire to become charter members on 29 October 1920. John passed away on 25 October 1953, and his wife died 17 February 1955. They are buried in Woodlawn Cemetery in Acton.

The Joanna Andersen Clan

Around 1890, **Joanna Ericksen Andersen**, wife of Anders Andersen, came to Concord from Norway. She was born ca. 1842 in Hedmark, Norway. It is not clear whether her husband died in Norway or in the US, but when she became a member of Trinitarian on 6 January 1895, she was joined by her son Edward and her daughter Annie, but not her husband. Certainly by the time of the 1900 census, she was a widow living with her daughter Annie and her husband. She later moved in with her son Edward and his family. Although she probably attended the Scandinavian Branch, there is no record that she or her children supported it financially, although her sons, John and Edward, gave substantial sums toward the building on Lang Street. She and Anders had many children who stood to become charter members of the church, including: Edward, Annie, Olava, and John.

Joanna's son **Edward (Edval) Andersen** was born 1 March 1871 in Romedal (just south of Løten), Hedmark, Norway. He became a member of Trinitarian on 6 January 1895 alongside his mother. On 5 December 1903, he married **Matilda Petersen**, in a ceremony officiated by Rev. Ole O. Thorpe. Edward petitioned for citizenship on 23 February 1916, stating that he had arrived in Boston on the vessel Samaria on 19 September 1891. They lived in Acton during the early

years of the church, but moved to Carlisle before 1930. Matilda died on 12 March 1931, and Edward married **Thora Jörgensen**, another charter member, in 1932. He died 1 April 1960.

Joanna's daughter **Annie Andersen** was born 5 June 1880 in Lillevoldsie (near Romedal), Hedmark, Norway. She became a

Annie (Anderson) and Anders Christoffersen 1945

member of Trinitarian on 6 January 1895 alongside her mother. On 9 November 1898, Ole O. Thorpe officiated at her wedding to Anders Christoffersen. Anders does not appear to have been a member of Trinitarian, nor is there any record that he attended the Branch, and he

is not listed as one of the charter members, but he clearly attended the church and helped purchase the lot upon which the original parsonage was built. They had seven children: Carl, Edwin, Allen, Margaret, Ella, Alton and Adelaide. Ella Mildred Christoffersen, born 1 November 1906, married Henry Alvin Johnson on 26 September 1936 in the Lang Street church, with Rev. Otto Rafos presiding. Ella Johnson became a member of the church on 9 November 1924, and her husband Henry

Ella (Christoffersen) Johnson 1945.

became a member shortly before their marriage in April 1926. Henry passed away in 1952, but the congregation enjoyed Ella's friendship for many years, until her death in 2000.

Olivia (Andersen) and Christian Monsen.

Joanna's daughter **Olava (Olivia) Andersen** (1876-1968) married **Christian Monsen** on 23 November 1895, officiated by Ole O. Thorpe. Christian was born ca. 1875 in Romedal, Hedmark, Norway, and arrived in the US in 1887. Both became members of Trinitarian on 2 May 1915, and they supported the Scandinavian Branch. He served as a trustee of the unincorporated society that bought the property, and not only contributed, but put his own financial welfare on the line for the new building until the property was conveyed to the church in 1922. He was personally heavily involved in the construction and financing of the facility. The Monsens lived on School Street in Acton, and had three children: **Mabel**, Olga, and Christian. Mabel became a member of Trinitarian on 6 May 1917 as part of the Scandinavian Branch. She stood with her parents to become charter members on 29 October

Mabel Monsen Holm 1970.

1920. On 27 October 1923, Mabel married Ludvig Holm, son of John Holm and Marie Mikkelsen. This was the first marriage held in the Lang Street church, officiated by Rev. Olaf Johnsen. Ludvig attended the Scandinavian Branch, at least during the years 1913-1914, but there is no record that he ever became a member of Trinitarian or, for that matter, the Free Church at Lang Street. One of Mabel and Ludvig's children, Marion (Holm) Christiansen, attends Faith EFC today. Christian died on 17 October 1961, and Olivia passed away in 1968. Mabel died in 1975.

Joanna's son **John Andersen** (born 6 September 1882) came to the United States with his mother in 1890, when he was only eight years old. He was married to **Olga Osberg** in 1914 by Rev. George Tewksbury of Trinitarian Congregational Church. They settled on a farm in South Acton.

John and Olga (Osberg) Andersen 1945.

He and Olga did not become members of Trinitarian until 3 November 1918, but they actively supported the new church, and stood to become charter members. John petitioned for citizenship on 13 January 1919, which was granted on 12 May of the same year. John was one of the men tasked with the details of constructing the new church at Lang Street, and after John Swen died, he served as a life elder until his own death in 1974. He and his wife Olga had eight children: Esther (m. Alfred Davis), Henry, Ralph, Willard, George (m. Ruth), Walter (m. Ruth Ann), James, and Helen (Esterbrook). Helen, Esther and her husband, George and Walter and their wives all became active members of the church as well. Walter was one of the trustees who co-signed the original mortgage for the church building at Acton.

As a side note, another of Joanna's sons, Hans Andersen, married Marta Maria Monsen, sister of Christian Monsen. Hans donated generously to the building effort in 1920. Most of the Andersen family are buried in Woodlawn Cemetery, Acton. Joanna, the matriarch of this amazing family, died 24 November 1921, barely a year after the church was founded.

Anton and Pauline Hoff

Anton Hoff was born 1 November 1875 in Norway, the son of Anders Hoff and Oleanna Severensen. His wife, Pauline Christiansen, was born ca. 1877, daughter of Christian Christiansen and Christine Olsen. He arrived in the United States on 31 March 1896 on the ship Scythia, having listed his last residence as Kristiania (Oslo). He petitioned for citizenship on 1 April 1899 (at which point he was living on Cabot

Street), and took the oath on 15 November 1901. His witnesses were Christian Petersen and William H. Hunt, the husband of Elizabeth Hunt. Anton and Pauline were married on 3 February 1900 by Ole O. Thorpe, and settled originally on Walden Street in Concord, working as a farm laborer. Shortly after their marriage they began sponsoring the newly-formed Young People's Society, which met in their home, and which was attended by many who became charter members in the new church. By 1910 they had moved to Barrett's Mill Road where they remained until sometime before 1930 when they moved to Carlisle. Anton became a member of Trinitarian on 2 May 1915, and was heavily involved in the Scandinavian Branch, acting as their treasurer for many years. They had five daughters: Olga, Cornelia, Alice, Florence and Esther. Olga and Alice became members of the church in 1924. Olga married Oscar Olsen ca. 1930. They had two children who became members of the church, Peter and Pauline. Pauline married Joe Tavilla. Alice eventually married Arthur Thoresen; their children were William, Allen, and George Thoresen, all of whom eventually became members of the church. Esther eventually married Raymond Waterman, with whom she had a son, Leonard. Leonard was the church sexton for many years. In 1919, Anton was one of the six men who were elected to head up the effort to purchase the land on Lang Street and construct the church building upon it. Although Anton stood as a charter member, Pauline did not become a member until 1950, shortly after Anton's death.

Esther (Hoff) Waterman

Olive Andersen

Olive S. Andersen (1886-1968), no relation to Joanna Andersen, was already a widow in 1920. She is listed in the 1920 census as a domestic servant living with Sydney and Mary Coolidge on Main Street in Concord. She arrived from Norway ca. 1890. There is no indication that she was a part of Trinitarian or the Scandinavian Branch, but she contributed to the new building and stood to become a charter member.

By 1930 she was living on her own on Laws Brook Road in Acton. She was on the membership roll until 1968.

Martin Helsjer Family

Martinus Olsen Helsjer/Helsher (1851-1944) was from Helgøya, an island in Lake Myøsa near Hamar, Hedmark, Norway. This area was very active during the Hauge revivals, and was the location of the print shop where Hauge's materials were printed and disseminated throughout the country. Martin arrived in the United States ca. 1873, making him one of the first Norwegians to settle in Concord. He and his wife **Emily** were married on the Fourth of July, 1904 by Rev. L.J. Pedersen of the Norwegian Evangelical Free Church of Roxbury. This was Martin's third marriage. His previous wives, Ellen (1852-1894) and Julia (1865-1897) had died early. Although his name does not show up in the scant records of the Scandinavian Branch, he was a member of Trinitarian since 1 July 1894, and he donated money to the building effort in 1920. He appears to have been a good friend of many of the people of the congregation. He vouched for more than one person on their naturalization petitions. He died in 1944 and is buried in Sleepy Hollow Cemetery in Concord.

Thore and Lena Johnsen

Thore Johnsen, son of John and Lisabet Johnsen, was born ca. 1868 in Norway, and emigrated to the United States in 1892. He became a citizen in 1900. He worked as a farm laborer for many years, living on Monument Street and eventually Lowell Road, rising through the ranks to foreman by 1910. By 1920 he had purchased his own farm on Lorraine Road in Concord. On 3 December 1898, Rev. Ole O. Thorpe married him to **Lena** Boresen, daughter of Bore and Eli (Nelsen). She was born in 1873, and came to America in 1895. Lena became a member of Trinitarian 3 January 1897, and Thore joined 6 May 1917. From at least 1910 the couple were active supporters of the Scandinavian Branch, and they both stood to become charter members of the new church. Thore died in 1940, and Lena a few years later.

Samuel and Karen M. Lee

Karen Lee
1945

Samuel Lee, son of Amund Simeonsen and Karen Jansen, was born 18 June 1869 in Lillehammer, Norway. He arrived in Boston on 27 April 1888 on the ship Catalonia. He married (1) Inga Nyborg on 26 September 1891, by Rev. Grindall Reynolds of First Parish in Concord, and (2) Karen Marie Rud(?) on 1 September 1894 by Rev. J.P. Andersen. Samuel and **Karen M. Lee** lived most of their lives together on Grove Street in Concord. Karen became a member of Trinitarian on 4 September 1898, and actively supported the Branch as well as the new church on Lang Street.

Samuel worked as a carpenter. After multiple petitions in 1905 and 1915, he became a naturalized citizen sometime after 1920. Anton Hoff was a witness for both of his declarations of intent. Although Samuel never became a member of the church alongside his wife, he did

Inga (Lee) Cahill 1970

contribute to the new building, and in 1925 the congregation sent a special letter of thanks to Mr. and Mrs. Lee for all they had done for the church in the previous year. Their daughter Inga married John P. Cahill in 1919, and became a member in 1924. Inga Cahill was financial secretary of the church from 1927 until 1959, and was the pianist and organist at least from 1938 until 1959. She organized and led the String band from 1927 until at least 1945. Karen died 16 August 1948 in Concord.

The Jörgensen Sisters

Thora Jörgensen was born 8 March 1874 in Råde, Østfold, Norway. She arrived in the United States at the Port of Boston on 10 May 1910 on the ship Saxonia. She was a domestic servant for the family of Philip Davis on Lowell Road in Concord. She became a member of Trinitarian on 3 May 1914, but had begun to actively support the Branch at least a year earlier. She gave substantial gifts for the new building, and stood to become a charter member on 29 October 1920. She declared her intention to become a citizen on 11 December 1924, and took the oath of citizenship on 17 October 1927. In 1932 she married **Edward Andersen** after his first wife Matilda died.

Thora Jörgensen Andersen
1945

Matilda Jörgensen, Thora's younger sister, was born in 1879 or 1880 in Norway, and arrived in the US in 1907. She was a domestic servant for Horton and Fannie Edmands in 1920, and Sarah Goodwin in 1930. She died in 1958. Both sisters joined the Scandinavian Branch ca. 1913, both became members of Trinitarian on the same date (3 May 1914), and both gave significant gifts toward the building of the church on Lang Street in 1920 ($350 and $400 respectively, worth $4,000 to $5,000 in today's dollars).

Matilda Jörgensen.

Christian and Karen Martinsen

Christian Albert Martinsen was born 24 November 1877 in Løten, Norway. His future wife, **Karen Elise Andreasen**, was born 16 September 1879 in Ebru, Hedmark, Norway. Karen came to the United States in 1901, and Christian arrived on 27 April 1902. Both settled in Concord. They married 20 June 1903, and had four boys and four girls. In 1910 and 1920 they lived on Bedford Court in Concord, and Christian was employed as a leather harness maker. In 1930 he opened a shoe repair shop on Hubbard Street. Christian petitioned for citizenship on 26 October 1907, and Rudolph Petersen and Christian Olsen acted as witnesses (Rudolph was one of the prime movers for the construction of the Lang Street church). Christian was one of the original church trustees named on the deed when the church property was purchased from Olaf Westby. Christian and Karen began supporting the Branch as early as 1913, and became members of Trinitarian on 2 May 1915. They stood to become charter members of the new church, where they served until their deaths in May 1966 and February 1979, respectively.

Karen Martinsen 1970.

Olaf and Selma Stensby

Olaf Stensby was born 23 March 1881 in Løten, Norway, the son of Christian Stensby and Anne Olsen. He arrived in Boston on 12 April 1906 on the ship Ivernia out of Liverpool. When he petitioned for citizenship on 29 October 1907, Rudolph Petersen vouched for him. He joined Trinitarian and the Branch on 3 January 1909 and on 26 September 1910 Ole O. Thorpe officiated at his wedding to **Selma** Berg, daughter of Ole Gulbransen and Bertha Jensen. Selma joined Trinitarian and the Branch on 5 March 1911. By 1920 they were living on Walden Street with three children: Bertha, Leif and Esther. They became charter members, but their names were removed a year later by their request. No reason for their request was recorded in the minutes. Selma died in 1931, and by 1940 Olaf was living in Concord with his son Leif and his family.

John Swen Family

John Swen, born 27 April 1884 in Fåberg (near Lillehammer) Norway, arrived in America on 1 May 1903. He petitioned for citizenship on 25 October 1905. He was a single carpenter and lumber

John and Pauline (Knudsen) Swen. Courtesy Marion Purinton.

dealer living on Monument Street in Concord. He became involved in the Scandinavian Branch shortly after he arrived in Concord. He became a member of Trinitarian on 3 January 1909. **Pauline Knudsen**, another charter member of the church, was born in 1892 in Norway, and emigrated to the US in 1904. She became involved in the Scandinavian Branch in 1911, becoming a member at Trinitarian on 5 March 1911. John and Pauline were actively involved with the Young People's Society which met at the home of Anton and Pauline Hoff for many years. John was directly involved in much of the construction of the church. In 1923 John and Pauline married, presumably in the Lang Street Church. Pauline died in 1938, and John married Dorothy Wilbur on 26 September 1940 in Falmouth, ME. Over the years, he acted in various positions of leadership at the church, and had a real servant's heart for the house of God. In addition to acting as chairman, deacon, and elder for life, for many years he volunteered as sexton. He was also a long-time member of the String Band. He died 27 April 1953.

Ole and Elizabeth Hansen

Ole Herman Hansen was born in Fredrikstad, Norway on 7 May 1889, son of Hans and Emelie Johansen. He traveled from Kristiania to Boston via Liverpool, arriving on 25 April 1907. On 10 December 1910 he married **Elizabeth** Johanna Kittelsen, after which they settled on Elsinore Street in Concord. He declared his intention to become a US citizen on 25 April 1914, and took the oath of allegiance on 1 October 1919. He worked as a carpenter for John Bent on Old Marlboro Rd. He and Elizabeth's names were crossed out in the membership roll ca. 1923, but with no specific date or reason.

The Petersen Brothers

Lars and Olive Petersen.

Lars Petersen, born in 1852 in Åmot, Hedmark, Norway, was one of the earliest Norwegian settlers in Concord, having arrived ca. 1871. He and his wife Oline (Olive) Olsen were married 13 February 1875 by Rev. Grindall Reynolds at First Parish in Concord. Petersen lived as a farmer on Monument Street. He and his wife joined Trinitarian on 1 July 1877, and by 1896, he was a deacon. He met Ole O. Thorpe at the railroad station when the latter arrived in Concord in 1879, and he spoke at Rev. Thorpe's funeral in 1927. His wife passed away in 1915. He was an active supporter of the Branch from the very beginning. Choosing to remain with Trinitarian, he never actually became a member of the new church. However, he was a huge help to the congregation: he acted as one of the trustees that bought the Lang St. property before the church was incorporated, and he served as trustee until 1922, when the property was formally conveyed to the church. He then returned to Trinitarian. Later, he sold another parcel of land on Lang Street to the congregation, upon which they built the original parsonage for the pastor. Petersen died on 27 June 1947, and is buried in Sleepy Hollow Cemetery in Concord.

Rudolph Petersen, born ca. 1863, arrived in 1878, also pre-dating Ole Thorpe. He too was a farmer on Monument Street. He was married to Inga Marie Andersen on 18 February 1888 by Rev. William DePew at Trinitarian. He and his wife joined Trinitarian on 3 January 1892, shortly before the creation of the Scandinavian Branch, but he actively supported it throughout its existence. Like Lars, he never became a member of the Free

Rudolph Petersen.

Church, but was still deeply involved both financially and personally in the construction. He served as secretary/clerk of the church until its incorporation with the Commonwealth of Massachusetts, and the Lang St. property was formally conveyed to the church in 1922. Even after this he continued attending the evening services and contributing to the Free Church until at least 1929. He died in 1937 and is buried in Sleepy Hollow Cemetery in Concord.

Olaf Westby

Olaf Westby was born 25 March 1884 in Kristiania (Oslo), Norway, the son of Jens Westby and Elise Olsen. He came to the US through New York City, arriving on 21 March 1907. He joined the Scandinavian M.E. church, and attended there for a few years before joining Trinitarian on 3 July 1910. He married Eline (Eleanor, or Elaine) Eilertsen on 30 March 1910 in Concord, officiated by Rev. Ole O. Thorpe. When he petitioned for citizenship on 14 November 1910, Rudolph Petersen and Emil Thorpe vouched for him. Olaf and Eline were active in the Scandinavian Branch from 1910, but did not become members of the Free Church when it was founded (it is not known whether they attended). They lived on Lang Street, and owned the vacant lot on which the original tent meetings were held in the summer of 1919. He sold it to the trustees for the new building in 1919 for $600, but donated half the value of the lot, so the net cost to the church was only $300. His wife died in 1923, and sometime after 1925 he moved to Littleton where he lived out his final days.

The Thoresen and Purinton Clans

No list of Faith families would be complete without mentioning the Thoresen clan, though none of them were charter members. Christian Mikkelsen, son of Mikkel Thoresen and Anne Christensdatter, was born in Løten, Norway on 19 February 1855 or 1856. He and his wife Mathea (Marta) arrived in the United States around 1882 and settled in Concord, where most of their children (except Arthur) were born. They joined Trinitarian on 4 November 1894, shortly after the Scandinavian

Branch was formed. Around 1900, they moved to Lowell, and by 1920 they were living in Billerica. Eventually they moved back to Concord, where they show up in the 1930 census. Their children were Anna, Carl, Henry, Julia, Edwin, Thomas, Mina, Olga, Helen, and Arthur. Of these, five were prominent in the history of Faith: Carl, Henry, Thomas, Olga, and Arthur.

Henry Thoresen (1888-1957) contributed to the building at Lang Street in 1920, although he never became a member.

The youngest, Arthur Thoresen (1901-1960), married Alice Hoff, the middle daughter of Anton and Pauline Hoff, who hosted the Young People's Society for many years. Arthur and Alice had three sons, William, Allen, and George, all of whom were active members at Lang Street. George married Eleanor McColl. It was their daughter, Catherine, who died unexpectedly in 1972 after having her wisdom teeth out.

Alice (Hoff)
Thoresen
1945

Olga Thoresen (1896-1979) married March Purinton, Sr. (1899-1981). They and their two sons and their wives, March Jr (1924-2018) (m. Marion), and Richard "Rit" (1925-1997) (m. Helen) were all active members and held many important offices in the church at Lang Street. Rit and Helen were the parents of Steve (m. Lorraine), Susan (m. Nick Lamonakis), and Carol Anne. March and Marion were the parents of Karen (m. Pete Hanson), David (m. Kim), and Carl (m. Sue).

Olga (Thoresen) and March
Purinton, Sr.

Thomas Edward "Ted" Thoresen (1892-1974) and his wife Ruth had five children: Ruth Helen (1918-1983) (m. Clough Vettrus) , Thomas Jr. (1920-2008) (m. Marion), Esther (1930-) (m. Stuart

Thomas "Ted" and Ruth Thoresen

Edna Thoresen

Scott), Robert (1932-2018) (m. Barbara), and Paul (1936-) (m. Sandra). Thomas Jr. and Marion had three children, one of whom was Linda (m. Bob Specht).

Carl and Edna Thoresen were the earliest of the Thoresen clan to formally join the church, having been accepted into membership on 9 April 1925.

The 1970 church directory shows seventeen entries for the Thoresen and Purinton families!

William H. and Elizabeth Hunt[1]

Elizabeth Middleton McEuen, the daughter of Dr. Thomas and Ann M. McEuen, was born 14 November 1829 in Philadelphia PA, and baptized in the Episcopal Church on 6 January 1830.[2] She lived with her parents until at least her twentieth birthday,[3] and it appears that the family was relatively well off. Her husband's niece, Mary Jacobs, described her as "a very cultivated woman with an unusual education for those days."[4] Her father was a physician, having earned his MD from the University of Pennsylvania in 1821. Her mother was an artist who died in St. Thomas, British West Indies in November 1850. Shortly after her mother's death, it appears that Elizabeth left home for New York City. While there, she gave birth to a son, Theodore Baker, on 3 June 1851. There is no record of the birth, and no record of a marriage, but in the 1855 Massachusetts state census, she and her son are found living in Framingham in the household of Rev. Samuel T. Robbins, a Unitarian minister.[5] In this census they are listed as Elizabeth and Theodore Baker. Sometime after this she and her son moved to Monument Street in Concord, living near the farm owned and operated by Daniel and Clarissa Hunt.

It appears that Elizabeth was shunned by the proper folks in Concord. She was not welcomed at the First Parish church, as seen in this excerpt from Leslie Perrin Wilson's article:

> In 1922, artist Edward Emerson Simmons—a son of the Reverend George Frederick Simmons and Mary Emerson Ripley Simmons—published his autobiography, *From*

Seven to Seventy: Memories of a Painter and a Yankee, the first chapter of which dealt with his early life in Concord. Discussing his mother's independence, Simmons—who grew up in and next to the Old Manse—wrote: "A woman had come to Concord, with no husband, and given birth to a child. This, for New England at that time, was a terrible scandal. The boy was my age [Simmons was born in Concord in 1852]. All the other boys whispered behind his back as if he had been in jail, although by this time his mother was properly married to a young farmer up on Barret's Hill [Punkatasset]. No one ever spoke to her in church or bowed. My mother, very quietly, every summer, put on her best clothes and walked the mile or more up the hill to call." Although Elizabeth Baker's son was not born in Concord, Simmons's chronology and most of the circumstances in his account strongly suggest that he referred to Mrs. Hunt in this passage. While Simmons is not an especially reliable source, there is probably some kernel of truth in his assessment of Elizabeth Baker's social standing. Whether or not she was truly a widow, and whether or not her son was illegitimate (as Simmons insinuated), the attitudes of the time likely cast suspicion on the respectability of a woman living and raising a child on her own.[6]

William Henry Hunt was the youngest son of Daniel and Clarissa Hunt, direct descendants of William Hunt who settled in Concord between 1636 and 1640. The elder William had purchased a large plot of ground on Punkatasset Hill on what is now Monument Street from Peter Bulkeley, the founder and first minister of Concord. Daniel Hunt was the 6th generation Hunt to own this plot of ground, but, although the family was well-known and respected in town, they were not wealthy except for the land they owned, and by this time Daniel was struggling to keep the farm profitable:

> "His major difficulty was that he had both many children to feed, clothe, and educate and, because of the size of his family, insufficient resources to improve upon increasingly outdated methods of managing his farm. Moreover, he did not have enough sons to ease the burden of farm work and to help generate surplus for market. He was locked into a hard way of life, characterized by intense labor and by little leisure to develop the higher sensibilities."[7]

William Henry was born in 1839, and like all the others, was baptized in the First Parish Church (Unitarian). He remained a member there until his death in 1927. First Parish was the church which most of the respected and important people of town attended.

Although Daniel did his best to provide for his children, including their education, his resources were limited, and being the youngest, William did not benefit from any formal education beyond his time at the District School No. 7 up the road from the farm. He was also not in line to inherit much of his father's estate. William was always conscious of his lack of schooling, and he made up for it by being a voracious reader and learner. Later, when he was more financially stable, he traveled extensively in Europe and learned French (perhaps encouraged by his wife, who learned Norwegian?).

The family of Daniel Hunt was well acquainted with grief and issues of the day. Their second son, Charles Francis, had died at six months, and when William was six years old, his oldest sister Martha died of apparent suicide by drowning in the Concord River. She was 19, and a teacher in the district school system. Martha was very literate, intelligent, well-educated, and had high aspirations, but struggled with her lot in life in a society which gave women limited options outside of the family, teaching children, or factory work. It appears that despair at her bleak prospects drove her to self-destruction.

In spite of the family's concerns, William and Elizabeth struck up a romance, and were soon engaged. Elizabeth was thirty, and William was twenty. The family was not happy with the prospects of William marrying a woman ten years older than he, especially an outsider who already had a child, but they eventually reconciled to the union. They were married on 25 November 1859 by Rev. Grindall Reynolds of the First Parish church.[8] They lived in the house Elizabeth had been occupying, the old Ripley's schoolhouse building near Daniel's farm. In 1861, they had a son, Willie, who died after only a few days.[9] Barely a month later, William's other sister, Ellen, drowned in the Concord River in an apparent suicide.

During the Civil War, William enlisted in Company G of the 47th Massachusetts Volunteer Militia, and served proudly for the Union, although he did not see any real action due to illnesses. After the war, he returned to Concord and concentrated on helping out on the family farm. William began to be more involved in the affairs of the town, and local Agricultural societies. As Elizabeth became more involved in the social life of the town, her respectability improved, and in 1868 she joined

> ...the Concord Female Charitable Society (Charitable Society records, Vol. I.a.8), a Concord women's organization founded in 1814 to provide aid to the local needy, to encourage their religious and moral development, and to offer members the opportunity to socialize. She paid her dues, attended meetings at the homes of leading ladies of the town—among them Mrs. Ebenezer Rockwood Hoar, Mrs. Francis Gourgas, and Mrs. George Merrick Brooks—and served as the society's North Quarter manager from 1884 to 1886.[10]

From 1867-1869, Elizabeth was paid as the organist for First Parish church, in spite of their earlier spurning. However, she never joined First Parish, choosing instead the First Baptist Church in Waltham. Her son Theodore also served as the First Parish organist, at least in 1871.[11]

By 1872 William had acquired the farm from his father (mainly because his older two surviving brothers were uninterested). In 1873 both Daniel Hunt and Elizabeth's father Thomas McEuan had died, leaving William and Elizabeth in a better financial position to put resources into the farm. Soon he was investing in new equipment, and hiring laborers to help with the work, something that his father had been unable to do. Many of these new laborers and domestic servants were recent immigrants from Norway.

William's memories of his childhood on the farm—listening to his parents and older siblings talk about slavery and the loss of his sisters—would certainly have made him sensitive and compassionate to the less fortunate. He was also still acutely aware of the need for good education. In Elizabeth, William saw both intellect and worldly wisdom. Elizabeth, for her part, had experienced what it was like to be an outcast, on the outside of society's inner circle. These experiences helped shape their lives together, and affected the way they treated their employees. William worked the farm alongside the hired hands, earned their respect, and enjoyed warm relationships with them. He developed a reputation as a successful experimental farmer. Elizabeth learned Norwegian and developed a keen sense of concern for the welfare of the immigrants.

By 1878, William and Elizabeth were able to entrust the farm to the hired help and traveled through Europe for about two years. They probably visited Theodore, who by this time was studying music in Germany.[12] In 1881, Theodore earned his doctorate from Leipzig Conservatory. His dissertation was on the music of North American Indians. In 1892, he came back to America where he became literary editor for the music publisher G. Shirmer, Inc. based in New York City. Shortly afterward he translated the traditional Dutch hymn, "We Gather Together To Ask The Lord's Blessing" into English. Later, he published numerous famous works, including Baker's Biographical Dictionary of Musicians (1900).[13]

When they returned to America, William and Elizabeth built a large new house, made major improvements to the farm, and assumed a much larger role in town affairs. From the 1880s onward, William served variously on the Board of Assessors, Selectman, the Overseer of the Poor, Road Commissioner, and member of the School Committee.

On 7 April 1894 William and Elizabeth hosted a special ninetieth birthday party for William's uncle, Deacon Francis Hunt, who at the time was one of the oldest residents of Concord and the oldest member of Trinitarian Church.[14] The following year Elizabeth served on the canvassing (fundraising) committee for the renovation of the Trinitarian meeting house along with Pastor Tewksbury and his wife. At the laying of the cornerstone on 21 May 1898, she sang a hymn of her own composition, which was placed in the time capsule with other documents.[15] She also composed and sang a dedicatory hymn at the first service in the new auditorium on 18 December 1898.[16]

While William always remained a member of the First Parish Unitarian Church, Elizabeth joined Trinitarian Congregational Church on 31 December 1886. The records state that she was accepted into membership by transfer from the First Baptist Church of Waltham. A search of the records at First Baptist Church of Waltham did not uncover any mention of her membership or baptism, however. It would be interesting to know when she first started attending a Baptist church, since she was baptized as an Episcopalian and had identified herself with the Unitarian church once she reached adulthood. One possibility is that she began attending the Waltham church because she had been ostracized at First Parish, and was converted back to the orthodox faith there. One might also speculate that she converted first (perhaps through the revival meetings that Moody held in Boston in 1877?), and sought fellowship with like believers, but did not feel comfortable in Concord because of her previous treatment. Regardless, she must have developed a preference by this time for Trinitarian doctrine, since she would have been required to submit to believer's baptism, or at least affirm personal trust in the Trinity and in Christ's atonement, in order to be accepted into membership at a Baptist church.

One indication of the intensity of her faith is found in the records of Trinitarian for the summer of 1889, when some expressed disaffection for then-pastor William DePew. At a special meeting to consider a resolution of dismissal, many spoke for and against the motion. Some of the criticism centered around his handling of the Scripture (e.g., treating the Garden of Eden allegorically), and his entrance into political commentary on the so-called New Departure.[17] Mrs. Hunt got to the heart of the matter: "Do we desire to have the gospel preached or no?"[18] It's not clear whether she was speaking for or against dismissal, but her focus was on the faithful proclamation of the Gospel.

Another indication of her fidelity is found in the tribute given her by the pastor when she died on 3 August 1903. In his annual report that year, he made mention of her "warm adherence to the doctrines of our faith:"

> The last to leave us was Mrs. Elizabeth Hunt, whose removal at the age of seventy-three closed a record of peculiar activity and usefulness in the service of Christ, her membership dating from 1886 by transfer from the First Baptist Church in Waltham. Her mental strength and culture, her warm adherence to the doctrines of our faith, her discriminating and appreciative judgment as a listener to pulpit discourse, her ability and faithfulness as a Sunday school teacher, her interest in the Maternal Association, of which she was a long time the secretary, and in the Woman's Board Auxiliary—all helped to emphasize her value to us, and now accentuate the greatness of our loss. In material and spiritual ways—in her presence, her influence, her gifts—she was an unfailing help in the work of the church. By gradual decline her earthly way glided gently into the heavenly, verifying in full at length the lines copied by her own hand, and sent to our pastor two or three years ago:

"My future from my past unlinking,
Each dying year untwined the spell;
The visible is swiftly sinking —
Uprises the invisible!"[19]

Elizabeth was buried on 5 August in Sleepy Hollow Cemetery in Concord. After her death, William eventually sold off all of his property and traveled extensively, coming back to live on Walden Street and sometimes at the Colonial Inn. For his last few years, he lived with his nephew and niece (Chandler and Emily Hunt) in Belmont until his death in 1926. In his will he endowed the town of Concord with $25,000 which was used toward the building of what is now known as the Hunt Recreation Center on Stow Street, just around the corner from Ole O. Thorpe's house on Hubbard Street.

It is easy to see how William and Elizabeth's experiences would have made them sympathetic with those servants in her own household, and given Elizabeth the desire to improve their lot both materially and spiritually. Although we cannot be sure about her involvement with the 1879 Norwegian class at Trinitarian, it is clear that she was actively teaching Sunday School until her death in 1903. There is also no doubt that she was fondly remembered by the early members of the Evangelical Free Church.

Appendix B:
Pastoral Staff

Dates	Senior Pastor
1894-1901	Ole O. Thorpe (ordained 1894)
1901	Sigvert Andersen (started in August)
1902-1906	Pulpit supply by N. B. Ursin, L. J. Pedersen (Boston), Ole Thorpe, George Tewksbury and others
1906-1908	Nikolai Berg (N.B.) Ursin
1908-1912	Ole O. Thorpe
1912-1914	Theodor Jensen
1914	Ole O. Thorpe (interim, 4 months), with help from Pastor Tewksbury and Dr. Emrich
1914-1919	Adolph Olsen Huseby (started Christmas, 1914)
1919-1921	E.M. Andersen (evangelist)
2/1921-4/1922	Olaf Thompsen
5/1923-8/1935	Olaf M. Johnsen
9/1935-6/1940	Otto T. Rafos
9/1/1940-fall 1947	Harry P. Odland
1/18/1948-3/1/1952	Gunnar Gundersen
3/1/1952-5/30/1952	Dr. Paul Jewett (interim)

11/2/1952-9/6/1959	Hyland T. Richmond
10/25/1959-8/27/1961	Donald Barnes
12/1961-8/31/1962	Dr. Charles F. Pfeiffer (interim)
9/1/1962-1/1965	Robert Westa
1/1965-7/1965	Dr. Roger Nicole (interim)
8/1/1965-9/30/1972	Gordon W. Condit
11/26/1972-7/15/1973	Edson Fast (interim)
7/15/1973-1/31/1979	Kenneth Spence
3/1979-3/1980	Dr. Royce Gruenler (interim)
3/1980-2/14/1982	David Fife
2/28/1982-9/12/1982	Dr. Kenneth McCowan (interim)
9/12/1982-5/1/1988	Dr. Martin Crain
1988-8/28/1989	Don Fisher (interim)
8/27/1989-9/18/2005	Douglas Welch
6/1/2006-present	Dr. Brad Johnson

Dates	*Associate Pastors*
2004-2006	Brad Johnson
2013-present	Dan Kasey

Dates	*Youth Pastors*
1967-1970	David McBride, Youth Director (part-time)
1974-1977	A. Raymond Randall, Jr., Youth Director (part-time)
1977-1981	William Lupole, Youth Pastor
1983-1983	Elliot & Lynda Cook, Youth Directors (part-time)
1984-1985	David Pattison, Youth Director (part-time)
1985-1987	David Pattison, Pastor of Youth and Young Adults
1988-2004	Brad Johnson, Pastor of Youth and Family Life
2004-2006	Dan Kasey, Youth Director (part-time)
2006-2013	Dan Kasey, Pastor of Youth Ministries
2013-present	Christian Waltmire, Pastor of Youth Ministries

Appendix C:
Demographics

A Profile of Faith

By any measure, Faith Evangelical Free Church has changed a great deal over the years. Unfortunately, no church directories from the church's first 50 years remain. For those years, it is necessary to look at the membership roll for our analysis. Those who choose to join the church formally tend to be older, and the membership list does not contain any information about children, so it becomes impractical to attempt any historical analysis of age distribution.

The Early Years

As the names make clear, the Scandinavian Branch at Trinitarian and the Norwegian Zion Evangelical Free Church on Lang Street, Concord, were ethnic congregations founded by Norwegian immigrants, specifically to evangelize and disciple Norwegians. No thought was given to ethnic diversity; in fact, their Norwegian heritage was celebrated. As one daughter of a charter member explained:

> In the church, we were all the same, all the families were the same, we were all going in the same direction in our knowledge. We were all children together, knew each other, grew up together and still carry on those associations after all these years. In fact, I went to Arlington a couple of weeks ago to meet a friend I probably hadn't seen for 25 years and we had a great time reminiscing about our childhood days in the Evangelical Free Church.[1]

It is difficult to create a financial profile of the church even at the present time, but it is possible to list some impressions. For example, we know that the average household income in Massachusetts in 1920 was $3270 per year. Many of the regular attenders and members at Lang Street were farmers (mostly working as hired farm hands, plus some who saved enough money to buy their own land to cultivate), retailers, carpenters, etc. Most of the single women were domestic servants.

According to the 1907-1916 records of the Scandinavian Branch[2], the typical benefactor pledged $.50 or $1.00 per week, with some couples giving $2.00 a week. This is probably in addition to their tithes and pledges to Trinitarian Congregational, the mother church.

However, it appears that some people who took an interest in the church had more resources at hand. Almost $10,000 was pledged and donated for the construction of the new church on Lang Street from the fall of 1919 up to the dedication of the building in November 1920.[3] Of this, almost $2,000 was donated by five people. Of those, $550 was donated by two young sisters, Thora and Mathilda Jörgensen, who were both domestic servants, and became charter members in 1920.

Geographically, the charter members were mainly clustered in the Norwegian neighborhoods around Concord Center, West Concord (Concord Junction, as it was then known), and South Acton. In the maps below, the shaded area represents the primary service area of the church as defined by the distribution of charter members of the church. The house icons represent the locations of the original church at Lang Street, and the new church in Acton. Subsequent maps are scaled to fit all current attenders as of 2019, with the original service area indicated by gray box.

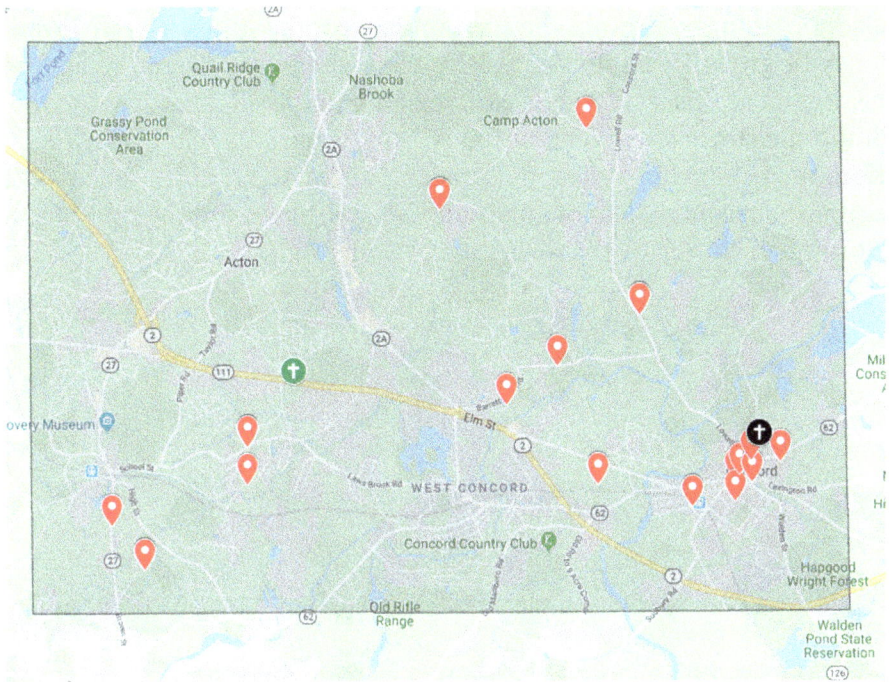

Charter members, 1920

After the War - 1945

When the war ended in 1945, and the church was celebrating its twenty-fifth anniversary, the membership list still contained many Norwegian names, such as Andersen, Mikkelsen, Monsen, Thoresen, and Purinton (not a Norwegian name, but the matriarch of which was Olga Thoresen[4]). Eighteen of the original twenty-nine charter members were still active in the church. There were about twice as many members, many of whom were children of original members and regular attenders, and they still tended to cluster around Concord, West Concord, and Acton.

1970

By 1970, the fiftieth anniversary of the church, the vast majority of the membership had drifted westward to West Concord and Acton, while also spreading out toward the surrounding communities. The westward focus of growth also illustrates the huge shadow of Grace Chapel in Lexington at this time. While Norwegian names still dominate the roll, other surnames like Wentworth, Wilson, Stuart, Putnam, McGuerty, Korhonen, Goodemote, and Comeau, make their appearance. The church is becoming less of an ethnic enclave, but is still thought of as a Norwegian church by the townsfolk of Concord.

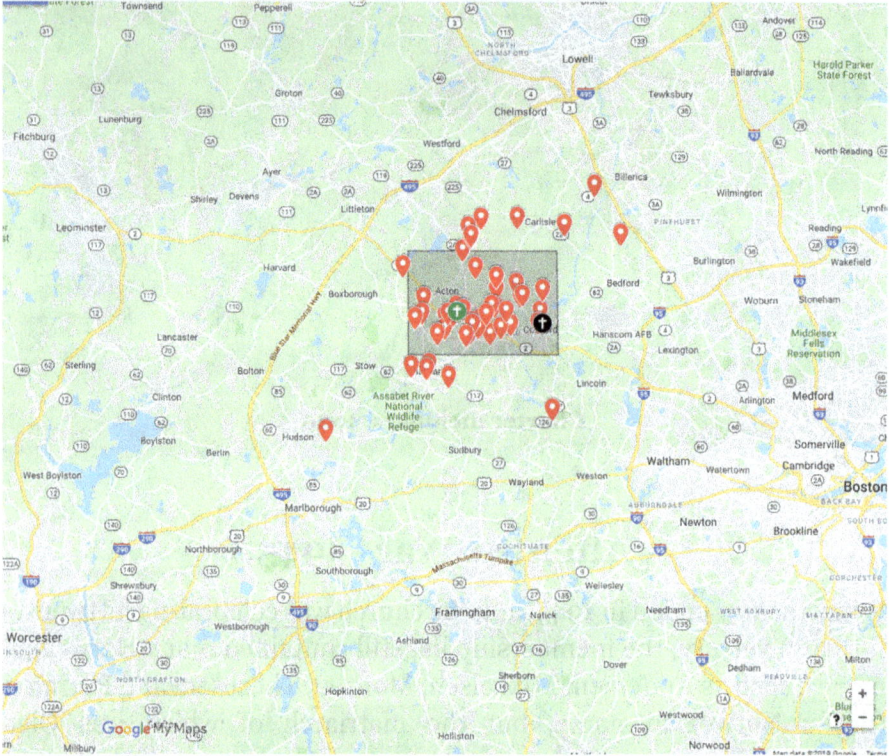

Church families, 1970

1980

By 1980, four years after the move to Acton, almost the only Scandinavian names on the membership roll are members of the Thoresen/Purinton clan. The original ethnic character of the church is

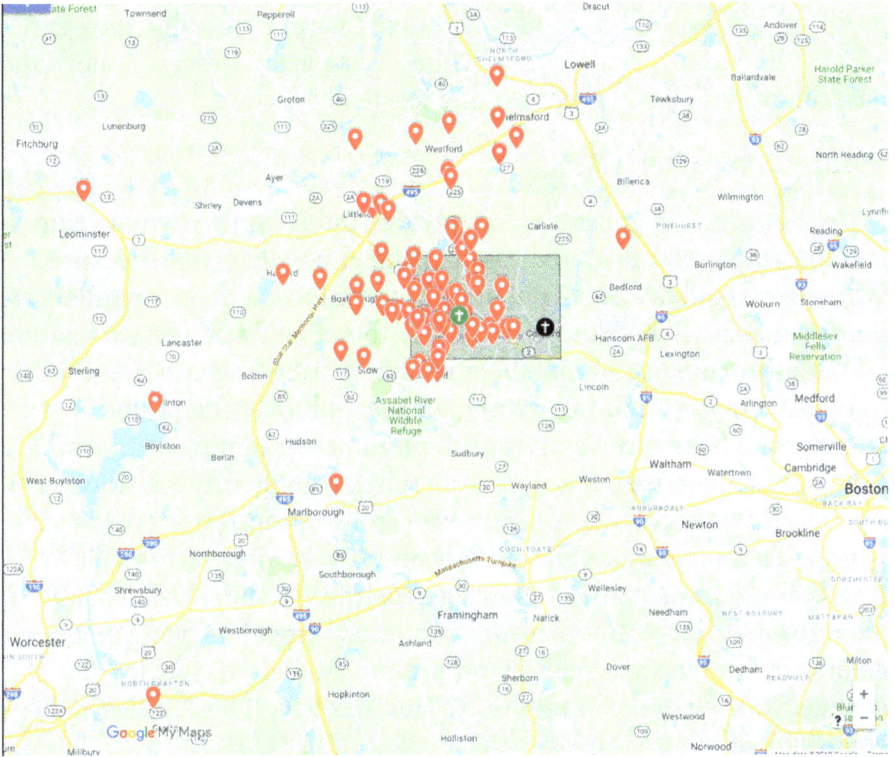

Church families, 1980

all but gone, although the congregation is still almost uniformly white, and of European descent, much like the surrounding communities. Geographically, the church draws mainly from Acton, West Concord, and Maynard, with a significant minority coming from the outlying surrounding communities such as Westford, Chelmsford, Littleton, and Stow. There are no member families in Concord Center. As expected with better mobility compared to the 1920s, people tend to drive further for church, as the distribution of members shows in comparison to the original 1920 area on the map.

1985 Demographic Analysis

In 1985, as part of a feasibility study for expanding the facilities, an analysis was conducted of the membership demographic changes (age and financial) between 1976 and 1985. Excerpts of the methodology used and analysis of the results are quoted here. Ethnically, the church was still almost uniformly white European descent, but the Scandinavian makeup is continuing its steady decline.

Family Characteristics

In reviewing the number of giving units, only actual church membership was considered. Data included members only because the 1976 records did not break out attendance information by members vs. non-members. It had to be assumed, therefore, that the correlation between the number of members regularly attending and the number of non-members attending remained constant over the period. It may come as a surprise to some that the number of family units who are members had increased by 47% from thirty-eight to fifty-six since 1976. Average Sunday attendance increased from 143 to 169 over this same period. This increase, while not apparently significant, may be so, in fact, because immediately following construction there was most likely an unusually large number of temporary attenders who were not committed to the church. Likewise, the nature of the family unit changed during the same period. The following chart reflects these changes.

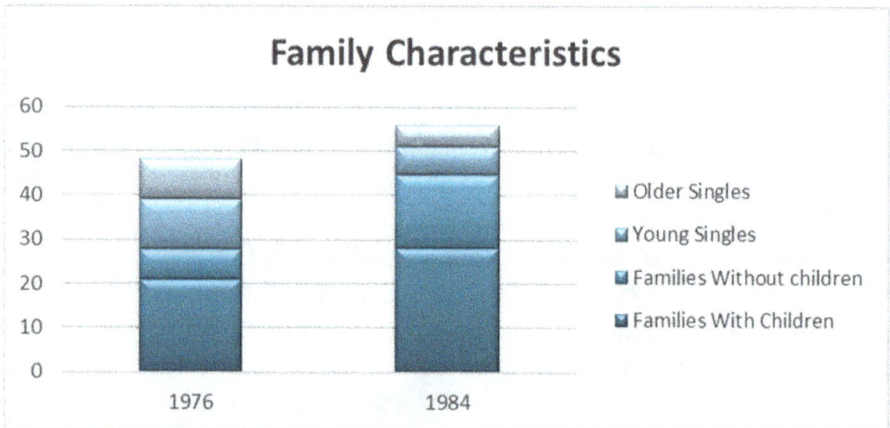

An interesting fact not depicted in the above chart: while the number of families with children living at home decreased as a percent of the total, the actual number of children increased from forty-eight to sixty.

Changes in Age Composition

One of the most significant changes during the period 1976-1985 was the shift in age groups that made up the church membership. A summary of this shift is shown below. In 1985 recent college graduates made up only 1% of the congregation:

Age Composition

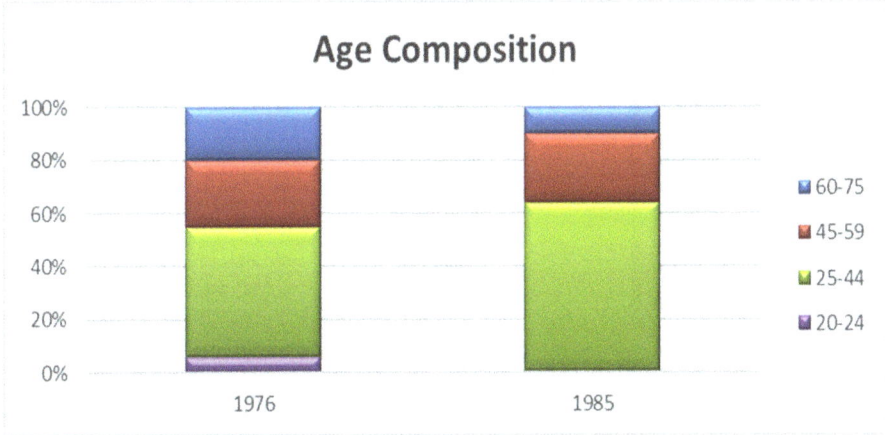

Occupational Changes

As part of the demographic analysis, the feasibility committee looked at the occupational mix and estimated financial information of the members. They were explicit as to how this information was calculated:

> A worksheet was prepared which listed all 1976 members, as well as those 1985 members who were not members in 1976. [For each member columns were added for number of children, occupation, and age in 1976 and 1985.] Data regarding the number of children and occupation were known. Ages were arrived at through consensus by committee members, but appear in brackets of five years. It is important to understand that no attempt was made to analyze or guess any particular person's salary. The potential income figures used below were predicted based on (a) estimated ages, (b) U.S. labor department figures, and (c) setting a wage for an average person in an occupational class at an estimated age. Wage changes from 1976 to 1985 were extrapolated using the price inflation index issued by the U.S. labor department.

Potential earnings for the entire congregation were totaled and total actual giving for each year was presented as a percentage of the total potential earnings. Results are shown in the following two charts:

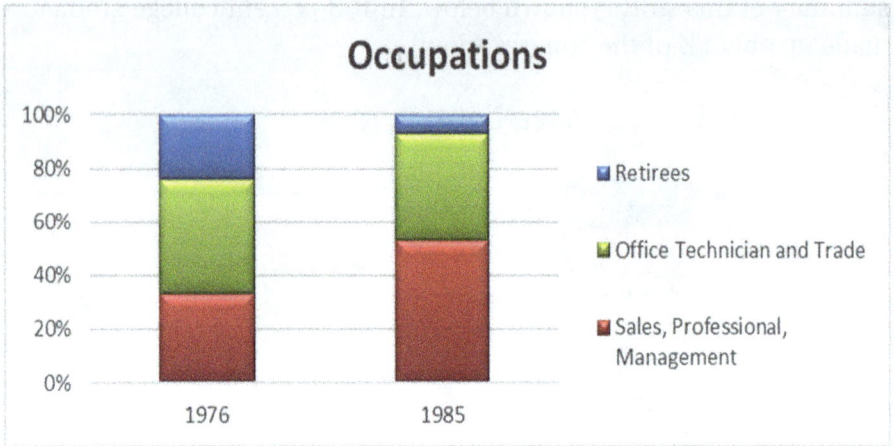

Occupations

Legend:
- Retirees
- Office Technician and Trade
- Sales, Professional, Management

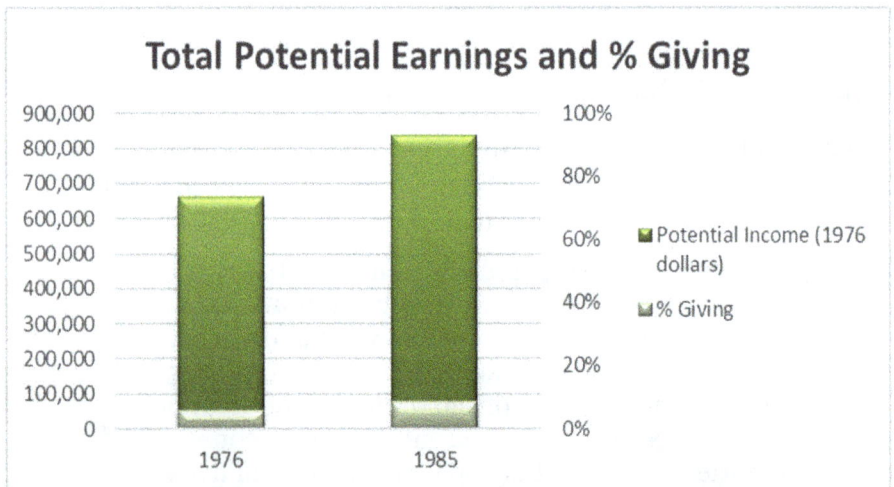

Total Potential Earnings and % Giving

Legend:
- Potential Income (1976 dollars)
- % Giving

This analysis revealed a number of interesting things about the church:

- Over time, the congregation was becoming less diverse in terms of age—the older generation was passing away. After an early influx of young college graduates in the late '70s, those young people were aging, and new graduates were not joining.
- The congregation was becoming more upwardly-mobile and professional.

- Giving as a percentage of gross income was increasing, indicating a higher level of commitment to tithing and supporting the church.

The Turn of the Twenty-First Century

Age diversity: people in their twenties in the 1970s had become middle-aged by the turn of the century. Their children were in the youth group, which was flourishing. But there were almost no young couples or recent college grads. The nursery did not have many babies. In short, the congregation was aging.

When the author joined the church in 1977, it was in the midst of an influx of young college graduates. The church was intentionally trying to reach out to the younger generation (baby boomers) at that time, and mild friction sometimes occurred as the older generation grew uncomfortable with some of the ministry changes taking place. However, they understood the need to be relevant to all age groups.

Over the years, that older generation passed on, and the young graduates from the late 70s aged. The church continued to cater to the needs of the boomer generation. However, the younger generations that followed found nothing to attract them. In fact, it was common for one or two young visitors visit for a few weeks then move on when they found nothing to keep them there. After they left, a few others might come, and the cycle would repeat. There was never a critical mass for effective ministry to that age group.

Recognizing this as a serious concern, the church began to pray. Around the time that Pastor Dan Kasey arrived, the Lord answered those prayers—younger families began to attend and settle in. New babies were born, or attended with their young families. Many of those families chose to keep their babies with them, at least during part of the service. Eventually, some older attenders grumbled that the baby noise was a distraction during the service. On one particularly noisy Sunday morning service, Pastor Brad stopped in the middle of what he was saying and remarked, "Do you hear that noise? That is an answer to prayer!" All grumbling immediately ceased!

As of 2018, there are about sixty children under the age of twelve involved in children's ministries.

Today

The effects of gentrification of the Concord/Acton area are evident, as families have begun moving west. Today the church draws people from the north and west of Acton, with very little to the east. There is still a central core from Acton, West Concord, and Maynard, but it is less pronounced than before. Some people to the far west are older members who moved there over the years. Others were attracted from Devens from the days when Fort Devens was an active military base. Others include younger families who have settled to the north and west where property is more affordable. The new church plant, Life Church in Ayer (blue marker in the map below) is well positioned to serve the western population.

Only six active members remain who were members when the church worshiped at Lang Street prior to 1975. There are currently no active members living in Concord Center, where the church once stood, although there are some living in West Concord.

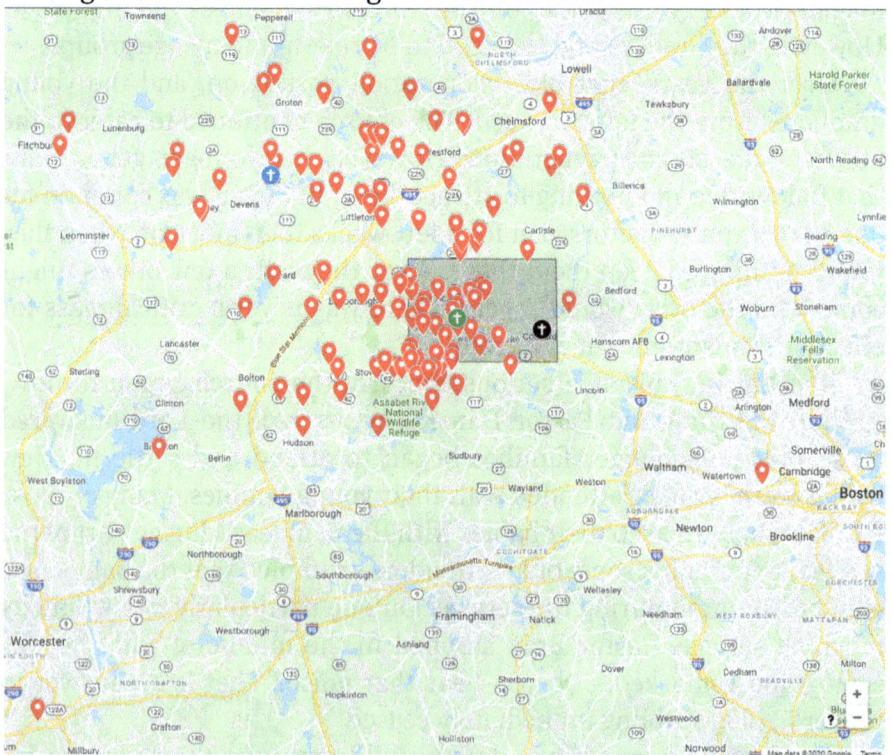

Church families, 2019

Ethnically, the makeup of the church is becoming more diverse. There are almost no Scandinavian names on the church membership roll. Although the vast majority of the congregation is still of white European descent, there are some people whose roots go back to every continent on the planet, including those of Brazilian, Haitian, African, and Asian ancestry. The ethnic makeup of the church is not much different than the town of Acton and some of the surrounding towns.

Using a methodology similar to the 1985 study, the age spread of current regular attenders and members looks better than it did around the turn of the 21st century. Based on the church's focus on teen ministry, it should be expected that the majority of constituents would be in their forties and fifties. The number of people in their twenties and thirties is much improved from fifteen years ago. The low number of college age attenders is expected, because there are few colleges in the immediate area.

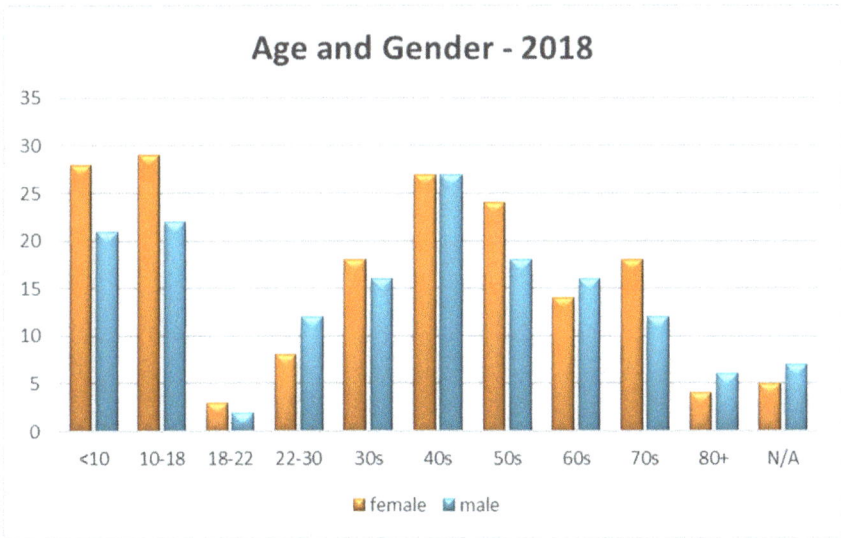

Age and Gender - 2018

Appendix D:
Statements of Faith

This appendix provides official Statements of Faith from various times in the history of FEFC, showing the evolution of the formulation through the years. It should be noted that although the expression of belief changed over time, the core beliefs of the congregation remained consistent.

Norwegian-Danish EFCA (1912)

This statement of faith was adopted by the national association when it was incorporated in the state of Minnesota, and represents the beliefs of the churches of the combined western and eastern associations.[1]

1. We believe that the Bible, the Old and New Testament, is the Word of God and is the only infallible rule and guide for faith, life, and doctrine.

2. We believe in the triune God: Father, Son and Holy Spirit, one God in three persons, in accordance with the apostolic faith.

3. We believe that all men by nature are sinners, aliens and strangers to God, and as a result thereof under condemnation.

4. We believe that Jesus Christ gave Himself as a Redeemer for all mankind, and those who repent from their sins and believe on Him shall be granted forgiveness and be adopted as children of God.

5. We believe that as many as by faith receive Jesus Christ as their Savior and Lord are born again and are given the witness of the Holy Spirit, and become children and heirs of God, and joint-heirs with Christ.

6. We believe that Christian churches should be organized in conformity with the teachings of the New Testament, and only those who have the witness of the Holy Spirit that they are children of God, and live accordingly, should be considered eligible to church membership.

7. We believe that Jesus Christ is the Lord and head of the Church, and that every local church has the right, under Christ, to decide and govern its own affairs.

8. We believe that the Lord has given His Church two sacraments: baptism and communion. (1) Baptism in the name of the Father, Son, and Holy Spirit. Freedom of conscience is given as to age and mode. (2) Communion should be administrated only to true believers, in accordance with the Word of God.

9. We believe that Jesus Christ who ascended into heaven, shall come again in great power and glory.

10. We believe in the resurrection of the dead, both the righteous and the unrighteous, and that everyone shall give an account to a righteous God for his life and conduct on earth.

11. We believe that there is eternal glory for those who believe on Jesus Christ and faithfully endure to the end, and eternal condemnation for those who die in impenitence and unbelief.

12. We believe that the sole duty of the Christian Church is to proclaim the Gospel to the whole world, and to assist charitable institutions, to work for righteousness and temperance, for unity and cooperation with all believers, and for peace among all people and nations on the whole earth.

Norwegian Zion Evangelical Free Church (1920)

1. We believe in a personal God, Father, Son and Holy Spirit—John 1:14; 14:26.

2. We believe in the verbal inspiration of the Bible—2 Tim 3:16; 2 Pet 1:21.

3. We believe that man was created in the image of God, and that he fell—and through his fall all have become sinners before God—Gen 1:27; Rom 3:23.

4. We believe that through the obedience and sufferings of Christ, and through His blood, redemption was wrought for all that would receive and believe—John 3:16; 1 Pet 1:18-19; Heb 9:36.

5. We believe that without regeneration by the Holy Spirit man is forever shut away from God—John 3:3; Mat 18:2-3.

6. We believe in the resurrection from the dead, and that both the just and the unjust shall give an account to God for their works—2 Cor 5:10; John 5:28-29.

7. We believe that Christ has a visible Church on earth, and that He is the head of the same—and every one that is born of the Spirit belongs to the Church—Mat 16:18; Eph 2:19-22; Acts 2:42.

8. We believe in baptism in the name of the Father and of the Son and of the Holy Spirit. As to age and method we give conscious liberty—Mat 28:19.

9. In that we confess these words to be the teaching of the Bible we declare ourselves willing to cooperate with all that have participated in the same faith, and with same will we work together in grace for the advancement of His kingdom.

Evangelical Free Church of America (1950)

(adopted into the Evangelical Free Church of Concord constitution in 1960)

The Evangelical Free Church of America believes:

1. The Scriptures, both Old and New Testaments, to be the inspired Word of God, without error in the original writings, the complete revelation of His will for the salvation of men, and the Divine and final authority for Christian faith and life.

2. In one God, Creator of all things, infinitely perfect and eternally existing in three persons, Father, Son and Holy Spirit.

3. That Jesus Christ is true God and true man, having been conceived of the Holy Ghost and born of the Virgin Mary. He died on the cross a sacrifice for our sins according to the Scriptures. Further, He arose bodily from the dead, ascended into heaven, where at the right hand of the Majesty on High, He is now our High Priest and Advocate.

4. That the ministry of the Holy Spirit is to glorify the Lord Jesus Christ, and during this age to convict men, regenerate the believing sinner, indwell, guide, instruct, and empower the believer for godly living and service.

5. That man was created in the image of God but fell into sin and is therefore lost and only through regeneration by the Holy Spirit can salvation and spiritual life be obtained.

6. That the shed blood of Jesus Christ and His resurrection provide the only ground for justification and salvation for all who believe, and only such as receive Jesus Christ are born of the Holy Spirit, and thus become children of God.

7. That water baptism and the Lord's Supper are ordinances to be observed by the Church during the present age. They are, however, not to be regarded as means of salvation.

8. That the true Church is composed of all such persons who through saving faith in Jesus Christ have been regenerated by the Holy Spirit and are united together in the body of Christ, of which He is the Head.

9. That only those who are thus members of the true Church shall be eligible for membership in the local church.

10. That Jesus Christ is the Lord and Head of the Church, and that every local church has the right under Christ to decide and govern its own affairs.

11. In the personal and premillennial and imminent coming of our Lord Jesus Christ and that this "Blessed Hope" has a vital bearing on the personal life and service of the believer.

12. In the bodily resurrection of the dead; of the believer to everlasting blessedness and joy with the Lord, of the unbeliever to judgment and everlasting conscious punishment.

Faith Evangelical Chapel Constitution (1981)

(based on the 1950 EFCA Statement of Faith, but with additional detail and Scripture references. Point 1 elaborates on the belief of plenary verbal inspiration of Scripture. In point 4 an attempt was made to provide more balance between Calvinist and Armenian views of regeneration. Point 6 elaborates on the active obedience of Christ)

1. We believe that the Scriptures, both Old and New Testaments, are the inspired Word of God, without error in the original writings. The nature of God's Word and His supervision of its transmission is such that an accurate translation of the text we have today preserves its God-breathed character. We therefore affirm that God's Word is available to His people today and that it is the complete revelation of His will for salvation and the divine and final authority for all Christian faith and life. (Luke 24:27, 44; John 5:39; Romans 15:4; II Timothy 3:16; II Peter 1:21)

2. We believe in one God, Creator of all things, infinitely perfect and eternally existing in three persons, Father, Son, and Holy Spirit. (Matthew 28:18-19; Mark 12:29; John 1:14; II Corinthians 13:14)

3. We believe that Jesus Christ is true God and true man, having been conceived of the Holy Spirit and born of the Virgin Mary. He died on the cross, a sacrifice for our sins, according to the

Scriptures. Further, He arose bodily from the dead, ascended into heaven, where at the right hand of the Majesty on High, He now is our High Priest and Advocate. (Matthew 20:28; Romans 3:25,26; II Corinthians 5:14; Hebrews 10:5-14; Hebrews 7:25; I Corinthians 15:20)

4. We believe that the ministry of the Holy Spirit is to glorify the Lord Jesus Christ, and during this age to convict sinners, regenerate the believer at salvation, indwell, guide, instruct, and empower the believer for godly living and service. (John 14:16-17, 16:7-15; Romans 8:9; I Corinthians 6:19; Galatians 5:16; I Corinthians 12:13; Ephesians 2:22, 4:30, 5:18; II Thessalonians 2:7; I John 2:20-27)

5. We believe that man was created in the image of God but fell into sin and is therefore lost and only through regeneration by the Holy Spirit can salvation and spiritual life be obtained. (Genesis 1:26, 2:17; Psalms 14:1-3, 51:5; John 3:6; Romans 3:10-19, 8:6-7; Ephesians 2:1-3; I John 3:8; John 3:36)

6. We believe that, in order to effect justification and salvation, Jesus Christ lived a sinless life, fulfilling the demands of the Law, and died on the Cross, bearing the penalty of the Law, as the federal representative of sinful men, and that the shed blood of Jesus Christ and His resurrection provide the only ground for justification and salvation. Only those who receive Jesus Christ are born of the Holy Spirit, and thus become children of God. (Leviticus 17:11; Isaiah 64:6; Matthew 26:28; John 3:7-18; Romans 5:6-9; II Corinthians 5:21; Galatians 3:13; Ephesians 1:7; Titus 3:5-7)

7. We believe that water baptism and the Lord's Supper are ordinances to be observed by the Church during the present age. They are, however, not to be regarded as means of salvation. (Matthew 28:19; Acts 10:47-48, 16:32-33, 18:7-8; I Corinthians 11:26)

8. We believe that the true Church is composed of all such persons who through saving faith in Jesus Christ have been regenerated by the Holy Spirit and are united together in the Body of Christ

of which He is the head. (Matthew 16:16-18; Acts 2:42-47; Romans 12:5; I Corinthians 11:3; Ephesians 4:3-10)

9. We believe that only those who are thus members of the true Church shall be eligible for membership in the local church. (Acts 2:41-42,47)

10. We believe that Jesus Christ is the Lord and Head of the Church, and that every local church has the right under Christ to decide and govern its own affairs. (Matthew 16:16-18; I Corinthians 11:3)

11. We believe in the personal and premillennial and imminent coming of our Lord Jesus Christ and that this "Blessed Hope" has a vital bearing on the personal life and service of the believer. (John 14:1-3; I Corinthians 15:51-52; Philippians 3:20; I Thessalonians 4:13-18; Titus 2:11-14)

12. We believe in the bodily resurrection of the dead; of the believer to everlasting blessedness and joy with the Lord, of the unbeliever to judgment and everlasting conscious punishment. (Luke 16:19-26, 23:42-43; II Corinthians 5:8; Philippians 1:23; II Thessalonians 1:7-9; Revelation 20:11-15)

Evangelical Free Church of America (2008)

EFCA Statement of Faith Adopted by the national EFCA conference on June 26, 2008

(Adopted by Faith Evangelical Free Church on September 23, 2009)

The Evangelical Free Church of America is an association of autonomous churches united around these theological convictions:

God

We believe in one God, Creator of all things, holy, infinitely perfect, and eternally existing in a loving unity of three equally divine Persons: the Father, the Son, and the Holy Spirit. Having limitless knowledge and sovereign power, God has graciously purposed from eternity to redeem a people for Himself and to make all things new for His own glory.

The Bible

We believe that God has spoken in the Scriptures, both Old and New Testaments, through the words of human authors. As the verbally inspired Word of God, the Bible is without error in the original writings, the complete revelation of His will for salvation, and the ultimate authority by which every realm of human knowledge and endeavor should be judged. Therefore, it is to be believed in all that it teaches, obeyed in all that it requires, and trusted in all that it promises.

The Human Condition

We believe that God created Adam and Eve in His image, but they sinned when tempted by Satan. In union with Adam, human beings are sinners by nature and by choice, alienated from God, and under His wrath. Only through God's saving work in Jesus Christ can we be rescued, reconciled, and renewed.

Jesus Christ

We believe that Jesus Christ is God incarnate, fully God and fully man, one Person in two natures. Jesus—Israel's promised Messiah—was conceived through the Holy Spirit and born of the virgin Mary. He lived a sinless life, was crucified under Pontius Pilate, arose bodily from the dead, ascended into heaven, and sits at the right hand of God the Father as our High Priest and Advocate.

The Work of Jesus Christ

We believe that Jesus Christ, as our representative and substitute, shed His blood on the cross as the perfect, all-sufficient sacrifice for our sins. His atoning death and victorious resurrection constitute the only ground for salvation.

The Holy Spirit

We believe that the Holy Spirit, in all that He does, glorifies the Lord Jesus Christ. He convicts the world of its guilt. He regenerates sinners and in Him they are baptized into union with Christ and adopted as heirs in the family of God. He also indwells, illuminates, guides, equips, and empowers believers for Christ-like living and service.

The Church

We believe that the true church comprises all who have been justified by God's grace through faith alone, in Christ alone. They are united by the Holy Spirit in the body of Christ, of which He is the Head. The true church is manifest in local churches, whose membership should be composed only of believers. The Lord Jesus mandated two ordinances, baptism and the Lord's Supper which visibly and tangibly express the gospel. Though they are not the means of salvation, when celebrated by the church in genuine faith, these ordinances confirm and nourish the believer.

Christian Living

We believe that God's justifying grace must not be separated from His sanctifying power and purpose. God commands us to love Him supremely and others sacrificially and to live out our faith with care for one another, compassion toward the poor, and justice for the oppressed. With God's Word, the Spirit's power, and fervent prayer in Christ's name, we are to combat the spiritual forces of evil. In obedience to Christ's commission, we are to make disciples among all people, always bearing witness to the gospel in word and deed.

Jesus Christ's Return

We believe in the personal, bodily, and premillennial[2] return of our Lord Jesus Christ. The coming of Christ, at a time known only to God, requires constant expectancy and, as our blessed hope, motivates the believer to godly living, sacrificial service, and energetic mission.

Response and Eternal Destiny

We believe that God commands everyone everywhere to believe the gospel by turning to Him in repentance and receiving the Lord Jesus Christ. We believe that God will raise the dead bodily and judge the world, assigning the unbeliever to condemnation and eternal conscious punishment, and the believer to eternal blessedness and joy with the Lord, in the new heaven and the new earth to the praise of His glorious grace. Amen.

Acknowledgements

As with any book, this was not the effort of one person. This work began simply as an attempt to create a detailed timeline documenting the early years of the church in preparation for Faith's upcoming centennial celebration in 2020. As things progressed, many people encouraged me to build on that work, especially Pastor Brad Johnson.

Special thanks to Leslie Perrin Wilson and Conni Manoli of the Concord Free Public Library William Munroe Special Collections for their patience and helpful suggestions while researching the records of the Trinitarian Congregational Church and information on the Hunt family. Steve Neth, museum technician for the Minute Man National Historical Park, spent many hours with me wading through old records on the Hunt farm on Punkatasset Hill, as well as the Elisha Jones House where the church bell hung for a time.

Tom Cairns, the EFCA archivist, and Roger Swanson, who volunteers his time in the archives, are both amazing people. They embraced this project with enthusiasm, and made themselves totally available to me during my visit to the home office. Tom already had many books and artifacts waiting for me when I arrived, and gave me a detailed tour and full access to the archives. Roger dropped what he was doing whenever I had old documents to scan for later translation. Their help was invaluable to fill in gaps in the narrative.

Thank you also to Hans Christiansen who donated many hours of his time reading difficult handwriting and translating the early Norwegian records of the church for me. Carolyn Light, Sally Abbott, and Tim Mullane provided helpful feedback and suggestions, without which this account would be much less interesting. Sally Abbott also provided important history about Joy Bible Study and its beneficial relationship with the church.

In addition, Linda Specht, Barbara Thoresen, Janet Stuart, Steve Purinton, Karen Hanson, Marion Purinton, Mike and Julie Miller, Ken Spence, and Gordon Condit provided valuable insight into the later Lang Street and early Acton years. Ann Brannon went above and beyond in her willingness to share her own very personal experiences.

A special thank you is in order for Karen Mullane, who volunteered many hours of her time as editor. She has done a truly remarkable job taking my rambling thoughts and turning them into prose that people will (hopefully!) be willing to read! She is truly a gifted editor, and a great friend.

Thank you also to George Plesko, who contributed his time for the book cover design. I am in awe of his design skills!

But the strongest thanks have to go to my beloved wife Kris, who not only encouraged me in the work, but put up with the mountains of papers, books and photographs that were strewn throughout the house during the writing. Often I would take a stack of books back to the church, only to return with a larger pile than before! Thank you for being my best friend, my partner, my girlfriend, and the love of my life for all these forty years!

Notes

Prologue: Fertile Soil at Home and Abroad

[1] This greatly simplified overview of nineteenth century events is much more ably described in Frederick Hale, "Norwegians, Danes and the Origins of the Evangelical Free Tradition" *Norwegian-American Studies*, Vol. 28, 1979, and David M. Gustafson, "D.L. Moody and the Norwegian-Danish Evangelical Free Church", Trinity Evangelical Divinity School.

[2] Wikipedia contributors, "Moody Church," *Wikipedia, The Free Encyclopedia,* https://en.wikipedia.org/w/index.php?title=Moody_Church&oldid=905565211 (accessed February 19, 2020). A few years after Moody's death, the Chicago Avenue Church was renamed the Moody Church in his honor. In 1925 the church moved to its present location at the corners of North Avenue, Clark Street and LaSalle Street. The location of the Chicago Avenue Church is now the site of the women's dormitory of Moody Bible Institute.

[3] Franson went on to found the Scandinavian Alliance Mission in 1890, which, in 1949, became The Evangelical Alliance Mission (TEAM), from which Faith EFC has supported many missionaries through the years.

[4] Rev. M. W. Montgomery, *A Wind From the Holy Spirit in Sweden and Norway*, (Bible House, NY: American Home Missionary Society, 1884), 23-24.

[5] R. Arlo Odegaard, *With Singleness of Heart: Pioneers and Pioneering for Christ in Home Mission Fields*, (Minneapolis: Free Church Press: 1971), 101.

[6] Ibid.

[7] Hale, 105-6. "Adiaphora" in this context refers to non-essential but permissible beliefs or practices which are not essential to the Christian faith.

Chapter 1: The Scandinavian Mission Society

[1] *Church Manual and Year Book of the Norwegian Evangelical Free Church (Congregational), Lang Street, Concord, Massachusetts* (Concord: Norwegian Evangelical Free Church, 1932).

[2] Leslie Perrin Wilson, "A Concord Farmer Looks Back: The Reminiscences of William Henry Hunt", *The Concord Saunterer, New Series*, Volume 10 (2002), p72.

[3] John Whittemore Teele, ed., *The Meeting House on the Green: A History of the First Parish in Concord and Its Church. 350th Anniversary, 1635-1985*, (Concord: The Parish, 1985), 129. This book contains an excellent summary of the history of many Concord churches up to the date of publication. It even contains a short section on the Evangelical Free Church at Lang Street.

[4] "U.S. Passport Applications, 1795-1925", database with digital images, *Ancestry* (https://www.ancestry.com/interactive/1174/USM1372_216-1345 : accessed 2 October 2019),

imaged passport application 1097 for William H Hunt, accompanied by his wife; citing *"Selected Passports.* National Archives, Washington, D.C."

⁵ Allen French, Correspondence with William Henry Hunt and working papers for Social Circle memoir of Hunt, including letter from Hunt's niece Mary R. Jacobs and Jacobs' responses to Social Circle biographical form on Hunt; *Allen French Papers*, Box 6, Folders 10-13, Minute Man National Historical Park Archives, Concord.

⁶ *Sabbath School Secretary Record Book* (Concord: Trinitarian Congregational Church, 1869-1882). Concord Free Public Library (CFPL) Special Collections, Trinitarian Congregational Church in Concord Records, 1686 (bulk 1826-2006), Vault A30, Unit C1.

⁷ "Massachusetts, State and Federal Naturalization Records, 1798-1950", database with digital images, Ancestry (https://www.ancestry.com/interactive/2361/007774861_00998 : accessed 2 October 2019), imaged certified declaration of intention 145-165, for Ole O. Thorpe on 30 October 1884; citing *"Naturalization Records.* National Archives at Boston, Waltham, Massachusetts." He applied for citizenship on October 30, 1884, and took the oath of allegiance on October 25, 1887.

⁸ "Massachusetts, Marriage Records, 1840-1915", database with digital images, *Ancestry* (*https://www.ancestry.com/interactive/2511/41262_b139541-00404* : accessed 2 October 2019), imaged marriage records for Ole O. Thorpe; citing *"Massachusetts Vital Records, 1840-1811,* New England Historic Genealogical Society, Boston, Massachusetts."

⁹ *Records of the Trinitarian Congregational Church Concord, Massachusetts, Book III*, Trinitarian Congregational Church: 1902 September-1928 December 3. CFPL Special Collections, Trinitarian Congregational Church in Concord Records.

¹⁰ Concord Historical Commission, *Highlights of Concord's Historic Resources*, (Town of Concord, Massachusetts, 1995), 47.

¹¹ The William Henry Hunt Recreation Center on Stow Street was built with funds given to the town in the will of Elizabeth Hunt's husband William, upon his death in 1927.

¹² For more information on the Wright Tavern during this period, see Groundroot Preservation Group, *The Wright Tavern 1747 Concord MA Historical Structural Report (Groundroot, 2014);* CFPL Special Collections, First Parish in Concord Records 1695-2014, Vault A30 Unit A1, Box 18, Folder 1, "Real Estate"; see also Bessie K. Hudson, *The Wright Tavern* [carbon copy of typescript] (1938?), also in the same collection. During this period the building was rented out to various tenants. In 1875 the building was sold to George M. Brooks, who sold it seven years later to Ebenezer R. Hoar and Reuben N. Rice, each of whom donated their half interest to First Parish in 1886. There is no extant information on renters from this time. Interestingly, Mrs. Hudson gave $10 toward the building of the Lang Street Church!

¹³ Montgomery, 23-24.

¹⁴ S.K. Didriksen, "Letters to his friends in Norway concerning his trip to America and efforts to evangelize Norwegians in Boston Area", *Morgenrøden*, 1885, p30. From the Papers of Fredrik Franson, Billy Graham Center Archives, Wheaton, Ill, Collection 87, Box 3, Folder 28.

¹⁵ Odegaard, 126-127.

¹⁶ *The Sixty-Fourth Report of the American Home Missionary Society*, presented to the Executive Committee, at the Annual Meeting, June 3, 1890, (New York: The American Home Missionary Society, 1890), 112; also, Odegaard, 130.

¹⁷ *Second Congregational Church Records, 1868-1902*, Trinitarian Congregational Church. Includes reports and accounts. p77. CFPL Special Collections, Trinitarian Congregational Church in Concord Records. Prior to its incorporation in 1891, Trinitarian Congregational Church was

known as the Second Congregational Church of Concord.

[18] Arne Hassing, "Methodism From Norway to America", *Norwegian American Studies*, Vol. 28, 1979, pp 196-197, https://www.naha.stolaf.edu/pubs/nas/volume28/Nor-Am%20Studies%20Vol%2028%20Article%20Eight.pdf, accessed 31 July 2019.

[19] Methodist Episcopal Church, New England Conference, *Official Minutes of the Ninetieth Session of the New England Conference of the Methodist Episcopal Church Held in Trinity Church, Worcester, April 10-16, 1889* (Boston, MA: Alfred Mudge & Sons, 1889). Found at Hathi Trust Digital Library, https://catalog.hathitrust.org/Record/008699889. Accessed 2 October 2019.

[20] Methodist Episcopal Church, New England Conference,, *Official Minutes of the Ninety-Eighth Session, 1894*; and *Official Minutes of the One Hundred and First Session, 1897*. Found at Hathi Trust Digital Library, https://catalog.hathitrust.org/Record/008699889. Accessed 2 October 2019.

[21] Teele, 129-130.

[22] *Women's Missionary Society 75th Anniversary Program* (1964), Faith Evangelical Free Church archives.

[23] *The Sixty-Fourth Report of the American Home Missionary Society*, presented to the Executive Committee, at the Annual Meeting, June 3, 1890, (New York: The American Home Missionary Society, 1890), 112. https://books.google.com/books?id=estMAAAAMAAJ&-lpg=PP2&ots=29O6Q7PEZA&dq=The%20Sixty-Fourth%20Report%20of%20the%20-American%20Home%20Missionary%20Society&pg=PP2#v=onepage&q=The%20Sixty-Fourth%20Report%20of%20the%20American%20Home%20Missionary%20Society&f=false. Accessed 2 October 2019.

[24] *Second Congregational Church Records, 1868-1902*, 161.

[25] Ibid., 184.

[26] Odegaard, 44.

[27] *Congregational Meeting Minutes, 1891-1899*, Norwegian Evangelical Free Church of Boston, Massachusetts, 60-61, Norwegian Heritage Collection, Box 10, Folder 5, EFCA Archives, Minneapolis MN.

[28] Robert A. Watson, *A History of the Trinitarian Congregational Church 1826-1988*, (Concord: Trinitarian Congregational Church, 2000), 28.

[29] Odegaard, 133.

[30] Second Congregational Church Records, 1868-1902, 285.

Chapter 2: *Skandinaviske Trefaldigheds Menighed*

[1] *Church Business Meetings, 1919-1943*, 1-2, Faith Evangelical Free Church archives, translated by Hans Christiansen.

[2] *Second Congregational Church Records, 1868-1902*, Trinitarian Congregational Church, 293-296.

[3] Odegaard, 116.

4 *Treasurer's Ledger, 1896-1904*, Norwegian Evangelical Free Church of Boston, Massachusetts, EFCA Archives, Minneapolis, MN.

5 *Annual Reports of the Trinitarian Congregational Church, Concord Mass, For the Year Ending September 1 1899* (Concord: Trinitarian Congregational Church, 1899), *14-15*, CFPL Special Collections, Trinitarian Congregational Church in Concord Records.

6 Olga Hoff Olsen, personal letter to Rev. Doug Welch, 6 May 1992.

7 *Second Congregational Church Records, 1868-1902*, Trinitarian Congregational Church, 399-400.

8 Ibid., 402-404.

9 Ibid., 405.

10 *Annual Reports for the Trinitarian Congregational Church, Concord, Mass, for the Year Ending September 1, 1901*, 15.

11 *Treasurer's Ledger, 1896-1904*, Norwegian Evangelical Free Church of Boston, Massachusetts, EFCA Archives. Rev. Andersen was reimbursed $1.00 for travel expenses from Concord.

12 *Annual Reports of the Trinitarian Congregational Church, Concord Mass, For the Year Ending September 1 1904* (Concord: Trinitarian Congregational Church, 1904), 17-18.

13 *Rapport over Forhandlingerne med Vestens og Østens Evangeliske Frikirke Foreningers Aarsmøder 1903*, (Chicago, Evangelisten Publishing Society, 1903), 59-60. Trinity International University Digital Archive, http://collections.carli.illinois.edu/cdm/landingpage/collection/tiu_efcadir, accessed 6 September 2019.

14 *For den Skandinaviske Trefaldigheds Menighed Concord Mass, 1907-1916*, Faith Evangelical Free Church archives, labeled *Faith Evangelical Church Accounts 1907-1916*. The records commence with December of 1907.

15 Rasmus Malmin, O.M. Norlie, and O.A. Tingelstad, *Who's Who Among Pastors in all the Norwegian Lutheran Synods of America, 1843-1927*, Third Edition, (Minneapolis, MN: 1928, Augsburg Publishing House), p615. Includes is picture and short biography, which states that he served in Concord from 1906-1908.

16 *Annual Reports of the Trinitarian Congregational Church, Concord Mass*, various annual reports for the years 1903-1907.

17 *Records of the Trinitarian Congregational Church Concord, Massachusetts Book III*, Trinitarian Congregational Church, 1902 September - 1928 December 3, 177, 180-181.

18 Ibid., 203.

19 Dr. Emrich was also an active supporter of the Swedish "Mission Friends" pietist movement in Massachusetts, which eventually grew into what is today known as the Evangelical Covenant Church.

20 Malmin, et al., 269.

21 *Records of the Trinitarian Congregational Church Concord, Massachusetts Book III*, Trinitarian Congregational Church, 1902 September - 1928 December 3, 224.

22 *For den Skandinaviske Trefaldigheds Menighed Concord Mass, 1907-1916*.

23 *Annual Reports of the Trinitarian Congregational Church, Concord Mass, For the Year*

Ending September 1 1918 (Concord: Trinitarian Congregational Church, 1918), 25.

[24] *Annual Reports of the Trinitarian Congregational Church, Concord Mass, For the Year Ending September 1 1919* (Concord: Trinitarian Congregational Church, 1919), 29.

[25] Odegaard, 132.

[26] *Annual Reports of the Trinitarian Congregational Church, Concord Mass, For the Year Ending September 1 1904* (Concord: Trinitarian Congregational Church, 1904), 18.

[27] *Annual Reports of the Trinitarian Congregational Church, Concord Mass, For the Year Ending September 1 1911* (Concord: Trinitarian Congregational Church, 1911), 38.

[28] David M. Gustafson, "D.L. Moody and the Norwegian-Danish Evangelical Free Church", Trinity Evangelical Divinity School, p21-22. Accessed on 30 May 2019 at https://www.academia.edu/19608158.

[29] While this might not seem like much, the dues were normally allocated to missionary support. In doing this, they were committing themselves to the establishment of a new church as a missionary effort.

Chapter 3: A Place to Call Home

[1] *Aarsrapport for De Evangeliske Frikirke-Foreningers Aarsmøder, 1917,* (Chicago: Evangelisten Publishing Society, 1917). Trinity International University Digital Archive, http://collections.carli.illinois.edu/cdm/landingpage/collection/tiu_efcadir, accessed 6 September 2019.

[2] *De Norske Evangeliske Frimenigheders Blad*, 9, No. 6 (June 1919), 5. EFCA Archives, Minneapolis MN, Norwegian Heritage Collection, Box 4, Folder 8.

[3] "Minutes of the Eastern Evangelical Free Church Association, 28th Annual Meeting", *De evangeliske Frikirkeforeningers Årsrapporter 1919,* (1919), 18-24. Trinity International University Digital Archive, http://collections.carli.illinois.edu/cdm/landingpage/collection/tiu_efcadir, accessed 6 September 2019.

[4] Odegaard, 132.

[5] *Church Business Meetings, 1919-1943*, 1-2, translated by Hans Christiansen.

[6] "Another Norwegian Church", *Concord Enterprise*, 8 October 1919, 5.

[7] "To The Public", *Concord Enterprise*, 22 October 1919, 1.

[8] Odegaard, 528.

[9] *Records of the Trinitarian Congregational Church Concord, Massachusetts Book III.*

[10] Part of the original Norwegian constitution and a complete English translation is available in the church archives. In the original constitution, calling a pastor required ⅔ of the cast votes. There was no quorum requirement. Elders, which essentially had the same role as the Pastor, served for 2 years, while Deacons served for 3 year terms.

[11] *Troesbekjendelse og Konstitution, Den Norske Evangeliske Frimenighed, Jersey City, New Jersey,* 1891, Norwegian Heritage Collection, Box 8, Folder 30, EFCA Archives.

[12] *WMS 75th Anniversary Program*, FEFC Archives.

[13] "USS Britannia (1862)," *Wikipedia, The Free Encyclopedia,* https://en.wikipedia.org/w/-index.php?title=USS_Britannia_(1862)&oldid=857636132 (accessed January 6, 2020).

[14] Ruth R. Wheeler, *North Bridge Neighbors, History of Area B,* Minute Man National Historic Park Archives, (Concord: 1964), p13.

Chapter 4: The Norwegian Evangelical Free Church

[1] Odegaard, 49.

[2] Middlesex So. District Registry of Deeds, Book 4492 - Page 240.

[3] *Church Business Meetings, 1919 to 1943,* Jan 20, 1930, 66.

[4] Cornelia Martinsen Lawrence and Clara Martinsen Murphy interviews, 1985, interviewed by William Bailey, CFPL Special Collections, *The Renee Garrelick Oral History Program Collection.* https://concordlibrary.org/uploads/scollect/OH_Texts/martinsen.html, accessed 2 October 2019.

[5] "Evangelical Free Church!", *Concord Enterprise,* 8 August 1923, 8.

[6] *Church Business Meetings, 1919 to 1943,* Jan 20, 1930, 75-76.

[7] Ibid, 81.

[8] Odegaard, 133.

[9] Interestingly, it took a special meeting, on June 14, 1936, for the pastor to be accepted as a member of the church. Apparently this was not automatic. Later, at a congregational meeting on April 14, 1941, "it was voted to give Pastor Odland the privilege to vote at our meetings."

[10] *Church Business Meetings, 1919 to 1943,* Jan 20, 1941, 138.

[11] It appears from the minutes that there may have been some concern about finances at this time: "Discussed matter of calling a new pastor now or not. Motion made and seconded to see about taxes on parsonage and also about payments on house before we do anything definite."

[12] *Church Register, 1944-1955,* Norwegian Zion Evangelical Free Church of Concord, Mass., p159-160.

[13] *Annual Reports, 1953,* Evangelical Free Church of Concord, Secretary's Report.

Chapter 5: The Evangelical Free Church of Concord

[1] *Annual Reports,* 1958, Pastor's Report.

[2] Judith V. Dunn, *Malcolm R. Dunn, "In God I Trust",* (1996: Little Guy Press, Auburn, Maine), 19. Copy in the possession of Marion Purinton.

[3] *Church Business Meetings, 1919 to 1943,* 94-95.

[4] In the 1961 Constitution and Bylaws, Elders served for life. Deacons has essentially the same duties as elders, plus communion responsibilities, and served for three years. The vote to call a pastor was changed to ¾ of members voting. The quorum for all meetings (including pastoral call) was 15 members. An earlier draft of the revised bylaws indicated that the church's covenant with the pastor should be renewed every two years by mail-in ballot. However, this

provision did not appear in the final draft.

⁵ Dunn, 32.

⁶ Ibid., 43-44.

⁷ *Business Meetings, 1955 to 1964* (Concord: Evangelical Free Church, Lang Street, Concord, Massachusetts), 223-224.

⁸ *Business Meetings, 1955 to 1964*, p267-268.

⁹ Ibid.

¹⁰ *Business Meetings, 1955 to 1964*, 262.

¹¹ Dunn, 43-44.

¹² *Annual Reports*, Pastor's Report, 1965.

¹³ *Official Board Meetings: Record of Executive Board Meetings, June 1965-June 1972* (Concord: Evangelical Free Church of Concord), 94-96. Interestingly, all of the nominated committee members left the church or moved away by the time the move to Acton was completed.

¹⁴ Ibid., 116-117.

¹⁵ Ibid., 118-120.

¹⁶ *Annual Reports*, 1971, Secretary's Pen report.

¹⁷ *Evangelical Free Church, Lang Street, Concord Massachusetts, Record of Business Meetings, 13 October 1964-21 September 1982*, 159-163.

¹⁸ Ibid., 172.

¹⁹ *Official Board Meetings: Record of Executive Board Meetings, June 1985-June 1972* (Concord: Evangelical Free Church of Concord), 140.

²⁰ *Evangelical Free Church of Concord, Record of Executive Board Meetings, August 1972 - January 1983*, 1-2.

²¹ *Evangelical Free Church, Lang Street, Concord Massachusetts, Record of Business Meetings, 13 October 1964-21 September 1982*, 175-6.

²² Ibid., 177.

²³ Ibid., 193-5.

²⁴ *Annual Reports*, 1995, Pastor Doug Welch's report.

²⁵ Kenneth Spence, Phone conversation with the author, 20 November 2018.

Chapter 6: Faith Evangelical Chapel

¹ *Evangelical Free Church, Lang Street, Concord Massachusetts, Record of Business Meetings, 13 October 1964-21 September 1982*, 208-210.

² Dunn, 32, 44.

³ *Evangelical Free Church of Concord, Record of Executive Board Meetings, August 1972 - January 1983*, 60-1.

4 In prior years the church would gather in a field on Monument Street near Punkatasset Hill for the sunrise, then go back to the church at Lang Street for a breakfast (Steve Purinton remembered that Roland Johnson and his son Arthur, who lived across the street from K-Mart in Acton, would walk the seven miles to Punkatasset for the sunrise service—about a 2-and-a-half hour walk!)

5 *Evangelical Free Church, Lang Street, Concord Massachusetts, Record of Business Meetings, 13 October 1964-21 September 1982,* 211.

6 Ted Thoresen was the father of Helen Vettrus, Bob, Thomas E (Jr.), Paul, and Esther Thoresen, and the brother of Olga (Thoresen) Purinton, wife of March Purinton Sr.

7 *Faith Evangelical Chapel Annual Reports,* 1978, Pastor's Report.

8 Pew Research Center, "The Rise in Dual Income Households", June 18, 2015. http://www.pewresearch.org/ft_dual-income-households-1960-2012-2, accessed 2 October 2019.

9 *Evangelical Free Church of Concord, Record of Executive Board Meetings, August 1972 - January 1983,* 145-6.

10 *Business Meeting Minutes* (Acton: Faith Evangelical Free Church), minutes from business meeting held July 25, 1982.

11 *Annual Reports,* 1986, Missions Report.

Chapter 7: Faith Evangelical Free Church

1 *Annual Reports,* 1995, Missions Report. Letter sent to all the missionaries of Faith Evangelical Free Church.

2 Henry T. Blackaby and Claude V. King, *Experiencing God: Knowing and Doing the Will of God;* (Nashville: Lifeway Press, 1990), inside back cover.

3 *Annual Meetings, 1982-1999* (Acton: Faith Evangelical Free Church), Special Business Meeting minutes, 6/18/1997.

4 *Board Meeting Minutes, 1985-1999* (Acton: Faith Evangelical Free Church), Annual Business Meeting minutes of Jan 23, 1999.

5 *Annual Reports,* 2003, Elders' Report.

Chapter 9: The Birth of a Church

1 Roy A. Thompson, *Looking Back Seventy Years: A Historical Glimpse of the Evangelical Free Church of America* (Minneapolis: Free Church Press, 1954), 1.

2 L.J. Pedersen, *The Norwegian Evangelical Free Church of Boston, Mass. (Congregational): A Brief Historical Sketch,* (Boston: Eastern Press, 1935), 9.

3 *Church Business Meetings, 1919-1943,* 4.

4 *Treasurer's Ledger, 1896-1904,* Norwegian Evangelical Free Church of Boston, Massachusetts, EFCA Archives.

5 The building at 50 Cedar Street is now being considered as a historic landmark of Boston.

See Boston Landmarks Commission Study Report, "St. James African Orthodox Church, https://www.boston.gov/sites/default/files/document-file-07-2018/7.11.18_version_saint_-james_african_orthodox_church_study_report_262.18_.pdf, accessed 29 April 2019.

[6] *Church Business Meetings, 1919-1943*, 87-88. It is not clear whether the "Home Mission Fund" is a reference to the Massachusetts Home Missionary Society or a Home Missions fund from the Eastern Evangelical Free Church Association.

[7] *De Norske Evangeliske Frimenigheders Blad*, 9, No. 6, (June 1919), 5. Trinity International University Digital Archive, http://collections.carli.illinois.edu/cdm/landingpage/collection/tiu_efcadir, accessed 6 September 2019.

[8] Ibid.

[9] Ibid., 9, No. 7, (July 1919), 3.

[10] Ibid., 9, No. 8, (August 1919), 2.

[11] Ibid., 9, No. 12 (December 1919), 3.

[12] Ibid., 10, No. 1 (January 1920), 3.

[13] Ibid., 10, No. 3 (March 1920), 4.

[14] Ibid., 10, No. 12 (December 1920), 3.

Chapter 10: Church Planting Insights

[1] Ed Stetzer, "5 Reasons Established Churches Should Plant Churches", *Christianity Today*, June 14, 2014, online, https://www.christianitytoday.com/edstetzer/2014/june/5-reasons-established-churches-should-plant-churches.html, accessed 2 October 2019.

[2] Jeffrey C. Farmer, Church Planting Sponsorship: A Statistical Analysis of Sponsoring a Church Plant as a Means of Revitalization of the Sponsor Church, (New Orleans Baptist Theological Seminary, 2017), https://caskeycenter.files.wordpress.com/2017/05/church-revitalization-through-church-planting-sponsorship-powerpoint.pdf, accessed 2 October 2019.

Chapter 11: Stages of Church Life and Church Health

[1] Russell Burrill, "Can Dying Churches Be Resuscitated?", *Ministry*, December 2002, https://www.ministrymagazine.org/archive/2002/12/, accessed 2 October 2019. Dr. Burrill is writing specifically for the Seventh-Day Adventist Church, but he is drawing from the experience of other denominations as well.

[2] Dan Bilefsky, "Where Churches Have Become Temples of Cheese, Fitness and Eroticism", *New York Times July 30, 2018*, https://www.nytimes.com/2018/07/30/world/canada/quebec-churches.html?rref=collection%2Fbyline%2Fdan-bilefsky&action=click&-contentCollection=undefined&region=stream&module=stream_unit&version=latest&contentPlacement=2&pgtype=collection, accessed 2 October 2019.

[3] R. Albert Mohler, *The Briefing*, 14 August 2018, https://albertmohler.com/2018/08/14/briefing-8-14-18, accessed 2 October 2019.

[4] A simple web search for "church life cycle" shows the ubiquity of this view. The five stages listed here are my simplification of the concept.

[5] Burrill, citing George Barna's report, *Turnaround Churches* (Ventura, Calif.: Regal Books, 1993).

[6] Ibid.

Chapter 12: Report Card

[1] *Annual Reports of the Trinitarian Congregational Church, Concord Mass, For the Year Ending September 1 1914* (Concord: Trinitarian Congregational Church, 1914), 39. Concord Free Public Library Special Collections, Concord, MA.

[2] *Annual Reports of the Trinitarian Congregational Church, Concord Mass, For the Year Ending September 1 1919* (Concord: Trinitarian Congregational Church, 1919), 29. Concord Free Public Library Special Collections, Concord, MA.

[3] Odegaard, 132.

[4] *Church Business Meetings, 1919 to 1943*, 80.

[5] Ibid., yearly report for 1928, 69.

[6] *Annual Reports of the Trinitarian Congregational Church, Concord Mass, For the Year Ending September 1 1918* (Concord: Trinitarian Congregational Church, 1918), 25. Concord Free Public Library Special Collections, Concord, MA.

[7] *Church Business Meetings, 1919 to 1943*, 59, 61.

[8] *Annual Reports*, 1948, Pastor's Report.

[9] *Annual Reports*, 1949, Sunday School Report.

[10] *Annual Reports*, 1950, Pastor's Report.

[11] *Annual Reports*, 1951, Pastor's Report.

[12] *Annual Reports*, 1958, Pastor's Report.

[13] *Annual Reports*, 1959, Pastor's Report.

[14] *Business Meetings, 1955 to 1964*, Minutes of 30 June 1964, , 291-294.

[15] *Annual Reports*, 1971, Pastor's Report.

[16] *Westwood Evangelical Free Church Business and Board Meeting Minutes, 1954-1967*, congregation meetings of 13, 22 and 27 September 1954. EFCA Archives.

[17] Linda Specht, email correspondence with the author, 27 October 2018.

[18] *Annual Reports*, 1974, Pastor's Report.

[19] *Annual Reports*, 1978, Pastor's Report.

[20] *Annual Reports*, , 1980, Pastor's Report.

[21] *Annual Reports*, 1981, Moderator's Report.

[22] *Annual Meetings, 1982-1999*, Business Meeting Minutes of 5/18/82.

[23] Ibid., Faith Evangelical Chapel Business Meeting Held January 29, 1983.

[24] *Annual Reports*, 1985, Pastor's Report.

[25] *Board Meeting Minutes, 1985-1999*, Business Meeting Minutes, January 24, 1987.

[26] Ibid., Business Meeting Minutes, May 26, 1987.

[27] Ibid., Congregational Meeting, September 28, 1988.

[28] All quotes from this section are taken from correspondence between Ann Brannon and the author, dated 13 September 2019. This very personal account is related here by permission of Ann Brannon and her children.

Chapter 13: Insights from Surveys and Evaluations

[1] Church Body Life Evaluation, 1997, given over the course of five weeks. Original survey, raw results and summary report in the possession of the author.

[2] 10 Indicators of a Healthy Church evaluation, 2004, given to the pastors, elders and deacons. Spreadsheet of results in the possession of the author.

[3] Ten Indicators of a Healthy Church evaluation, 2007, given to the leadership. Spreadsheet of results with includes comparison to 2004 results is in the possession of the author.

Chapter 14: Insights from Pastoral Transitions

[1] *Church Business Meetings, 1919 to 1943*, Jan 20, 1941, 106-108.

[2] *Business Meetings, 1955 to 1964*, 83.

[3] Ibid., 84-86.

[4] Ibid., 87-88.

[5] Ibid., 89-91.

[6] Ibid., 92-93.

[7] *Business Meetings, 1955 to 1964*, 2 February 1960, 110-111. It appears that the church had 97 members on the roll, of which 20 were inactive.

[8] *Business Meetings, 1955 to 1964*, 223-224.

[9] *Board Meeting Minutes*, 1985-1999; Business Meeting Minutes of January 24th, 1987.

[10] *Annual Meetings*, 1982-1999, May 26, 1987.

[11] Ibid., Business Meeting Minutes, May 26, 1987.

Chapter 15: Insights from Attendance

[1] *Church Business Meetings, 1919*-1943, p291-4.

[2] *Church Business Meetings*, 1919-1943, p42.

3 Based on raw data from church registers and membership committee reports in Faith EFC archives.

4 Rev. Ken Spence, conversation with the author, 20 November 2018, "We just kind of rattled around in the sanctuary!"

5 Based on raw attendance figures in Faith EFC archives from the fall of 1976 to the present. Averages are based on running four-week averages to smooth out special conditions such as cancellation of services due to weather. Spreadsheet showing how the data was processed is in the possession of the author.

Chapter 16: Lessons Learned

1 Jim Van Yperen, *The Shepherd Leader*, (ChurchSmart Resources, 2004), 20.

2 *Board Meeting Minutes, 1985-1999*, Business Meeting Minutes, January 24, 1987.

3 Vanderbloemen and Bird, *Next: Pastoral Succession That Works,* (Grand Rapids: Baker Books, 2014), 9.

4 Ibid., 134-135.

Epilog: Looking Ahead

1 Joseph Belcher, D.D., *George Whitefield: A Biography, With Special Reference To His Labors In America*, (New York: American Tract Society, 1857), p317.

Appendix A: Biographical Sketches

1 Much of the following account is based on the excellent research and article by Leslie Perrin Wilson, "A Concord Farmer Looks Back: The Reminiscences of William Henry Hunt", *The Concord Saunterer, New Series*, Volume 10 (2002).

2 "Pennsylvania and New Jersey, Church and Town Records, 1669-2013", database with digital images, Ancestry (https://www.ancestry.com/interactive/2451/40162_264360-00011 : accessed 2 October 2019), image for Elizabeth Middleton McEuan, baptized 6 January 1830; cited "Historic Pennsylvania Church and Town Records. Philadelphia, Pennsylvania: Historical Society of Pennsylvania."

3 "1850 United States Federal Census", database with digital images, *Ancestry* (https://www.ancestry.com/interactive/8054/4205118_00296 : accessed 2 October 2019), image for "Year: 1850; Census Place: Philadelphia Locust Ward, Philadelphia, Pennsylvania;Roll: M432_814; Page: 145A; Image: 296."; cited "Seventh Census of the United States, 1850; (National Archives Microfilm Publication M432, 1009 rolls); Records of the Bureau of the Census, Record Group 29; National Archives, Washington, D.C."

4 Wilson, p72.

5 "Massachusetts, State Census, 1855", database with images, *Ancestry* (https://www.ancestry.com/interactive/4472/41265_307603-00408 : accessed 2 October 2019), image for inhabitants of Framingham, Middlesex, Massachusetts, p27; cited

"Massachusetts. 1855–1865 Massachusetts State Census [microform]. New England Historic Genealogical Society, Boston, Massachusetts".

6 Wilson, p78-79.

7 Wilson, p69.

8 "Massachusetts, Marriage Records, 1840-1915", database with images, *Ancestry* (https://www.ancestry.com/interactive/2511/41262_B139090-00070 : accessed 2 October 2019), image for Massachusetts Marriage Records for Elizabeth Baker; cited "Massachusetts Vital Records, 1840–1911. New England Historic Genealogical Society, Boston, Massachusetts."

9 Ibid.

10 Wilson, p79.

11 Leslie Perrin Wilson, "Theodore Baker of Concord: An Archival 'Aha!'", *The Concord Journal*, Thursday, July 7, 2005, p23.

12 Wilson, "Theodore Baker of Concord".

13 Wikipedia contributors, "Theodore Baker," Wikipedia, The Free Encyclopedia, https://en.wikipedia.org/w/index.php?title=Theodore_Baker&oldid=783006716 (accessed March 28, 2019).

14 *Concord Enterprise*, 15 April 1897, p5.

15 *Concord Enterprise*, 25 May 1898, p5.

16 *Concord Enterprise*, 15 April 1898, p1.

17 The "New Departure" was a movement among the Democratic Party to re-invent themselves after the Civil War.

18 *Second Congregational Church Records, 1868-1902*, Trinitarian Congregational Church, 143-145. Includes reports and accounts.

19 *Annual Reports of the Trinitarian Congregational Church, Concord Mass, For the Year Ending September 1 1903*, (Concord: Trinitarian Congregational Church, 1903), 14-15.

Appendix C: Demographics

1 Connie Martinson Lawrence, interviewed by Renee Garrelick 18 November 1992, CFPL Special Collections, Renee Garrelick Oral History Program Collection, https://concordlibrary.org/special-collections/oral-history/lawrence_c, accessed 3 October 2019.

2 *For den Skandinaviske Trefaldigheds Menighed Concord Mass, 1907-1916*, Faith Evangelical Free Church archives, labeled *Faith Evangelical Church Accounts 1907-1916*.

Faith Evangelical Church Accounts 1907-1916.

3 Church Business Meetings, 1919-1943, pp17-21.

4 Although there were no Thoresen's in the list of charter members, Henry Thoresen (brother of Olga Thoresen, who was wife of March G. Purinton, Sr.) contributed to the construction of the Lang Street church building in 1920.

Appendix D: Statements of Faith

[1] Greg Strand, "EFCA Statement of Faith: Introduction", Appendix 2, online at *Evangelical Free Church of America*, https://www.efca.org/sites/default/files/resources/docs/2013/04/sof-proposed-revision-introduction.pdf, (accessed 30 May 2019).

[2] In the summer of 2019 the EFCA statement of faith was amended to replace the word "premillennial" with "glorious", thus no longer requiring a premillennial view of Christ's return. As of the writing of this book, Faith EFC has not yet amended the church's constitution to reflect this change. The amendment will be discussed and a vote is planned sometime during the centennial year, 2020. Since the Faith EFC delegates to the national conference voted in favor of the change, its acceptance by the congregation is likely.

Bibliography

The following is a list of the major sources used for this book. Because this is not intended to be a thorough genealogical treatise, genealogical sources are not listed here, although some appear in the chapter endnotes. Unless otherwise indicated, all sources related to Trinitarian Congregational Church are housed in the Concord Free Public Library.

(1919-1920). *De Norske Evangeliske Frimenigheders Blad.* Brooklyn, NY: Norwegian Evangelical Free Church and 2nd Norwegian Evangelical Free Church. Retrieved from EFCA Archives, Norwegian Heritage Collection, Box 5 Folder 8

(1922, May 6). *LaCrosse Tribune and Leader-Press.* Retrieved from https://newspaperarchive.com/la-crosse-tribune-may-06-1922-p-2/

(1977-<ongoing>). *Renee Garelick Oral History Program Collection.* Concord: Concord Free Public Library Special Collections. Retrieved from https://concordlibrary.org/special-collections/oral-history

(1917). *Aarsrapport for De Evangeliske Frikirke+Foreningers Aarsmøder, 1917.* Trinity International University Digital Archive. Chicago: Evangelisten Publishing Society. Retrieved September 6, 2019, from http://collections.carli.illinois.edu/cdm/landingpage/collectio

n/tiu_efcadir

Belcher, J. D. (1857). *George Whitefield: A Biography, With Special Reference To His Labors In America.* New York: American Tract Society. Retrieved September 21, 2019, from http://www.gutenberg.org/files/44140/44140-h/44140-h.htm

Bilefsky, D. (2018, July 30). Where Churches Have Become Temples of Cheese, Fitness and Eroticism. *New York Times.* Retrieved September 21, 2019, from https://www.nytimes.com/2018/07/30/world/canada/quebec -churches.html?rref=collection%2Fbyline%2Fdan- bilefsky&action=click&contentCollection=undefined&region=s tream&module=stream_unit&version=latest&contentPlaceme nt=2&pgtype=collection

Blackaby, H. T. (1990). *Experiencing God: Knowing and Doing the Will of God.* Nashville: Lifeway Press.

Burrill, R. (2002, December). Can Dying Churches be Resuscitated? *Ministry.* Retrieved September 21, 2019, from https://www.ministrymagazine.org/archive/2002/12/

Concord Historical Commission. (1995). *Highlights of Concord's Historic Resources.* Town of Concord, Massachusetts.

den Skandinaviske Trefaldigheds Menighed. (1907-1916). *Faith Evangelical Church Accounts, 1907-1916.* Concord: Trinitarian Congregational Church. Retrieved from Faith EFC Archives

Dunn, J. V. (1996). *Malcolm R. Dunn, "In God I Trust".* Auburn, ME: Little Guy Press, Inc. Retrieved from In possession of Marion Purinton

Eastern Evangelical Free Church Association. (1919). Minutes of the 28th Annual Meeting. Chicago: Evangelisten Publishing Society. Retrieved September 6, 2019, from http://collections.carli.illinois.edu/cdm/landingpage/collectio n/tiu_efcadir

Evangelical Free Church of Concord. (1941-1975). *Annual Reports.* Concord: Evangelical Free Church of Concord. Retrieved from Faith EFC Archives

Evangelical Free Church of Concord. (1955-1964). *Business Meetings.* Concord: Evangelical Free Church of Concord. Retrieved from Faith EFC Archives

Evangelical Free Church of Concord. (1964). *Women's Missionary Society 75th Anniversary Program.* Concord: Evangelical Free Church of Concord. Retrieved from Faith EFC Archives

Faith Evangelical Free Church. (1964-1982). *Record of Business Meetings.* Concord: Evangelical Free Church of Concord. Retrieved from Faith EFC Archives

Faith Evangelical Free Church. (1972-1983). *Record of Executive Board Meetings.* Acton: Faith Evangelical Chapel. Retrieved from Faith EFC Archives

Faith Evangelical Free Church. (1976-2018). *Annual Reports.* Acton: Faith Evangelical Free Church.

Faith Evangelical Free Church. (1982-1999). *Annual Meetings.* Acton: Faith Evangelical Free Church. Retrieved from Faith EFC Archives

Faith Evangelical Free Church. (1985-1999). *Board Meeting Minutes.* Acton: Faith Evangelical Free Church. Retrieved from Faith EFC Archives

Farmer, J. C. (2017). *Church Planting Sponsorship: A Statistical Analysis of Sponsoring a Church Plant as a Means of Revitalization of the Sponsor Church.* New Orleans: New Orleans Baptist Theological Seminary. Retrieved September 21, 2019, from https://caskeycenter.files.wordpress.com/2017/05/church-revitalization-through-church-planting-sponsorship-powerpoint.pdf

First Parish in Concord. (1695-2014). *Records.* Concord: Concord Free Public Library Special Collections. Retrieved from Vault A30, Unit A1

French, A. (n.d.). *Allen French Papers*, Box 6, Folders 10-13. Concord: Minute Man National Historical Park Archives. Retrieved from Correspondence with William Henry Hunt and working papers for Social Circle memoir of Hunt, including letter from Hunt's niece Mary R. Jacobs and Jacobs' responses to Social Circle biographical form on Hunt

Gustafson, D. M. (n.d.). *D. L. Moody and the Norwegian-Danish Evangelical Free Church*. Retrieved May 30, 2019, from Academia.edu: https://www.academia.edu/19608158/D._L._Moody_and_th e_Norwegian-Danish_Evangelical_Free

Hale, F. (1979). Norwegians, Danes and the Origins of the Evangelical Free Tradition. *Norwegian-American Studies, 28*. Retrieved September 21, 2019, from https://www.academia.edu/19608158/D._L._Moody_and_th e_Norwegian-Danish_Evangelical_Free

Hassing, A. (1979). Methodism From Norway to America. *Norwegian-American Studies, 28*, 192-216. Retrieved July 31, 2019, from https://www.naha.stolaf.edu/pubs/nas/volume28/Nor-Am%20Studies%20Vol%2028%20Article%20Eight.pdf

Hudson, B. K. (1938?). *The Wright Tavern*. Carbon Copy of Typescript, Concord. Retrieved from Concord Free Public Library Special Collections

Jonswold, O. M., & Nelsen, N. W. (Eds.). (1919-1920). *De Norske Evangeliske Frimenigheders Blad*. Retrieved from Evangelical Free Church of America Archives

Lawrence, C. M. (1985, April 18). New Perspectives in Concord's History. (W. Bailey, Interviewer) Concord Free Public Library. Retrieved September 21, 2019, from https://concordlibrary.org/uploads/scollect/OH_Texts/marti nsen.html

Malmin, R. N. (1928). *Who's Who Among Pastors in all the Norwegian Lutheran Synods of America, 1843-1927* (Third Edition ed.). Minneapolis: Augsburg Publishing House.

Methodist Episcopal Church, New England Conference. (1889). *Official Minutes of the Ninetieth Session of the New England Conference of the Methodist Episcopal Church Held in Trinity Church, Worcester, April 10-16, 1889*. Boston: Alfred Mudge &

Sons. Retrieved from https://catalog.hathitrust.org/Record/008699889

Mohler, R. A. (2018, August 14). *The Briefing.* Retrieved from https://albertmohler.com/2018/08/14/briefing-8-14-18

Montgomery, R. M. (1884). *A Wind From the Holy Spirit in Sweden and Norway.* Bible House, NY: American Home Missionary Society. Retrieved September 21, 2019, from https://archive.org/details/windfromholyspir00mont

Norwegian Evangelical Free Church. (1919-1943). *Church Business Meetings.* Concord: Norwegian Evangelical Free Church. Retrieved from Faith EFC Archives

Norwegian Evangelical Free Church. (1932). *Church Manual and Year Book of the Norwegian Evangelical Free Church (Congregational), Lang Street, Concord, Massachusetts.* Concord: Norwegian Evangelical Free Church. Retrieved from FEFC Archives.

Norwegian Evangelical Free Church. (1944-1955). *Church Register.* Concord: Norwegian Evangelical Free Church. Retrieved from Faith EFC Archives

Norwegian Evangelical Free Church of Boston. (1896-1904). *Treasurer's Ledger.* Boston, Massachusetts: Norwegian Evangelical Free Church of Boston. Retrieved from Evangelical Free Church of America Archives, Minneapolis MN

Odegaard, R. A. (1971). *With Singleness of Heart: Pioneers and Pioneering for Christ in Home Mission Fields.* Minneapolis: Free Church Press.

(1965-1972). *Official Board Meetings: Record of Executive Board Meetings.* Concord: Evangelical Free Church of Concord. Retrieved from Faith EFC Archives

(1889, 1894, 1897). *Official Minutes of the New England Conference of the Methodist Episcopal Church.* Boston: Alfred Mudge & Sons. Retrieved September 21, 2019, from https://catalog.hathitrust.org/Record/008699889

Olsen, O. (1992, May 6). Correspondence with Rev. Doug Welch. Retrieved from Faith Evangelical Free Church Archives

Pedersen, L. J. (1935). *The Norwegian Evangelical Free Church of Boston, Mass (Congregational): A Brief Historical Sketch.* Boston: Eastern Press. Retrieved from Faith Evangelical Free Church Archives

(1903). *Rapport over Forandlingerne med Vestens og Østens Evangeliske Frikirke Foreningers Aarsmøder 1903.* Trinity International University Digital Library. Chicago: Evangelisten Publishing Society. Retrieved September 6, 2019, from http://collections.carli.illinois.edu/cdm/landingpage/collectio n/tiu_efcadir

(1890). *Sixty-Fourth Report of the American Home Missionary Society.* The American Home Missionary Society. Retrieved September 21, 2019, from https://books.google.com/books?id=estMAAAAMAAJ

Specht, L. (2018, October 27). Email correspondence with the author.

Spence, R. K. (2018, November 20). Phone conversation. (M. J. Young, Interviewer)

Stetzer, E. (2014, June 14). 5 Reasons Established Churches Should Plant Churches. *Christianity Today.* Retrieved September 21, 2019, from https://www.christianitytoday.com/edstetzer/2014/june/5-reasons-established-churches-should-plant-churches.html

Strand, G. (n.d.). *EFCA Statement of Faith: Introduction.* Retrieved May 30, 2019, from Evangelical Free Church of America: https://www.efca.org/sites/default/files/resources/docs/2013 /04/sof-proposed-revision-introduction.pdf

Teele, J. W. (Ed.). (1985). *The Meeting House on the Green: A History of the First Parish in Concord and its Church, 350th Anniversary, 1635-1985.* Concord: The Parish. Retrieved from Concord Free Public Library Special Collections

The General Association of the Congregational Churches of Massachusetts. (1897). *Minutes of the Ninety-Fifth Annual*

Meeting, Worcester, May 18-20, With the Statistics. Boston: Congregational Sunday School and Publishing Society, Congregational House. Retrieved from https://books.google.com/books?id=usCrcisQ_FAC&lpg=RA1-PA86&ots=CD6WfesqIz&dq=general%20association%20of%20congregational%20churches%20of%20massachusetts%201897&pg=PP1#v=onepage&q=general%20association%20of%20congregational%20churches%20of%20massachusetts

Thompson, R. A. (1954). *Looking Back Seventy Years: A Historical Glimpse of the Evangelical Free Church of America.* Minneapolis: Free Church Press. Retrieved September 21, 2019, from http://collections.carli.illinois.edu/cdm/ref/collection/tiu_efcalit/id/9271

Trinitarian Congregational Church in Concord. (1686-2006 (bulk 1826-2006)). *Record.* Concord: Concord Free Public Library Special Collections. Retrieved from Vault A30, Unit C1

Van Yperen, J. (2004). *The Shepherd Leader.* ChurchSmart Resources.

Vanderbloemen, W. a. (2014). *Next: Pastoral Succession That Works.* Grand Rapids: Baker Books.

(various). *Concord Enterprise.* Marlboro, MA: The Enterprise. Retrieved from https://newspaperarchive.com

Watson, R. A. (2000). *A History of the Trinitarian Congregational Church, 1826-1988.* Concord: Trinitarian Congregational Church.

Wheeler, R. R. (1964). *North Bridge Neighbors, History of Area B.* Concord: Minute Man National Historic Park Archives.

Wikipedia contributors. (n.d.). *Theodore Baker.* Retrieved March 28, 2019, from Wikipedia, the Free Encyclopedia: https://en.wikipedia.org/w/index.php?title=Theodore_Baker&oldid=783006716

Wilson, L. P. (2002). A Concord Farmer Looks Back: The Reminiscences of William Henry Hunt. *The Concord*

Saunterer, New Series, 10, 65-123. Retrieved September 21, 2019, from https://www.jstor.org/stable/i23392865

Wilson, L. P. (2005, July 7). Theodore Baker of Concord: An Archival Aha! *The Concord Journal*, p. 23. Retrieved from Concord Free Public Library Special Collection

(2014). *Wright Tavern 1747 Concord MA Historical Structural Report.* Concord Free Public Library Special Collections. Concord: Groundroot Preservation Group. Retrieved from Concord Free Public Library Special Collections

Index of Names

www.ingramcontent.com/pod-product-compliance
Lightning Source LLC
Chambersburg PA
CBHW051849090426

42811CB00034B/2275/J